RESTORATION LITERATURE

ENGLISH LITERATURE

Editor
PROFESSOR BASIL WILLEY
*formerly King Edward VII Professor of English Literature
in the University of Cambridge*

RESTORATION
LITERATURE

K. M. P. BURTON
FORMERLY FELLOW OF NEWNHAM COLLEGE, CAMBRIDGE

HUTCHINSON UNIVERSITY LIBRARY
LONDON

HUTCHINSON & CO. (*Publishers*) LTD
178–202 Great Portland Street, London, W.1

London Melbourne Sydney
Auckland Bombay Toronto
Johannesburg New York

★

First published 1958

Second edition 1965

*This book has been printed in Great Britain
by litho-offset by William Clowes and Sons Ltd,
London and Beccles*

ACKNOWLEDGEMENTS

I should like to record my thanks to the Council of St. John's College, Cambridge, for their permission to quote from MS. S.17 in the College Library, and to the following for their permission to make use of copyright material:

G. Bell & Sons, Ltd. (Samuel Pepys, *Diary*, ed. H. B. Wheatley).

Sir Basil Blackwell (Sir George Etherege, *Works*, ed. H. F. B. Brett-Smith).

The Bodley Head (Charles Cotton, *Poems*, ed. J. Beresford).

Professor R. L. Brett (*The Third Earl of Shaftesbury*).

Cambridge University Press (John Bunyan, *Grace Abounding, The Pilgrim's Progress, The Life and Death of Mr. Badman, The Holy War*, ed. J. Brown; Samuel Butler, *Hudibras* and *Characters*, ed. A. R. Waller; G. R. Cragg, *From Puritanism to the Age of Reason*; C. E. Raven, *John Ray*).

The Clarendon Press, Oxford (Gilbert Burnet, *History of My Own Time*, ed. O. Airy; *Characters from the Histories and Memoirs of the Seventeenth Century*, ed. D. Nichol Smith; *Critical Essays of the Seventeenth Century*, ed. J. Spingarn; John Dryden, *Essays*, ed. W. P. Ker; John Evelyn, *Diary*, ed. E. S. de Beer; Jonathan Swift, *A Tale of a Tub*, ed. Guthkelch and Nichol Smith; Thomas Traherne, *Centuries of Meditations*; The Marquis of Halifax, *Works*, ed. W. Raleigh).

Constable & Co., Ltd. (Sir Charles Sedley, *Works*, ed. V. de S. Pinto).

J. M. Dent & Sons, Ltd. (Aphra Behn, *Oroonoko, Shorter Novels*, Vol. II, Everyman's Library).

Duke University Press, Durham, N.C. (*Coleridge on the Seventeenth Century*, ed. R. F. Brinkley).

ACKNOWLEDGEMENTS

Harvard University Press, Cambridge, Mass. (L. Bernbaum, *The Mary Carleton Narratives 1663–1673*).

The Johns Hopkins Press, Baltimore, Maryland (*Critical Works of John Dennis*, ed. E. N. Hooker).

Macmillan & Co., Ltd. (Pope, *Poetical Works*, ed. A. W. Ward).

The Nonesuch Library Ltd. (Donne, *Complete Poetry and Selected Prose*, ed. J. Hayward).

Oxford University Press (John Dryden, *Poems*, ed. J. Sargeaunt).

CONTENTS

NOTE TO THE SECOND EDITION

When this book was written, W. P. Ker's edition of Dryden's *Essays* was the standard one, and all references in the text are to this. Since then, George Watson's edition, *Of Dramatic Poesy and Other Critical Essays*, has superseded Ker's; it therefore appears in the revised bibliography.

PREFACE

The title *Restoration Literature* is more convenient than accurate. The Restoration took place in 1660; the period covered by this book lasts from 1660 until just after the turn of the century. But dates make discouraging titles, and alternative descriptions have their disadvantages. *Pre-Augustan Literature* has an apologetic air, and suggests a period of preparation rather than achievement. *Literature of the Later Seventeenth Century* is correct, but unwieldy, and may well belong to a future volume in the Oxford Histories. In the end *Restoration Literature* seemed the most suitable, since it was succinct, and would act as a reminder that a new age was beginning, with an access of energy, different interests and preconceptions, and a great variety of occupations and writings, which only gradually blended into the more uniform tradition and decorum of the Augustan Age.

The conformation of this book will probably surprise the reader for whom this period calls to mind Milton, Dryden and Restoration comedy. I have omitted to discuss Milton because Dr. Daiches's book on Milton in this series comes very close to *Restoration Literature* in date of publication. Milton was, in any case, formed by an earlier age; he continued to uphold its traditions against the assaults of the later period. Dryden has been decentralized and dealt with piece by piece for a different reason. As long as 'pure' literature—the drama, fiction, lyric poetry—is considered to be the most important product of this age, it is logical that Dryden should be treated as its central and unifying figure—a writer who showed his genius in every kind, whose output towered above that of all competitors, and who was for over thirty years the acknowledged leader of the literary field. But in this book, the drama and other forms of 'pure' literature are regarded almost as the froth on the surface of an age that was vigorous, original and worth consideration in its more serious writings—those in which the author did not set out primarily to produce an entertaining work of art, but to accomplish a task in life. Literary genius was widely distributed over the field of morals, science, religion, politics and criticism. In such a landscape, Dryden appears as one peak within a large range of mountains. The emphasis falls on his critical work and on his satires, rather than on the whole Dryden as the grand old man of all literature. His achievements have tended to obscure those of his contemporaries; this book constitutes an attempt to redress the balance. If the result seems like *Hamlet* without the prince, I am sorry; it is really more like an attempt to criticize *Henry IV* as a whole play, instead of assessing it on Falstaff alone. Dryden was a character of genius, but neither the sole genius of the age nor its complete representative. He remains a writer whose work will continue to be read with pleasure and admiration. At the end of the book I shall briefly put him together again and indicate what qualities of his writing I have omitted. But if the pendulum seems to have swung too far away from Dryden for justice to be done, it must be remembered that 'our best writings, in this Life, are but *Essays*, which we leave to Posterity to review and correct', as Thomas Burnet remarked.

In quotations from seventeenth-century works, the original spelling and punctuation have been retained, but contractions have been expanded.

I am grateful to the following modern writers for a better understanding of the age: Professor J. W. Atkins, Dr. G. R. Cragg, Dr. D. G. James, Professor R. F. Jones, Professor D. Ogg, Canon C. Raven, Dr. M. Starkmann and Professor B. Willey. Their influence will be seen most obviously in the introductory chapter, where I have not always acknowledged specific debts. I am even more grateful both to Dr. Bradbrook and to Professor Willey in person for their most helpful and stimulating criticism. As General Editor, Professor Willey has patiently saved me from a variety of unscholarly errors. If any remain, he is not to blame.

I

INTRODUCTION

AT ITS best, literature from the Restoration until just after the turn of the century was characterized by hard-won honesty and realism. Although the period was not entirely cut off from the earlier world-picture, the beliefs of the age had been considerably modified by the new developments in religion and science. The better writers took modern life as their material; their images were concrete and their language racy and vigorous. With the exception of Milton, who was the product of an earlier age, its poets did not create new worlds of the imagination. The novel as we know it did not exist. The drama was mainly given up to entertainment and make-believe. 'Pure' art was pursued by men who imitated old forms without sharing the conviction of those who had devised them. The writers who still claim serious critical attention were men whose purposes were not single-mindedly artistic: the historians, political writers, satirists, preachers, philosophers. Halifax and Clarendon achieved moderation and detachment; Bunyan and Traherne demonstrated the value of the spiritual world; Thomas Burnet showed that modern science had enlarged men's sense of wonder at the universe; Dryden and Rochester criticized contemporary civilization; Locke showed how man, 'the glory, jest and riddle of the world', could remain balanced and tolerant in a disconcerting universe. With the exception of the preachers, they lacked the transcendence and the high seriousness which Arnold required of the poet, but within their own age their achievement was a triumph.

The nature of this triumph can only be seen by studying the course of events during the years 1660–1700. The relation of literature to the life of the time will not, of course, immediately put the critic in a position where he can make a final judgment on the literature, but it will enable him to understand it more completely. An examination of

11

the strains and stresses of the period, its material, intellectual and religious developments, is an indispensable preliminary to literary criticism.

HISTORICAL AND SOCIAL BACKGROUND

Sixteen hundred and sixty itself was a year of panegyric. For many men, the restoration of the monarchy in the person of Charles II, the rightful heir, meant the arrival of a golden age. John Evelyn's account of the King's progress to London on the 29th of May is typical:

> This day came in his Majestie *Charles* the 2d to London after a sad, and long Exile and Calamitous Suffering both of the King and Church: being 17 yeares: This was also his Birthday, and with a Triumph of above 20000 horse and foote, brandishing their swords and shouting with un-expressable joy: The wayes straw'd with flowers, the bells ringing, the streetes hung with Tapissry, fountaines running with wine. . . . I stood in the strand, and beheld it, and blessed God. And all this without one drop of bloud, and by that very army, which rebell'd against him: but it was the Lords doing, *et mirabile in oculis nostris*: for such a Restauration was never seen in the mention of any history antient or modern, since the returne of the *Babylonian* Captivity; nor so joyfull a day, and so bright, ever seene in this nation.
>
> *Diary* (ed. E. S. de Beer, 1955), vol. III, p. 246.

The country had great expectations. Charles was seen as the epitome of the virtues, and the symbol of strong fatherly government; his return meant the end of indecision and weak disputes. There may have been some flattery in Dryden's loyal address, *Astrea Redux*, but it was slight in comparison with the very genuine hopes expressed:

> And now times whiter Series is begun,
> Which in soft Centuries shall smoothly run. . . .
> Our nation, with united Int'rest blest,
> Not now content to poize, shall sway, the rest.
> Abroad your Empire shall no Limits know,
> But like the Sea in boundless Circles flow . . .

At home the hateful names of Parties cease,
And factious Souls are weary'd into peace. . . .
Oh Happy Age! Oh times like those alone,
By Fate reserv'd for great *Augustus* throne!
Poems (ed. J. Sargeaunt, 1913), p. 10.

To understand this almost hysterical optimism, it is necessary to look briefly at the events of the previous twenty years of civil wars and uneasy interregnum. Not only had the wars brought great material losses to the majority of people in the country, but the idealistic principles which were originally defended had given way to prudential motives. At first, Parliament stated that it was taking up arms to prevent the King from becoming a tyrant, and to defend Low Churchmen against the encroachments of Laudianism; and the King's party said they were taking up arms in defence of the known laws and the decencies of the Anglican liturgy and ceremonial. But liberty soon ceased to be the chief aim of the Presbyterians and the Parliament: the remains of the Lower House became as tyrannical as their picture of the King, and the Presbyterians tried to impose their religion on the whole country, precisely as Laud had done. The composition of the opposing forces altered. English Presbyterians and the Scots joined the King, who supported the cause of Presbyterianism against Cromwell's army of Independents. The Army's final aim was the destruction of the King. A war had to be won, however confused the causes for which it was being fought. When the King had been executed, none of the country's problems had been solved. The Commonwealth failed to bring security; in fact a series of disagreements drove Cromwell to rule as a virtual military dictator. At his death, Parliament and the Army renewed their struggle for power, which was only resolved by the recall of the expelled members of the Long Parliament. A dissolution was followed by new elections. The new House recalled the King.

For twenty years people had been promised a great deal, and none of the promises had been carried out. They were back where they started, after a disagreeable and frustrating interlude. Their chief reaction was a hatred of the enthusiastic pursuit of Causes, and a deep fear of change. The ideals set before the country had been destroyed by self-interest and treachery. It must have seemed as if the only absolutes left were those of power and wealth. In the private letters of such men as Sir Roger Burgoyne and Ralph Verney there is a characteristic note of disillusionment. The wars had brought out the worst in people. John Heydon wrote in 1658:

> It is manifest that we are fallen into the dregs of time; we live in the rust of the iron age, and must expect to feel, *ultima senescentis mundi delivia*, the dotages of a decrepit world. What is become of truth, sincerity, charity, humility, those *antiqui mores*? whither are they gone? did they attend *Astrea* into heaven, and have left such dangerous successours, as cruelty, pride, fraud, envy, oppression. . . .
>
> *Advice to a Daughter*, p. 200.

Clarendon wrote of the corruptions induced by encouraging children to betray their parents, servants their masters. Integrity had ceased to be an ideal, since craft met with so much better success. Charity was thought foolish, hard-heartedness and severity admired. Acquisitiveness had taken the place of generosity. Values and standards had disappeared. In consequence, many men mistrusted life as 'nasty, brutish and short'. Hobbes's pessimism was not peculiar; others also thought that man was purely self-centred and aggressive, needing the fear of punishment as a deterrent from crime. Only an inviolable authority could protect men from one another. This picture of life, fostered by years of misery and insecurity, led to a morality of self-protection. Material welfare and public order were the only things that mattered. An individual soul claiming to act on personal ideals was a public danger. The spiritual world was a mere phrase, without a referent. There was a spirit of cynicism which stripped man of his potential worth, and advised him to avoid putting his fingers into the fire in which so many of his predecessors had been burned. This mood can be seen not only in Hobbes's *Leviathan* (1651) but also in Francis Osborn's *Advice to a Son* (1658), one of the most popular books in the early part of Charles II's reign, according to Sir William Petty.

The Restoration was seen as a panacea for all these evils. Charles would bring stability to the country. There would be room for virtues to flourish in the State. Spiritual values could be reasserted, and men would be free to worship in their own way. Enterprise would find scope. England would once again take her rightful place in Europe, and build up her empire in east and west.

The new reign began well. The first Parliament was moderate and wise in handling the immediate problems caused by the change of power. The King wanted to introduce freedom of conscience, partly because he thought forms of creed and liturgy an indifferent matter. He ruled through the laws of the country. He encouraged intellectual activities, was a patron of the newly formed Royal Society, and took an interest in the practical application of new scientific and technological discoveries. There was a general trend towards material prosperity.

Disappointments soon outweighed these initial advantages. Men wanted their own religious beliefs tolerated, but they did not wish to tolerate those of others. The Anglican majority feared that dissent was synonymous with fanaticism and faction, and the Clarendon Code was promulgated to limit the civil liberties of the Dissenters. Public office was barred to them, and they were disfranchised. Charles's court, far from being an encouragement to virtue, was full of intrigue and profligacy; his courtiers were enjoying a period of dissipation after the moral restrictions of the Commonwealth. Even if only some of the stories related by Antony Hamilton in his *Memoirs of Count Grammont* are true, the court made a habit of casual affairs. John Evelyn, who was a sober man, not given to gossip, could not blind himself to the depravity and irresponsibility of the so-called nobility:

> I know none (amongst all our Court great-ones) . . . who dos naturaly care for our state. . . . All seeke their owne . . . I am a plaine country gentleman, yet heare, and see, and observe, as those in the valies best discerne the mountaines; this nation is ruin'd for want of activity on our parts; religion and gratitude on all . . . God give the repentance of David, to the sinns of David! We have all added some weights to this burthen; ingratitude, and luxurie, and the too, too soone oblivion of Miracles.
>
> Letters to Viscount Cornbury, 9th and 12th September 1665. *Diary and Correspondence of John Evelyn* (ed. W. Bray, 1906), vol. III, pp. 318–21.

Most of all, perhaps, men had hoped for security. What they had to endure was a series of foreign wars, the worst outbreak of the plague for centuries, the Fire of London, the raid of the Dutch Navy up the Medway, the Popish Plot, the Rye House Plot, secret treaties and heavy taxation, the dispute about the succession, Monmouth's rebellion. When Charles II died, they were faced with a King who was determined that England should return to the Roman Catholic Church.

They were slow to believe that it was worth taking action to improve their state. James's attacks on the liberty of institutions were tolerated for nearly three years, but the combined effects of the birth of a male heir to James, of his second Declaration of Indulgence, and of his attempt to coerce the constituencies into returning members who favoured his policy, finally drove them to take the decisive step of inviting William of Orange and Mary to the English throne. This revolution was a quiet affair; men did not rush to this Dutch prince as they had rushed to welcome Charles II. Holland—a recent enemy and a rival in trade—was not popular, but this was the lesser of two evils, since the continued reign of James II would mean subordination to France and to Rome.

The reign of William and Mary began with the Bill of Rights, which made the King subject to the laws, and removed many of his prerogatives; it also ensured frequent sessions of Parliament. The Toleration Act freed Dissenters from most of the penalties imposed by the Clarendon Code. During the nineties the wars with France made England into a mature and united nation, instead of a collection of factions. A professional army was created, which took the place of the undisciplined mercenaries. A large volume of shipping was built, and a powerful navy came into being. England's finances were put in order: the Bank of England was established, and a method was found of floating public loans on sound security. A modern system of direct and indirect taxation was set up, and the coinage was reformed.

The middle classes were conscious of a good deal of material improvement since the devastation of the Civil Wars. They found or created conditions in which their business could thrive. England was developing fast as a maritime and trading state, making wide use of her overseas possessions, and competing intensively with the Dutch, the French and the Portuguese in trading ventures. The younger sons of the aristocracy and the clergy found in trade and industry a respected occupation. The Dissenters, barred from the professions for nearly thirty years, thought that personal prosperity was a sign of divine approval, and were energetic in their efforts for commercial success. The skill and application of French Huguenot immigrants did much for the development of English industries.

London itself was obviously becoming more civilized. The Great

Fire was followed by the rebuilding of the city in stone: over fifty of its churches were designed by Sir Christopher Wren, and some of their woodwork was carved by Grinling Gibbons. The water supply was improved by the creation of new reservoirs at Highgate. Sewers were dug, and householders were forbidden to throw rubbish into the streets; they had to keep it for collection by the city scavengers. Shops were replacing the former stalls. Lamps were used instead of dim lanthorns for street lighting. In addition to the indoor theatres, with their sophisticated provision of scenery and machines, there were concert rooms where the music of such men as Purcell could be publicly performed. There was a flow of newspapers and cheap books. Coffee-houses were being set up, where men could meet and discuss public events, politics and the latest literature. London was the centre of intellectual life in England, and was acquiring a cosmopolitan reputation.

The bad state of the roads, and the slowness with which enclosures were being granted, retarded the development of the countryside. Yet stage-coaches made travelling easier. The Fens were successfully drained. Some new crops—notably French grasses and clovers—were introduced, and the use of artificial fertilizers was recommended. Methods of growing fruit and woodland trees improved. Well-laid-out gardens were developed at many of the great country houses. Evelyn's diary and Celia Fiennes's account of her tours on horseback give an excellent idea of the state of the country at this time.

Social improvements were foreshadowed. There were schemes for providing pensions for widows, and for providing for the families of sailors. Defoe suggested a great many reforms in his *Essay upon Projects* (1697); these included a scheme for personal accident insurance and one for contributory pensions for all who worked for their living. There was a general awareness of an expanding economy, in which risks could profitably be taken, and in which the welfare of the less fortunate could be considered.

By the end of the century there was a feeling that, despite the political struggle between Whigs and Tories, law and order had been established on a sound basis of respect for the rights of the individual. The Toleration Act and the Habeas Corpus Act protected the individual from injustice on the part of Church or State, and Locke's principles of government, based on the identification of the law with freedom, helped widely differing types of people to live in a society without a violent clash of interests.

RELIGIOUS BACKGROUND

The rough pattern of development in religious thought was from sectarian zeal to pious common sense at the end of the period. The first half of the seventeenth century had been characterized by a multitude of sects, each with its devotees. (An unfair account of the practices of some of these can be found in Thomas Edwards's contemporary pamphlet *Gangrena*.) In the second half of the century the important differences were not so much in doctrine and liturgy as in the relative intensity with which the beliefs were held. A graph could be made of all degrees between complete devotion and scepticism, revealing a preponderance of comfortable assent towards the end of the century. There were many distinguishable groups. The High Anglicans were trying to revert to some of Laud's tenets, and impose them on the nation, on the argument that it was ten to one that God spoke through a lawful Christian magistrate rather than through the conscience of a private person. There were the Latitudinarians, leniently orthodox, preaching calmness, and convinced that religious belief was an entirely reasonable activity. The Deists were a less respectable group, with their abolition of mysteries, and their simplification of Christianity to a belief that Christ was the Messiah; they defined faith as 'a firm persuasion founded on substantial reasons'. The Cambridge Platonists emphasized personal insight and responsibility, and reconciled religious zeal with charity to those who differed from them. The Dissenters adhered devoutly to their right to worship God as they thought best. The neo-Epicureans rejected both reason and the absolutes of religion, and exalted the senses, while the materialists denied the existence of spirit in man and the universe.

Three quotations will serve to illustrate some of these differences in intensity. The first is taken from Hobbes's *Leviathan*. Hobbes, it was said, believed in God Almighty Matter, and thought the law of the civil sovereign the only obliging rule of conduct and belief. There was no place in his life for divine sanctions or absolute values; everything was subordinated to the needs of the State, in the interests of preserving the peace. The extent of his disengagement from religious experience can be judged by the tone of the following passage:

> It is not hard to reconcile our Obedience to God, with our Obedience to the Civill Soveraign; who is either Christian, or Infidel. If he bee a Christian, he alloweth the beleefe of this Article, that *Jesus is the Christ*; and of all the Articles that are contained in, or are by evident consequence deduced from it: which is all the Faith Necessary to Salvation. And because he is a Soveraign, he requireth Obedience to all his owne, that is, to all the Civill Laws; in which also are contained all the Laws of Nature, that is, all the Laws of God: for besides the Laws of Nature, and the Laws of the Church, which are part of the Civill Law, (for the Church that can make Laws is the Common-wealth,) there bee no other Laws Divine. Whosoever therefore obeyeth his Christian Soveraign, is not thereby hindred, neither from beleeving, nor from obeying God. . . . And in case a Subject be forbidden by the Civill Soveraign to professe some of those his opinions, upon what just ground can he disobey? Christian Kings may erre in deducing a Consequence, but who shall Judge? Shall a private man Judge, when the question is of his own obedience? or shall any man Judg but he that is appointed thereto by the Church, that is, by the Civill Soveraign that representeth it?

> *Leviathan* (1651), chap. XLIII.

The individual has nothing to do but obey; he need not consult his conscience, and he must not presume to judge for himself.

The second quotation is from the sermons of Robert South, a moderate Anglican who believed in the essential reasonableness of religion:

> Reason therefore is undeservedly and ignorantly traduced, when it is set up and shot at, as the irreconcilable Enemy of Religion. It is indeed the very Crown and Privilege of our Nature; a Ray of Divinity sent into a mortal Body: *The Star that guides all wise Men to Christ*: The Lanthorn that leads the Eye of Faith, and is no more an Enemy to it, than an obedient Hand-Maid to a discreet Mistress. Those, indeed, whose Tenets will not bear the Test of it, and whose Ware goes off best in the dark Rooms of Ignorance and Credulity, and whose *Faith* has as much Cause *to dread a Discovery as their Works*; these (I say) may decry Reason; and that indeed not without Reason.

> *Sermons* (1715), vol. IV, pp. 291–2.

There is a certain complacency in this passage, and a tendency to by-pass difficulties. Those who hold differing views are patronized from a comfortable elevation. The writer has religious convictions, but they feel more like a pillow than a goad.

The tone of Richard Baxter has an urgency completely lacking in the other two. He was still a member of the Church of England in 1651, when this book was written:

> Even the Godly themselves deserve this reproof, for being too lazy Seekers of their everlasting Rest. Alas, What a disproportion is there betwixt our Light and our Heat? Our Professions and Prosecution? Who makes that haste, as if it were for Heaven? How still we stand? How idly we work? . . . Who would think that stood by us, and heard us pray in private or publick, that we were praying for no less than everlasting Glory? Should Heaven be sought no more earnestly than thus? Methinks we are none of us all in good sadness for our Souls. We do but dally with the Work of God. . . . The Plague of *Lot's* Wife is upon us, as if we were changed into lifeless and immovable Pillars: we are dying, and we know it, and yet we stir not; we are at the door of eternal Happiness or Misery, and yet we perceive it not: Death knocks, and we hear it not: Christ calls and knocks, and we hear not: God cries to us, *To day if you will hear my voice, harden not your hearts. Work while it is day, for the night cometh, when none shall work.*
>
> *The Saints Everlasting Rest* (12th ed., 1688), Part III, chap. 5, pp. 338–9.

He was certainly in earnest, and single-minded in pursuit of the welfare of men's souls.

As the period progressed, certain dominant trends could be distinguished. Calvinism declined; Deism grew up. High Anglicanism was watered down to Latitudinarianism. Reason was elevated; common sense tended to take the place of personal religious experience as a basis for belief. Enthusiasm was deprecated because it led to faction; mysteries and miracles were thought either dangerous or absurd. A comfortable assurance of salvation by a just God took the place of religious awe. Religion became altogether more simple. It was no longer a question of having to believe in a host of difficult dogmas: what was required was adherence to the central belief in a magnanimous God at the centre of a mathematical universe. Salvation depended on simplified faith, and on virtue; and virtue was easy, for it was now 'visibly the most enriching purchase, and by much the best bargain'.

The persecuting temper of the sixties, induced less by religious principle than by a fear that dissent involved political rebellion, gave way gradually to a reasonable extent of toleration. Persecution had clearly failed to achieve what was intended—the extermination of nonconformity—and recognition of this fact led to the passing of the Toleration Act in 1689.

By the end of the period there was a perceptible decline in the quality of religious experience described by the majority of writers. What they wrote on religion is of interest more as a symptom than in its own right; they failed to catch the imagination. Common sense had come in as a necessary antidote to the fanaticism of the previous age, but in the end genuine religious feeling declined so much that common sense was almost all that was left. Reason may have liberated men from persecution, but reason itself came to be a limitation. Passionate certainties were automatically suspect, and an atmosphere of religious *laissez faire* was established.

The growth of religious apathy was undoubtedly encouraged by the new view of God presented by the Anglicans. God, they said, was not in any sense terrible. No good man could behave as the Calvinist God was reputed to do, condemning the unborn to eternal damnation. Therefore, no Being identified with infinite goodness could possibly behave in this way. The Deists went further: the good God, they said, could not possibly visit Adam's sin on his descendants in the way supposed; Adam's sin had merely made men mortal. Or as Locke, who was not a Deist, put it in *The Reasonableness of Christianity* (1695):

> Much less can the righteous God be supposed, as a punishment of one sin, wherewith he is displeased, to put man under the necessity of sinning continually, and so multiplying the provocation.
>
> *Works* (1823), vol. VII, p. 6.

Men that were treated in this way would not think themselves fairly dealt with. But in fact men who had done their best to keep God's laws of conduct, and who had faith in God's promises, would attain eternal bliss; the sinners would cease to exist, but were not reserved for eternal torment. The worst that could happen was a simple cessation. The power of God to overawe men was declining. He became a figure scientifically deduced from self-evident facts; he was not described from religious experience. Dr. G. R. Cragg has summed up the situation:

With cool, dispassionate clarity, God was set forth as a necessary postulate, wholly reasonable and satisfying to the mind, and upheld by evidence conforming to the standards of the intellectual discipline which then commanded unquestioning assent. . . . They declared themselves in favour of an 'eternal Being', but He lacked the majesty and splendour of the God the Puritans had worshipped.

From Puritanism to the Age of Reason (1950), p. 121.

'God is, and is Almighty, to forgive' might stand as an epigraph for men's beliefs at this period.

The mathematical approach to the world, partly based on the Cartesian synthesis which professed to deduce its universe from the existence of God, naturally gave rise to an emphasis on the role of reason in religion. Many of the more extreme sectarians had made a cult of irrationality; by the end of the century there had been a complete swing of the pendulum, and reason was the only court of appeal. Locke played no small part in this change. All the truths disclosed by God were answerable to reason. Revelation was simply a means of communicating to the ignorant things which in themselves were eminently reasonable. The Deist Toland was only an extreme example of a general tendency when he stated that anything 'contrary to reason cannot be a miracle'; it must be a possible event, capable of explanation in terms of natural laws. Even the Scriptures were approved because they conformed to the canons of reason, not because they constituted the final authority. Reason, however, too often became a dignified euphemism for common sense or plausibility.

A creed which appealed to reason found previous dogmas unpleasantly over-complex; clarity and simplicity were what was required. 'The things we must believe are few and plain', as Dryden put it in *Religio Laici* in 1682. The drift of Scripture became more important than the minute analysis of a series of texts balanced one against another. Words in the Bible were now given their literal meaning, rather than an allegorical or mystical one. Moreover, there was a beginning of historical criticism of the Bible as a whole. Locke made a distinction between the worth of the Gospels and of the Epistles: the central truths of Christianity were expressed in the Gospels, while the Epistles were *ad hoc* writings, intended to meet the specific needs of groups of Christians in the early days of the Church. He freed men's reading of the Bible from the kind of fundamentalism which regarded every word as of equal importance, and had caused Bunyan so much distress. This was a distinction which made for genuine progress in the study of the Bible. In addition, the Deists attacked previous schools of Biblical criticism and interpretation. They accused the Fathers of dealing in impenetrable labyrinths of irrelevant learning, and recent theologians of hair-splitting, obscurantism and scholastic jargon. The importance of theology declined; morality tended to take its place. There had been a movement in this direction as early as 1662, when Convocation had issued a circular letter to the clergy, asking them to avoid preaching on speculative theology and confine themselves to the topic of moral duty.

In the long run, toleration was the outcome of political developments rather than of any widespread recognition of the rights of man to freedom of thought and freedom of speech. It came only gradually. At the beginning of Charles II's reign, it was thought that the Established Church would be lenient to the Dissenters. Charles himself did not care very much about doctrine, and he made a series of gracious speeches promising fair treatment, provided that the policy was endorsed by his Parliament. But when the Anglicans realized the strength of their own position, they took harsher measures against the Dissenters than had been expected, on the childish argument that those who had been intolerant could not expect to be tolerated. In fact, they feared civil disorder from those who would not subscribe to a State Church. Disunity, they thought, spelt weakness. Archdeacon Parker and Sir Roger L'Estrange were terrified of the sedition which had seemed in the past to be the inevitable outcome of religious faction. The Clarendon Code was an attempt to deprive Dissenters of all power to rebel.

Some men, however, came to realize that truth could be trusted to emerge triumphant in a conflict, and did not need the immoral protection of persecution. Men were, after all, prone to error; they should humbly acknowledge that they had no right to impose their views on others. Sir William Temple, Bishop Gilbert Burnet and William Penn were some of the advocates of this liberal view. Penn's *The Great Case of Liberty of Conscience* (1671) contained most of their cardinal propositions. Persecution could lead only to hypocritical worship. The

Gospel must persuade by its own virtues, not by the application of force. Force was anathema to the spiritual kingdom, and an invasion of the natural liberty of man. Moreover, it was impossible by any means of this kind to achieve religious unity.

These arguments were summed up and made effective by Locke's famous *Letters on Toleration* (1689–92). He stressed the uselessness of persecution as a method of spreading religious truth. 'I cannot be saved by a religion that I distrust, and by a worship that I abhor' (*Works*, 1823, vol. VI, p. 28). In religion, mathematical certainty was impossible; it was therefore an area in which no one could claim to dictate because he was in sole possession of the truth. The magistrate had no rights over the religious affairs of the individual. Locke's influence led directly to the passing of the Toleration Act, which made considerable concessions to individual liberty in religious matters. Atheists and Roman Catholics were, however, exempted from its provisions, on the grounds that they could not be trusted to be loyal to the government. In the main, the policy of persecution was dead.

The passing of the Act reflected the increasingly secular temper of the age. Religion mattered less. The confidence of the different groups was waning: it was mere vanity to assert that you had the truth while others had not. But the absence of vanity itself led to a mood of self-satisfaction. Men were progressive, enlightened, well balanced. The Church could now operate quietly in the background; it was no longer a dynamic force in men's lives. Some thirty years after the turn of the century Pope depicted what the Church had come to mean. He was describing the chapel in the rich man's villa:

> And now the Chapel's silver bell you hear,
> That summons you to all the Pride of Pray'r:
> Light quirks of Music, broken and uneven,
> Make the soul dance upon a Jig to Heav'n.
> On painted Ceilings you devoutly stare,
> Where sprawl the Saints of Verrio or Laguerre,
> On gilded clouds in fair expansion lie,
> And bring all Paradise before your eye.
> To rest, the Cushion and soft Dean invite,
> Who never mentions Hell to ears polite.

> *Poetical Works* (ed. A. W. Ward, 1930), *Moral Essays, Epistle IV.*

In the seventeenth century science was within the province of the normally intelligent man. It was only an ancillary subject at the universities, in spite of Puritan efforts to replace the trivium and quadrivium by a scientific and technological education. There were few professional scientists, and a vast number of amateurs, most of whom could contribute something to the growing stock of knowledge in its elementary stage of development, and all of whom realized the importance of scientific discovery to man's idea of the universe. The Royal Society, which had begun informally in the 1640s as The Invisible College, met regularly after the Restoration and published a series of transactions on a wide variety of subjects. Besides such specialists as Robert Boyle and Isaac Newton, its members included the Duke of Buckingham, Sir William Petty, navigator, economist and Professor of Music, Sandwich the naval Earl, Barrow the divine, Evelyn the country gentleman, Dryden and Pepys, and the tradesman John Graunt. Here the virtuosi had an opportunity of discussing their discoveries with a group of very able and live men who shared their interests, and receiving criticisms and suggestions which would send them back to make further observations in the light of which a body of really accurate data could be established. This interchange of ideas led to some of the speediest advances in scientific knowledge since the days of the Greeks.

The scientists rejected the religious theory of Nature's decay. According to this way of thinking, there had been a golden age, which had been lost to man because of his sin. Now mutability reigned, and everything created was deteriorating; the end of the world was close. The natural world should be despised; only the supernatural world was of value. It had been held that this world was not worth further study, and that experiments on physical substances were no fit work for a scholar. In the later seventeenth century the decay of Nature looked like an outmoded hypothesis. A feeling of vigour had been induced by the recent expansion of the known world by explorers, by the process of empire-building, and by the awareness that men's knowledge had been considerably widened in the recent past. Joseph Glanvill in his

Plus Ultra (1668) showed the extent of this increase. In geography, for instance:

> The *frozen North*, the *torrid Line*, and formerly *unknown South*, are visited . . . The *Earth* hath been rounded by *Magellan, Drake* and *Candish.* The *great Motion* of the *Sea* is *vulgar* . . . the *diversities* of *Winds stated,* and better understood: the *Treasure* of *hidden* Vertues in the *Loadstone,* found and used. The *Spicy Islands* of the *East*, as also *those* of the remote *South* and *North, frequented*, and the Knowledge of that *People* and those *Countries* transmitted to us, with their *Riches.* . . . Our *Navigation* is far *greater*, our *Commerce* is more *general*, our *Charts* more *exact*, our *Globes* more *accurate*, our *Travels* more *remote*, our *Reports* more *intelligent and sincere* . . .
>
> *Plus Ultra* (1668), pp. 49–50.

There was tangible evidence of an advance on the Ancients in the invention of the compass, the telescope and microscope, the barometer and printing. It became a little absurd to maintain that progress was impossible, and that history merely repeated itself. It seemed more sensible to hold that each age improved a little on its predecessors. Eventually, the riddles of the universe would be solved. A spirit of optimism was emerging that partly counteracted the earlier personal disillusionments. Wotton, in his *Reflections upon Ancient and Modern Learning* (1694), had come to believe that his own age would almost exhaust the possibilities of scientific discovery—'the next Age will not find very much Work of this Kind to do'. Newton had recently demonstrated the capacity of the human mind for fathoming the laws of Nature, in his brilliant application of mathematical principles to astronomy. Kepler had observed that the planets moved in ellipses; Newton had shown that this had to happen, if his assumed laws of motion and gravitation were correct. Deduction and induction fitted satisfactorily. It must be said that the scientists' pride in achievement was collective; individually they were humble, and there is no reason to doubt Newton's sincerity when he said:

> I do not know what I may appear to the world; but to myself I seem to have been only like a boy, playing on the sea-shore, and diverting myself, in now and then finding a smoother pebble or a prettier shell than ordinary, while the great ocean of truth lay all undiscovered before me.
>
> J. Spence, *Anecdotes* (1820).

Scientists were not only making a contribution to knowledge; they claimed to be doing a very great service to common life and the material needs of man. Robert Boyle set out firmly the utilitarian aims of the new experimental philosophy; it would teach men to master Nature:

> Though it be but too evident, that the barren Philosophy wont to be taught in the Schools, have hitherto been found of very little use to human Life; yet if the true Principles of that fertile Science were thorowly known, consider'd and apply'd, 'tis scarce imaginable, how universal and advantagious a change they would make in the World . . . And though I presume not to judge of other Mens knowledge, yet, for my own particular, I shall not dare to think myself a true Naturalist, till my skill can make my Garden yield better Herbs and Flowers, or my Orchard better Fruit, or my fields better Corn, or my Dairy better Cheese than theirs that are strangers to Physiology.
>
> *The Usefulnesse of the Experimental Naturall Philosophy* (1663), Part II, pp. 3–4, quoted R. F. Jones, *Ancients and Moderns* (St. Louis, 1936), p. 212.

He foresaw discoveries which would be of the greatest use in the practice of medicine, and in such trades as tanning, dyeing, brewing, metal-founding. Such work would be of far more benefit to mankind than the airy and baseless speculations of Aristotle had been.

Yet there was constant care taken to show that the experimental study of nature was not a substitute for the study of theology. In fact it was an adjunct to theology, since it gave opportunities for studying the wisdom of God as it was revealed in the creation. The more men understood of nature, the more intelligently they could praise God for His wonders. Boyle in this same treatise and Sprat in his *History of the Royal Society* (1667) made a strong plea for the religious stimulus given by such a study. 'They who would deter men from the scrutiny of nature tend to deprive God of much of the glory due to him' (Boyle, *op. cit.*, Part II, p. 15). The telescope and the microscope had helped to reveal the power and providence of God in designing the creatures in His immeasurable universe. The study of material things would certainly not make men less pious. The title of John Ray's book—*The Wisdom of God manifested in the Works of the Creation* (1691)— indicates a treatise given up to showing the real unity of the natural and the divine order. Ray interpreted the significance of physical structures and processes, showing how the plan of the universe reflected the mind of God. Nothing in the natural world came about by accident. He considered, for instance, how well the structure of various animals was related to their habitat or to their methods of acquiring food: water birds were web-footed, divers were shaped for swimming under water; the woodpecker had a long tongue with which to extract insects from holes in trees and in the ground. He remarked that animals reproduced themselves in numbers which were related to their vulnerability: birds of prey, having few enemies, could afford to have only two chicks, whereas birds like pigeons had a series of families in a season. He showed that the horizontally set tails of porpoises helped them to rise quickly to the surface to breathe; a fish's vertically set tail would have been of far less use to them. Ray was certain that it was the business of man to converse with Nature:

> It may be (for ought I know, and as some Divines have thought) part of our Business and Employment in Eternity, to contemplate the Works of God. . . . And therefore those who have Leisure, Opportunity, and Abilities, to contemplate and consider any of these Creatures, if they do it not, do as it were rob God of some part of his Glory, in neglecting or slighting so eminent a Subject of it, and wherein they might have discovered so much Art, Wisdom, and Contrivance . . . Think not that any Thing he hath vouchsafed to create, is unworthy thy Cognizance, to be slighted by thee. It is Pride and Arrogance, or Ignorance and Folly in thee so to think. There is a greater depth of Art and Skill in the Structure of the meanest Insect, than thou art able for to fathom or comprehend.
>
> *The Wisdom of God manifested in the Works of the Creation* (7th ed., 1717), pp. 170–80.

Such a book as this, first published in 1691, gave science a religious sanction which was later reflected in the work of as severe a moralist as Bishop Butler.

The basis of science in England in the later seventeenth century was Baconian rather than Cartesian. The emphasis fell on a combination of scepticism and experiment. Men must jettison authority and preconceived ideas. The dogmatism with which Aristotle's pronouncements had been cited as a *ne plus ultra* was suspect; nothing was to be taken for granted :

The *Peripateticks* may as well hope to stop the current of the Tide, or (with *Xerxes*) to fetter the Ocean, as to hinder the overflowing of free Philosophy: Me-thinks, I see how all the old Rubbish must be thrown away, and the rotten buildings be overthrown, and carried away with so powerful an Inundation. These are the days that must lay a new Foundation of a more magnificent Philosophy, never to be overthrown: that will Empirically and sensibly canvass the Phaenomena of Nature, deducing the Causes of things from such Originals in Nature, as we observe are producible by Art, and the infallible demonstration of Mechanicks: and, certainly, this is the way, and no other, to build a true and permanent Philosophy.

Henry Power, *Experimental Philosophy* (1663), p. 190, quoted R. F. Jones, *Ancients and Moderns*, p. 191.

The former explanations of the world seemed speculative and barren. Scepticism was generally encouraged. Boyle, for instance, refused to accept the previous fundamentals of chemistry. He rejected the four 'elements' of earth, air, fire and water, previously thought to be the basis of all matter, because he wanted to discover elements which could not be broken down into other substances. He also rejected the alternative alchemical principles of salt, sulphur and mercury. Instead of these suppositions, men wanted to establish a body of scientifically observed facts, from which later generations could deduce the laws of Nature:

The *true* knowledge of *general Nature*, like Nature it self in its noblest *composures*, must proceed *slowly*, by degrees almost *insensible*: and what *one* Age can do in so *immense* an Undertaking as *that*, wherein all the generations of Men are concerned, can be little *more* than to remove the *Rubbish*, lay in *Materials*, and *put* things in *order* for the Building. *Our work* is to *overcome prejudices*, to *throw aside* what is *useless*, and yields no advantage for *Knowledge* or for *Life* . . . We must *seek* and *gather*, *observe* and *examine*, and *lay up* in *Bank* for the Ages that come after. *This* is the business of the *Experimental Philosopher*.

Glanvill, *op. cit.*, p. 91.

The Royal Society began in 1665 to publish communications resulting from observations and experiments. Their members had noted the presence of microscopic living organisms on blighted leaves, birds' feathers, flies' feet, fishes' scales; they had devised a hygroscope for measuring the humidity of the air; they had observed a spot on one of the belts of Jupiter. Many members published, in addition, a series of books in which their experiments were organized in significant patterns. Boyle's *New Experiments and Observations touching Cold* (1665) and his *Experiments and Considerations touching Colours* (1664) were among the most stimulating of these. The habit of making experiments was growing at the universities. John Allsop, a Sizer at St. John's College, Cambridge, recorded some of these in his commonplace book for 1685. A study was being made of the properties of air, with the assistance of the recently invented air-pump. Demonstrations were made which showed that air was necessary to preserve flame, that air was required for the transmission of sound (a watch placed in a vacuum could not be heard ticking), that not only birds and animals but flies, worms and caterpillars depended on breathing air (this surprised the spectators), that air had powers of expansion :

> An experiment whereby to proue the Air hath vis elastica. A lambs bladder was taken which was large, well dryed and very lember, being about halfe full of air, was put into the receiuer, and the pump was set on work, and as the air in the receiuer was more and more exhausted, the imprisoned air in the bladder began to swell more and more, so that before all the air was exhausted, the bladder appeared as full as if it had been blowed with a quill.

> MS. S. 17, St. John's College Library.

The invention of new apparatus and the advances made in mathematics did much to make the methodical organization of experiments possible; they could now be planned strategically, instead of being undertaken in a haphazard and unrelated manner.

Possibly the most distinguished scientific achievements of the age are to be found in the work of Newton, Boyle and Ray. Only a mathematician can properly appreciate Newton's discoveries, but the layman can see something of the results. Newton took various disparate discoveries in the realms of mechanics and astronomy and combined them into a whole which explained not only the motions of the planets but also the fall of minute bodies towards the earth. Galileo and Descartes had suggested that bodies, far from needing a push to make them continue in motion, tended to go in one direction unless they were stopped (the doctrine of inertia, generally known as Newton's First Law of Motion); and Galileo had formulated Newton's Second Law of

Motion as well. Borelli had pictured, without reference to mathematics, a system by which the planets were pulled between the attraction of the sun and a centrifugal force which made them tend to fly off at a tangent. It had been suggested that the force of gravity operated between all bodies, however large or small. Picard had succeeded in making a more accurate measurement of the radius of the earth. But a collection of miscellaneous ideas and observations, however significant they may turn out to be, does not constitute a science. It was Newton who showed how to construct dynamics as a mathematical system. Starting from a few very simple principles (the three Laws of Motion, and the inverse square law of gravitation), he was able to deduce a theory which dealt with an astonishingly wide range of astronomical problems, and which fitted the observed behaviour of the planets, the moon and the tides. He also made important contributions to the study of light. He created the differential and integral calculus (simultaneously with Leibniz, and independently of him); this has been a weapon of fundamental importance both in pure mathematics and in science.

Boyle—described as the father of chemistry—collected a great body of concrete data. He realized the importance of repeating an experiment many times before he accepted the happenings for a fact, and of keeping a detailed record of procedure and results. His view of matter was that it was composed of an enormous quantity of minute particles, the behaviour and arrangement of which determined the different characteristics of physical bodies. Crystalline structure, for instance, was governed by the different chemical combinations of these minute particles. Things were fluid when their particles touched only at some points, and could glide easily over one another. Bodies had a particular colour because their texture and their surface disposition of particles modified the way in which light was reflected from them—as velvet looked a different colour when seen from different angles. His experiments on air and fire brought him considerably nearer to modern views than had seemed possible in a century so ridden by the alchemical theories of the transmutation of substances.

John Ray laid the foundations of modern zoology and botany. He found no precise or ordered knowledge of plants and animals, and worked very hard both in the field and in libraries to achieve accurate descriptions and systems of arrangement:

He studied, corrected and collated the existing literature; he collected, identified, investigated, described and classified mammals, birds, reptiles, fishes and insects, cryptogams and all known plants; he contributed richly to the advance of geology and made observations in astronomy and physics.

C. E. Raven, *John Ray* (1942), p. 12.

Moreover, he had a genius for asking the right questions, pointing to fundamental problems—some of which have still not been answered today. What mechanism ensured that migrating birds started at the right time and arrived in the right place thousands of miles away? How was it that a bird reacted 'instinctively' to the first sight of a hawk in the sky, and gave the alarm call? How did birds know when they had laid enough eggs in any one clutch? He made vast contributions to biological knowledge, many of which were not improved on or developed until the present century.

The discoveries of such men gave their contemporaries a new view of the universe. The period marked a transition from medieval to modern thought. In science, the feeling that everything had been said gave way to the feeling that everything was still to say. Here was this almost infinite universe, ready to be explored by man, who could now begin to come to terms with the most minute and the largest things in creation. But the new science had many critics who warned against the dangers of presumption. The stigma of Puritanism on the one hand and of atheism on the other was not easy to shake off—the Royal Society attempted to deal with the latter by never admitting the chief sinner, Thomas Hobbes, to membership. In their rasher moments, some of the scientists had claimed that a new moral philosophy might be formed on the basis of the study of nature. This was felt to be highly dangerous. Moreover, the experimenters appeared to undervalue reason, and in their wholesale rejection of Aristotle they were apparently setting matter above spirit. Peter Gunning, Bishop of Chichester, and Henry Stubbe, a doctor of medicine, attacked their presuppositions continually. The most comprehensive and intelligent criticism came from Meric Casaubon of Canterbury. He felt it was a serious error to call humanistic learning useless and scientific useful. The scientists were operating on a materialistic standard, and thinking of man's happiness in terms of his comfort and convenience, not in terms of his soul.

Concentration on the natural world would lead to neglect of the spiritual world. Casaubon spoke as one of the Ancients, sure that the religion and education of the past had done more to civilize man than science could ever hope to do. This attitude gave rise to many literary attacks on the new science, as a body of knowledge devoid of real judgment. These Moderns failed to see what was really important; they were using tradesman's standards to judge between the value of naturalism and humanism. Swift's attacks in *A Tale of a Tub* and in *Gulliver's Travels*, and Pope's in the *Essay on Man*, had been preceded by much satire in the period between 1660 and 1700, of which Eachard's account of the virtuoso, in his *Some Observations upon the Answer* (1671), is a fair example:

> The small Ingenioso or experimenteer; who having perhaps blown a glass, seen a paper-mill or a bell run, that knows within two houses where the best chymist in town dwells; and dined once where one of the Royal Society should have been; and looked another time into the door at Gresham, when the company was sitting: He comes down with a receipt of a miraculous sort of gingerbread, with a little pot of double refined jessamy, and a box-full of specific perfumed lozenges, and a little licensed essence of orange, and he calls the minister and the chief of the parish together, and he falls to his ingenious tricks and operations, and freezes a dish to the stool by the fire side; sets up half a dozen tobacco pipes, and then makes them fall into a mathematical astonishing figure: After this he desires to withdraw, and puts claret and beer together, and brings them out unmixt . . . He wonders . . . to what purpose is it to preach to people, and go about to save them, without a telescope, and glass for fleas.
>
> *Works* (1774), vol. I, pp. 264–5.

THE BACKGROUND OF CRITICISM

Neither literature nor criticism was the exclusive possession of professionals in this period. Gentlemen amateurs took a great interest in literary problems, not only patronizing less-well-off writers, but writing extensively themselves. The Duke of Buckingham, the Earls of Roscommon, Rochester and Mulgrave, Sir William D'Avenant, John Evelyn, Sir Robert Howard and Sir Charles Sedley all had works to their credit, and all took part in the kind of literary discussion that is reflected in Dryden's *An Essay of Dramatick Poesie* (1668). They interested themselves in the theory of criticism: Roscommon translated Horace's *De Arte Poetica* (1680), and composed an *Essay on Translated Verse* (1684); Mulgrave commended Boileau's doctrines to the public in his *Essay upon Poetry* (1682). The returning exiles—including Evelyn, Cowley, D'Avenant, Waller—brought with them a great affection for contemporary French culture. Luckily they were in contact not only with strict neo-classicism, but also with the liberalizing influences of Corneille and Saint-Évremond, who did not adhere to the worship of the Ancients and the Rules, but inaugurated a more historical and psychological method of criticism. (*See* J. W. Atkins, *English Literary Criticism: 17th and 18th Centuries*, 1951, chap. I.) When Saint-Évremond was exiled he spent long periods in England, in close contact with Buckingham, Hobbes, Waller, Cowley, and was often to be found discussing literature at Will's coffee-house. The Royal Society took a strong interest in the development and purification of the English language. The commoners who made a name by writing, such as Dryden, Wycherley, Shadwell, were taken up by literary courtiers, and given a wide circle of contacts, and an easy entrée into court circles. Dryden said that greatness was easy of access, and conversation free. London and Westminster covered a small area at the time, and men who had similar cultural standards could meet frequently for the exchange of ideas. Literary standards were a matter of concern to a large number of men within the capital.

Almost all the writers discussed in this book—with the exception of the enthusiasts—had contacts with this wide London group of men. They belonged to a live society, that had a heritage of the humanities as well as a strong interest in the new philosophy. Whatever was written for this public was certain to be discussed up and down the town, both before and after publication. Butler's *Hudibras* engrossed the attention of the court as soon as the first book came out, and the King walked about quoting couplets from it with great delight. Writers were strongly aware of the taste of this polite and socially distinguished society for which they were writing, and endeavoured to conform to it. The 'mob of gentlemen who wrote with ease' expected politeness, smoothness, finish. The products of creative energy must be ordered and perspicuous, though they must certainly not be dull. They admired the perfection of glaze on Waller's poetry, when he was writing on the late improvements in St. James's Park:

> Methinks I hear the musick in the boats,
> And the loud ECHO which returns the Notes. . . .
> Beneath, a shole of silver fishes glides,
> And plays about the gilded barges' sides:
> The Ladies, angling in the chrystal lake,
> Feast on the waters with the prey they take:
> At once victorious with their lines, and eyes,
> They make the fishes, and the men, their prize.

> Waller, *Works* (1744), pp. 130–1.

But they could also appreciate the hard hitting of Dryden against Shaftesbury in *The Medall*:

> Next this, (How wildly will Ambition steer!)
> A Vermin wriggling in th'Usurper's ear,
> Bart'ring his venal wit for sums of gold,
> He cast himself into the Saint-like mould;
> Groan'd, sigh'd, and pray'd, while Godliness was gain,
> The lowdest bagpipe of the Squeaking train.

> *Poems* (ed. Sargeaunt, 1913). p. 84.

They demanded entertainment, but it had to be on a reasonably intelligent level.

Correctness was to be balanced by the fire and power demanded by Longinus, whose treatise on the sublime, translated by Boileau, was now beginning to be valued. Energy was felt to be of great importance —or wit, as it was then called. (For the complex of meanings attached to this word the reader should consult E. N. Hooker, 'Pope on Wit', in *The Seventeenth Century from Bacon to Pope*, Stanford, 1951.) The greatest genius was lively and fruitful, possessed of a great soul, a '*vividia vis animi*'. David Abercromby in his *Discourse of Wit* (1685) emphasized that 'we never write wittily, but when our Imagination is exalted to a certain degree of heat, destructive to our cold dulness'. An invigorating spark was a pre-requisite of great writing; and this spark must not be quenched by the imposition of copy-book rules. Real genius evolved its own rules as it wrote, and created the standards which would form the taste of critics in the future— as Homer and Virgil themselves had done. As Sir William Temple put it:

> The Truth is, there is something in the *Genius* of Poetry too Libertine to be confined to so many Rules; and whoever goes about to subject it to such Constraints loses both its Spirit and Grace, which are ever Native, and never learnt, even of the best Masters. 'Tis as if, to make excellent Honey, you should cut off the Wings of your Bees. . . . They must range through Fields as well as Gardens, choose such Flowers as they please, and by Proprieties and Scents they only know and distinguish. They must work up their Cells with Admirable Art, extract their Honey with infinite Labour, and sever it from the Wax with such Distinction and Choyce as belongs to none but themselves to perform or to judge.
>
> Temple, *Of Poetry* (1690). *Critical Essays of the Seventeenth Century* (ed. J. E. Spingarn, 1908), vol. III, pp. 83–4.

There was need of art, but not of a cold application of the rules. The test of great writing was not its obedience to the critics, but its power to move the reader, as Horace had insisted. The shaping spirit of genius must find its own true form in each work of art.

Towards the end of the century, however, the city section of the public rebelled against the taste of the court, and demanded a literature which was useful and earnest rather than witty and energetic. Defoe, in his poem *The Pacificator* (1700), pleaded for a union between the men of sense and the men of wit—a demand which was partly met in the writings of Addison and Steele. Though Locke took no active part in this controversy, his sympathies clearly lay with the men of sense. The influence of the men of sense increased, partly because the public was replacing the patron as a source of income for the writer. Eighteenth-century literature became more middle-class in tone, blending sentiment and common sense.

The material of art was Nature; but Nature was a portmanteau word at the time. At its best level, the statement meant that art was concerned with truth—the permanent truths about man and the universe. It could mean straightforward 'realism'—a depiction of the scenes of London life. In the strict neo-classic sense it could mean adherence to the rules deduced from the practice of the Ancients. It could mean Reason; this concept tended to degenerate into common sense. In general there was a movement away from the Rules (which had been concerned in the main with the writing of epic and tragedy, forms less frequently employed in this period in England) towards a realization that the art of the Ancients had embodied Nature in ways which were admirable for their time, but which did not constitute a direct pattern for present-day methods of embodying Nature. Times had changed, and methods must; what should be imitated was the spirit informing the Ancients. There was the beginning of an appreciation of the fact that formal standards and practice varied, and should vary, from age to age, and from nation to nation; a view which was stated in Sprat's *History of the Royal Society* (1667). The French precepts of Rapin and Boileau should no more be preached as authoritative than those of the Romans. Sir Robert Howard, despite his use of rhyme in *The Indian Queen* (1665), attacked the practice as an unfortunate piece of French imitation which was unsuited to English drama, long before Dryden tired of it. Similarly he attacked the unities. Taste, not the rules, should arbitrate in literary matters. Dryden became the greatest exponent of this critical creed.

Not all the critics in this period were moving in such a civilized direction. Thomas Rymer showed the appalling depths to which the doctrine of Nature as reason or common sense could subside. He thought 'taste' was the mark of a quack; common sense was the sole test of literary merit. He criticized in detail plays by Shakespeare and Beaumont and Fletcher. He thought that many of Shakespeare's scenes would be far more telling without any words at all. He thought Beaumont and Fletcher showed a shocking ignorance of the manners of polite society in *The Maid's Tragedy*. He mildly approved the moral of *Othello*:

> First, this may be a caution to all Maidens of Quality how, without their Parents consent, they run away with Blackamoors . . .
> Secondly, This may be a warning to all good Wives that they look well to their Linnen.
>
> Rymer, *A Short View of Tragedy* (1692), ed. Spingarn *op. cit*, vol II, p. 221.

But he thought the play was totally marred by the glaring improbabilities of the plot and characters. Shakespeare had made havoc of his theme: 'the tragical part is plainly none other than a Bloody Farce'. It is heartening to know that such views were strongly criticized by Dryden and John Dennis.

Two controversies which seemed very important at the time need only brief treatment here: one because so little progress was made in the argument, the other because, though famous, it is hardly relevant to the state of criticism at the time. The first concerned the question of the relationship between morality and art, which was treated on a very simple level. Towards the end of the century there was a strong movement, championed by Jeremy Collier and Sir Richard Blackmore, to reject immorality outright as unsuitable material for art. The only interesting contribution to this controversy came from Wolseley, who in his preface to Rochester's *Valentinian* (1685) said that the excellence of a poet depended not on his material but on his treatment of it; creative genius could perfectly well use immorality as its subject and produce a work of art. The second controversy was that of the Ancients and Moderns, and was an offshoot of the movement to exalt the new philosophy above humanism. Sir William Temple, in his *Essay upon Ancient and Modern Learning* (1690), defended the Ancients' claims to greatness against the attacks of the Moderns. Unfortunately he based some of his arguments on the authenticity of the so-called *Epistles of Phalaris*. Richard Bentley had no difficulty in proving that these were not an authentic production of the Ancients. The controversy now takes its proper place in the general pattern of the rejection of authority during the period.

Much more interesting was the growth of historical and scholarly techniques in estimating the literature of the past. Edward Phillips, in his *Theatrum Poetarum* (1675), was aware of the uncouth state of the language in the time of Chaucer, yet he thought that both Chaucer and the Elizabethans had lasting excellencies and deserved to be read. What was once of real value must be so still: the fashions of the present time were no real criterion of worth. 'Custom and Opinion oft times take so deep a root that Judgment hath not free power to act.' John Dennis was aware of the part played by the conventions of the time and place in which works of art were composed. In his *Impartial Critic* (1693) he wisely attacked Rymer's attempt to force Greek conventions on modern English drama. England had a religion and customs which were

entirely different from those of ancient Greece, and the Greek Chorus
could not possibly be acclimatized on the English stage. Dryden put
this recognition of the importance of the social background of a work
of art to very good account when he was comparing the satirical scope
of Persius with that of Horace. He pointed out that Persius lived in the
time of Nero, and had gross vices to satirize, Horace in the more
civilized times of Augustus, when his target could only be follies and
absurdities. Similarly, he explained the development of French and
English drama along different lines in terms of the different characteristics of the two nations. These trends in criticism were reinforced by the
kind of scholarly work that Richard Bentley was doing, emending
corruptions in texts, annotating historical, geographical and anthro-
pological difficulties, and starting to compile a dictionary. The Moderns
might be scorned by Swift for their apparent pedantry, but they were
making a genuine contribution to the understanding of the literature of
the past. Criticism was beginning to look at literature in terms of its
environment, and to acknowledge the processes of change in tradition
and culture.

For modern readers of Restoration literature, probably the most
significant critical development is the changes in the style of prose and
poetry which were consolidated in the period. A variety of influences
combined to discredit the ornamental Ciceronian style of prose used
by John Donne or Sir Philip Sidney, and the tortuous metaphysical
conceits of the earlier seventeenth-century poets. The movement
towards the plain style in preaching dated from the previous century.
The arguments used ran roughly like this: if you do not want to teach
men, what are you doing in the pulpit? If you want to, why do you not
speak so as to be understood? The ornate style, intended at first for
educated audiences, had spread because of its prestige to parish
churches where it was entirely unsuitable. Not only Puritan preachers,
but Church of England divines like John Wilkins supported the plea for
a style devoid of rhetorical tricks many years before the Restoration.
The styles of Tillotson and South were the norm, where sense was more
apparent than decoration. John Eachard was attacking the few who had
not amended their ways, and who still adhered to the elaborate figures
of speech of an earlier age. He professed admiration for their art and
ingenuity:

It seems also not very easy, for a man in his sermon, to learn his parishioners how to dissolve gold; of what, and how the stuff is made. . . . Suppose then, that he takes for his text that of St. Matthew, *Repent ye, for the kingdom of God is at hand.* Now, tell me, Sir, do you not perceive the gold to be in a dismal fear, to curl and quiver at the first reading of these words? It must come in thus. The blots and blurs of your sins, must be taken out by the aqua-fortis of your tears: to which aqua-fortis, if you put a fifth part of sal-ammoniac, and set them on a gentle heat, it makes aqua-regia, which dissolves gold. And now 'tis out. Wonderful are the things that are to be done by the help of metaphors and similitudes.

Works (1774), vol. I, pp. 50–1.

The views of the Restoration period on the ideal style in preaching were summed up in Glanvill's *Essay concerning Preaching* (1678): plainness and clarity, free from vulgarity and from the abuses of eloquence.

Another influence which encouraged a plainer way of writing was that of the new philosophy. Bacon, the father of the experimental movement, had been Senecan rather than Ciceronian in style, curt and pithy. Hobbes, the originator of the mechanical philosophy in England, made a strong plea in his *Leviathan* for denotation rather than connotation in the allotted significance of words:

The Light of humane minds is Perspicuous Words, but by exact definitions first snuffed, and purged from ambiguity.

Leviathan, chap. V.

He was against the deceits of metaphor in expression. In 1664 the Royal Society set up a committee for 'improving the English tongue', with Dryden and Evelyn among its members. Its deliberations came to nothing, but their trend can be seen from Sprat's *History of the Royal Society*. This contains the classic plea for purging style of the abuses of rhetoric:

To return back to the primitive purity, and shortness, when men deliver'd so many *things*, almost in an equal number of *words*. They have extracted from all their members, a close, naked, natural way of speaking; positive expressions; clear senses; a native easiness; bringing all things as near the Mathematical plainness, as they can: and preferring the language of Artizans, Countrymen, and Merchants, before that, of Wits, or Scholars.

History of the Royal Society (1667). p. 113.

In his *Life and Writings of Cowley* (1668) Sprat praised Cowley for writing in precisely the familiar style desired: 'a natural easiness and unaffected grace where nothing seems to be studied yet everything is extraordinary'.

The long sojourn of many of the literary men in France was another factor in the simplification of style. French was by nature a more lucid language, and a demand for something of this perspicuity in English was made by the exiles on their return. Moreover, the run of popular pamphleteering that accompanied the struggle between King and Parliament in the forties had brought home to a variety of writers the necessity of expressing themselves so that they could be quickly understood. These factors combined to encourage the creation of a style which considered the convenience of the reader—a style that conveyed clear ideas in conversational language, a practical style that reflected the writer's grasp on reality. Later in the period it was claimed that the English language had reached its peak of development, because of the interest taken in letters by polite society.

Poetry was likely to suffer from this restrictive attitude to language. Mulgrave's *Essay upon Poetry* showed the new standards that were being advocated. The aim for the lyric was a combination of the natural and the correct:

> Th'expression easy, and the fancy high,
> Yet that not seem to creep, nor this to fly;
> No words transpos'd, but in such just cadance,
> As, though hard wrought, may seem the effect of chance.

In writing odes, though the poet is to be fired with passion,

> Though all appears in heat and fury done,
> The Language still must soft and easy run.

He was against figures of speech in poetic drama:

> *Figures* of *Speech*, which Poets think so fine,
> Art's needless Varnish to make Nature shine,
> Are all but Paint upon a beauteous Face,
> And in Descriptions only claim a place.

> Mulgrave, *Essay upon Poetry* (1682), ed. Spingarn,
> *op. cit.*, vol. II, pp. 288-91.

Sir William Temple commented on the deficiencies of such an ideal for the language of poetry:

> Besides these two Veins brought in to supply the Defects of the modern Poetry, much Application has been made to the Smoothness of Language or Style, which has been at the best but the Beauty of Colouring in a Picture, and can never make a good one without Spirit and Strength. ... The *French* Wits have for this last Age been in a manner wholly turned to the Refinement of their Language, and indeed with such Success that it can hardly be excelled, and runs equally through their Verse and their Prose. The same Vein has been likewise much Cultivated in our modern *English* Poetry. . . . with what Success, I leave to be judged by such as consider it in the former Heights and the present Declines both of Power and of Honour.
>
> Temple, *Of Poetry* (1690), ed. Spingarn, *ibid.*, vol III, pp. 102–3.

The position of poetry seemed to be in danger, particularly when so many complaints were being made against the style of Shakespeare. Rymer was horrified by his 'bombast circumstance'. Dryden found faults in his manner of expression: 'He often obscures his meaning by his words, and sometimes makes it unintelligible.' It was a bad habit in Shakespeare to coin new words and phrases, and to twist a word from a normal to an abnormal use. The ideal style for dramatic poetry, according to Dryden, was one characterized by 'purity of phrase, clearness of conception and expression, boldness maintained to majesty, significancy and sound of words . . . justly elevated' (*Essays*, ed. W. P. Ker, 1900, vol. I, p. 248). Words went by quickly on the stage, and the dramatist's first aim must be clarity. The limitations of this view can be seen by inspecting Dryden's versions of the plays of Shakespeare.

Dryden distinguished, however, between the style of drama and the style of epic. The style of epic should be more lofty, since it was not concerned with strong passions, or with dialogue, which demanded a greater degree of naturalness. The circumstances of their respective audiences differed; an epic was read in the study by someone who had leisure to digest it:

> There an author may beautify his sense by the boldness of his expression, which if we understand not fully at the first, we may dwell upon it till we find the secret force and excellence.
>
> *Ibid.*, vol II, pp. 165–6.

Dryden emphasized that only a man who had a taste for epic should pronounce on its style; it was impossible to appreciate the details if one disliked the genre. He pointed out that the practice of Homer, Virgil and Milton justified the use of the hardest metaphors and the strongest hyperboles:

> I will presume for once to tell them, that the boldest strokes of poetry, when they are managed artfully, are those which most delight the reader.
>
> *Ibid.*, vol II, p. 183.

He blamed the French for being frightened of using imagery in the epic; the result was that they had 'unsinewed' their poetry. In his justification of the lofty style in epic, Dryden was drawing on a wide variety of critical sanctions: the neo-classic doctrine of the Kinds; the practice of the authorities, ancient and modern; the circumstances, the practical differences between reading and playgoing; and personal taste. These blend into a valid and personal defence, not only representative of the different trends in the age, but also characteristic of Dryden at his best.

Dryden was not simply a better critic than any of his contemporaries; he was one of the great English critics. Anyone who reads his essays today is immediately conscious of a thinking mind, tackling literary problems with honesty and vigour, of a catholic response to literature, and of a width of practical experience in creative writing. He was essentially a free inquirer into the practice of art. His ideas were expressed in an easy, vivid and persuasive style. Like Corneille, his model in preface-writing, he spoke as a working poet and dramatist. Each preface was concerned with the immediate problems raised by the work of art which it preceded. Any principle relevant to those problems was discussed, but Dryden never attempted a systematic exposition of all his critical theories in isolation. The points were handled discursively, as they arose. It might seem that this method would create a disorganized impression in the reader, but in fact the impression made by the essays is one of self-consistency and synthesis. The same vigorous mind can be seen at work throughout.

His mind was open, and his judgments were wise. He knew the limits of the poet's art. He knew that a poet needed the power of invention, that he had to study the practice of his predecessors, that he must have judgment to criticize and improve on his own efforts, that he must have perfect control over his diction and numbers; yet he was aware that all these were not enough. They were a necessary basis, but very often the best turns of phrase were given, not wrought. When he was admiring a phrase of Virgil's, he commented:

> This was happiness, the former might be only judgement: this was the *curiosa felicitas*, which Petronius attributes to Horace; it is the pencil thrown luckily full upon the horse's mouth, to express the foam which the painter with all his skill could not perform without it. These hits of words a true poet often finds, as I may say, without seeking; but he knows their value when he finds them, and is infinitely pleased.
>
> *Ibid.*, vol. II, p. 151.

He knew that such effects could never be obtained by correction, and that a man who was for ever tinkering would drive all the life out of his poem. In the same way, he knew the limits of the reader's response. The public had to learn to like a truly original work. When it was first published, the greatest poetry always came as something of a disconcerting experience to the reader. Gradually it insinuated itself into the liking of the reader:

> The more he studies it, the more it grows upon him; every time he takes it up, he discovers some new graces in it.
>
> *Ibid.*, vol. II, p. 225.

According to this theory, Milton's *Paradise Lost* would one day achieve the admiration it deserved.

Reason played a great part in Dryden's judgments. Without falling into Rymer's mistake of using pure common sense as his standard, Dryden contrived to examine many artistic questions by the light of nature. In his *Essay of Dramatick Poesie* (1668), as Neander, he deprecated the declamations of contemporary French drama, in which the hero's passions were poured out a hundred lines at a time. An interchange of short speeches was more natural in moments of passion, and would be more likely to move the audience. He thought the French were wrong to despise tragi-comedy; it was not true to say that humour

was completely unwelcome after a serious and pathetic scene, for
contrarieties set each other off, and men were refreshed by change, and
relieved from tension. He pointed out absurdities created by the
doctrine of the unities, one of which was the assembly of an unlikely
collection of people in one place. But when, later on in the essay, he
passed from criticism of the French to praise of the English tradition in
the theatre, his reason was enriched by an imaginative response to the
plays. His estimate of Ben Jonson was sensitive and just:

> A most severe judge of himself . . . One cannot say he wanted wit, but
> rather that he was frugal of it . . . He managed his strength to more ad-
> vantage than any who preceded him. . . . Humour was his proper sphere.
>
> *Ibid.*, vol. I, pp. 81–2.

But when he came to speak of Shakespeare, it was with an emotion
stronger than sympathy:

> He was the man who of all modern, and perhaps ancient poets, had
> the largest and most comprehensive soul. All the images of Nature were
> still present to him, and he drew them, not laboriously, but luckily; when
> he describes anything, you more than see it, you feel it too.
>
> *Ibid.*, vol. I, pp. 79–80.

He felt that Shakespeare gave him the best opportunity, among the
moderns, for fulfilling the most important function of the critic—that of
commenting on the virtues and graces of authors so that others could
appreciate them. Some critics had tried to show their own worth by
finding fault, but in reality

> the chiefest part of [criticism] is, to observe those excellencies which
> should delight a reasonable reader.
>
> *Ibid.*, vol. I, p. 179.

This could not be done by a critic who lacked feeling, imaginative
insight and taste.

Dryden's own practice can be judged by the standards he described.
His appreciations of the beauties of ancient and modern writers were
genuinely illuminating. In an age which found Chaucer dry and old-
fashioned, he could see the excellence of Chaucer's character-drawing,

and his gift for pathos. Unlike Ovid, Chaucer could reject, in a moving scene such as the death of Arcite, anything that detracted from the dignity of the subject. His pilgrims were brilliantly conceived, all true to human nature, yet most delicately distinguished from one another; universal, yet particular. Each told a tale perfectly suited to his individuality. Dryden showed equal insight when discussing the character of Shakespeare's Caliban; such a person might seem unnatural, but Shakespeare had made him entirely plausible, with

> all the discontents and malice of a witch, and of a devil . . . the dejectedness of a slave is likewise given him, and the ignorance of one bred up in a desert island . . . His language is as hobgoblin as his person.
>
> *Ibid.*, vol. I, pp. 219–20.

He perceived that Aeneas was a hero who could justly be admired. His quality of piety included 'not only devotion to the gods, but filial love, and tender affection to relations of all sorts'. He was not merely dutiful, but moved by love. He was no second-rate champion, for, though he was not a bravo, he showed great courage in his battle with Turnus. He had been accused of being 'a St. Swithin hero, always raining'. But he wept for compassion, on seeing the portraits of his dead friends, in Carthage; for Palinurus, untimely lost; and in fear for the future of his people. Such a hero was not the dutiful milksop outlined by his detractors. In most of these criticisms the remarks are scattered over a series of pages, but in his appreciation of Theocritus, Dryden's method can be seen in its entirety. It is, moreover, one of the passages in which he shows real discrimination:

> That which distinguishes Theocritus from all other poets, both Greek and Latin, and which raises him even above Virgil in his *Eclogues*, is the inimitable tenderness of his passions, and the natural expression of them in words so becoming of a pastoral. A simplicity shines through all he writes: he shows his art and learning, by disguising both. His shepherds never rise above their country education in their complaints of love: there is the same difference betwixt him and Virgil, as there is betwixt Tasso's *Aminta* and the *Pastor Fido* of Guarini. Virgil's shepherds are too well read in the philosophy of Epicurus and of Plato, and Guarini's seem to have been bred in courts; but Theocritus and Tasso have taken theirs from cottages and plains. It was said of Tasso, in relation to his similitudes, *mai esce del bosco*: that he never departed from the woods; that

is, all his comparisons were taken from the country. The same may be said of our Theocritus: he is softer than Ovid; he touches the passions more delicately, and performs all this out of his own fond, without diving into the arts and sciences for a supply. Even his Doric dialect has an incomparable sweetness in its clownishness, like a fair shepherdess in her country russet, talking in a Yorkshire tone.

Ibid., vol. I, p. 265.

Dryden's mastery of the techniques of literary appreciation makes it difficult to remember that he was their first serious practitioner in English.

His manner was admirably adapted to the literary essay. His tone was civilized and generous, his style lucid, conversational and picturesque. He avoided any appearance of laying down the law; he argued gently with the reader, from the same level. He was continually slipping in the modest phrase which emphasized his undictatorial nature—'But, after all, to speak impartially. . . . 'Tis worth our consideration a little. . . . I write not this with the least intention to undervalue the other parts of poetry . . . I do not dispute the preference of Tragedy. . . . Ought they not rather, in modesty, to doubt of their own judgments . . .' He was inquiring, investigating, trying to reach a fair judgment. But he was by no means tentative; he could pronounce vigorously and unforgettably, in a sudden lively image:

Nothing but Nature can give a sincere pleasure; where that is not imitated, 'tis grotesque painting; the fine woman ends in a fish's tail.

Ibid., vol. II, p. 161.

Whereas poems which are produced by the vigour of imagination only have a gloss upon them at the first which time wears off, the works of judgement are like the diamond; the more they are polished, the more lustre they receive.

Ibid., vol. II, p. 225.

[The satire] of Horace was a pleasant cure, with all the limbs preserved entire; and, as our mountebanks tell us in their bills, without keeping the patient within-doors for a day.

Ibid., vol II, p. 94.

Perhaps his chief virtue as a critic was that he judged by taste and
reason, not by the Rules; but much of his attraction for the modern
reader lies in the quality of his own prose.

This period seems to be the first in which the reader can feel at all
well acquainted with the personalities of the time. In earlier periods
there are many facts available, out of which a composite historical
picture can be made of, say, the life of Sir Philip Sidney or Robert
Greene; and there are occasional survivals of more intimate documents, such as the Paston letters, or the Book of Margery Kempe. Not
until the later seventeenth century is there available the wealth of
diaries, autobiographies and memoirs which preserve the authentic
flavour of a wide group of personalities. The richest document in the
period is undoubtedly the diary kept by Samuel Pepys in shorthand
from 1660 until 1669, but there are many other highly rewarding
survivals: the diaries of John Evelyn and Sir John Reresby, the
spiritual autobiographies of Bunyan and Baxter, the Life and Times of
Clarendon, Gilbert Burnet, Anthony à Wood, the Lives of John
Aubrey and of Isaak Walton, the full-scale biographies of Sprat
describing Cowley, and of Lucy Hutchinson and the Duchess of
Newcastle describing their respective husbands, the Verney Papers, the
familiar letters of Rochester, Evelyn, Pepys, Dryden and John Locke.

These and other documents provide a close-up of men in this age
which is invaluable. Locke can be seen picking flowers in the Botanical
Gardens at Oxford and preserving them carefully between the Latin
exercises written by his pupils at Christ Church, or prescribing for the
illnesses of his friends, or filling in his amazingly neat and highly
organized commonplace books from his very wide reading. Evelyn can
be seen commenting on the Queen's 'languishing and excellent eyes',
and her unfortunate teeth which stuck out, or holding the candle while
Mr. Cooper drew the King's head from life to make a design for the
new coinage, or catching sight of Grinling Gibbons behind the window
of a poor cottage in Deptford, and bringing him to the King's notice,
or finding *Hamlet* old-fashioned and admiring the scenic effects of *The*

Indian Queen, or exploring Norwich with Sir Thomas Browne as his guide.

Clarendon gave vivid glimpses of the men of his time: of John Earle, the untidy scholar:

> No Man was more negligent in his Dress, and Habit, and Mien; no Man more wary, and cultivated, in his Behaviour, and Discourse; insomuch as He had the greater Advantage when he was known, by promising so little before he was known.
>
> *The Life of Edward Earl of Clarendon, written by himself* (1760), vol. I, p. 40.

and of Thomas Hobbes, who did not discuss his ideas with other men:

> It hath bin alwaies a lamentation amongst Mr *Hobbes* his Friends, that he spent too much time in thinking, and too little in exercising those thoughts in the company of other Men of the same, or of as good faculties; for want whereof his natural constitution, with age, contracted such a morosity, that doubting and contradicting Men were never grateful to him.
>
> *A Brief View of the Dangerous and pernicious Errors . . . in . . . Leviathan* (1676), p. 3.

John Aubrey's notes on Hobbes are a delight:

> In his old age he was very bald, which claymed a veneration; yet within dore he used to study, and sitt bare-headed: and sayd he never tooke cold in his head but that the greatest trouble was to keepe-off the Flies from pitching on the baldness . . .
> He had always bookes of prick-song lyeing on his Table: e.g. of H. Lawes &c. Songs: which at night when he was a bed, & the dores made fast, & was sure no body heard him, he sang *aloud*, (not that he had a very good voice) but to cleare his pipes: he did beleeve it did his Lunges good, & conduced much to prolong his life.
>
> MS. Aubrey, Bodleian Library, quoted D. Nichol Smith, *Characters from the Histories and Memoirs of the Seventeenth Century* (1918), pp. 184–5.

Burnet showed Charles II telling stories about himself until he had bored the whole court:

He went over these in a very graceful manner, but so often, and so copiously, that all those who had been long accustomed to them grew weary of them, and when he entered on those stories they usually withdrew: so that he often began them in a full audience, and before he had done there were not above four or five left about him: which drew a severe censure from Wilmot, earl of Rochester. He said he wondered to see a man have so good a memory as to repeat the same story without losing the least circumstance, and yet not remember that he had told it to the same persons the very day before. This made him fonder of strangers, for they hearkened to all his often repeated stories, and went away as in a rapture at such an uncommon condescension in a King.

History of My Own Time (ed. O. Airy, 1897), vol. II, p. 469.

All these, however, are overtopped by Pepys's diary, faithfully kept in Thomas Shelton's system of shorthand from the eyes of his household. Evelyn, his nearest competitor, was too prudent a man: he gave an excellent picture of his day, but he wrote down nothing that he would not wish to see published under his name. Pepys's diary is a masterpiece because he was completely truthful, in love with living, and in touch with so many of the currents of public affairs and with all sorts and conditions of men. His curiosity was inexhaustible, and his eye for detail as piercing as Defoe's. The reader becomes fascinated by his rise from obscurity and poverty in the service of his cousin, Edward Montagu, to his position as the indispensable Clerk of the Acts who kept a firm and expert hand on all naval affairs. Everything that affected Pepys went into the diary: his quarrels with his wife, his improvements to the house, the presents people gave him for services rendered, his playgoing, the current scandals, his own casual affairs with women, repented and repeated, the Fire of London, his good resolutions and how they were broken, his petty annoyances and every-day delights—all in glorious profusion, for his own satisfaction. It was a great grief to him when his eyesight finally deteriorated so much that he had to give up writing his diary.

He gave an unsurpassed picture of public affairs, great and small, in his day, all the more vivid for being interspersed with his own activities. He went with Montagu to The Hague with the expedition that fetched the King and the Duke of York back to England, and made sure of seeing the sights of the Low Countries while they waited for fair weather. He fired a cannon himself in the King's honour, 'but, holding my head too much over the gun, I had almost spoiled my right eye'. He listened to the King's stories of his escape from Worcester, at which he nearly wept, and discussed optics with Dr. Scarborough, and was kindly addressed by the Duke of York, with promises of future favour. He watched the Mayor of Dover giving the King a Bible when he landed, and heard the King say 'it was the thing that he loved above all things in the world'. This was recounted without irony, for the King had succeeded in impressing Pepys as a sober man. Five years later, Pepys showed what it was like to live through the Plague in London, with the Bills of Mortality rising every week, and the carts carrying the dead away even by daylight when the numbers grew too large to be handled by night. He gave a superb impression of the Great Fire, with the bustle of people trying to get their goods away to safety, and the city officials trying hard to blow up enough houses to make a gap that the fire could not bridge. Pepys took all his treasures to Bethnal Green, in a cart provided by the wife of one of his colleagues, riding in the cart in his night-gown; and put the rest of his household goods on a lighter near Tower Hill. It was made more difficult by the absence of his servant Mercer, who had gone to help her own mother with her goods, and by the dinner which was only the cold left-overs from the day before. He buried his wine and his parmesan cheese in the garden. The fire was an amazing spectacle:

> When we could endure no more upon the water, we to a little alehouse on the Bankside, over against the Three Cranes, and there staid till it was dark almost, and saw the fire grow; and, as it grew darker, appeared more and more, and in corners and upon steeples, and between churches and houses, as far as we could see up the hill of the City, in a most horrid malicious bloody flame, not like the fine flame of an ordinary fire. Barbary and her husband away before us. We staid till, it being darkish, we saw the fire as only one entire arch of fire from this to the other side the bridge, and in a bow up the hill for an arch of above a mile long: it made me weep to see it. The churches, houses and all on fire and flaming at once; and a horrid noise the flames made, and the cracking of houses at their ruine. So home with a sad heart.

> 2nd Sept., 1666. *Diary* (ed. Wheatley, 1893–9), vol. V, p. 421.

The fire reached the bottom of the lane where Pepys's house stood, but then slackened off. His feet were almost burned, walking through the town over the embers, and he was longing to buy some clean clothes to change into, and have a chance to wash off the filth of the past few days, and start on the tedious process of clearing up.

He took a great interest in the behaviour of the nobility, and was often shocked not only by their vices but by their lack of decorum. He saw the Duke and Duchess of York at the Cockpit, watching the King's players act *Claracilla*, and was disturbed by their 'unnatural dalliances there, before the whole world, such as kissing of hands, and leaning upon one another'. He commented on the unfortunate levity of the royal party at the launching of the *Royal Catherine*, when they teased the Maids of Honour who had been seasick on the way to Woolwich. He recorded court gossip about the current positions of the King's mistresses, and the favour shown to the Duke of Monmouth, and curious incidents like that at the court ball where 'a child was dropped by one of the ladies in dancing, but nobody knew who, it being taken up by somebody in their handkercher'. Next morning all the Ladies of Honour appeared on duty punctually, to show that they were not responsible, but one of them was taken ill in the afternoon, and the incident fastened on her—unjustly, as Pepys said later. But the story about the child was true:

> The King had it in his closett a week after, and did dissect it; and making great sport of it, said that, in his opinion, it must have been a month and three hours old; and that, whatever others think, he hath the greatest loss (it being a boy, as he says), that hath lost a subject by the business.
>
> 17th Feb., 1663. *Ibid.*, vol. III, p. 44.

He became fascinated by his work at the Navy Office, and took great pains to make himself expert. He studied mathematics in order to measure timber, and got up early to learn the multiplication tables. He learned how to tell good rope from old stuff disguised with a new covering of hemp, and how to select good timber for masts. He had himself taken round a number of ships and learned about their construction. He went into the system of contracts, and discovered that some merchants had a monopoly of supplies, and were supplying inferior goods at high prices. He found that the Governors of the Chatham Chest for disabled seamen were misappropriating the funds.

He fought for years against the entirely inadequate allocation of money for the Navy. He devised a filing system in his office, transcribed documents and kept memoranda. He met merchants to discuss prices, and was constantly inspecting the shipyards. He was a highly capable Civil Servant. The climax of his career within the period of the diary came when he successfully defended the Navy Office against the charges of neglect made when the Dutch had sailed up the Medway. At the bar of the House he made an admirable defence of the conduct of his office, which surprised him, for he had thought he would be frightened:

> I began our defence most acceptably and smoothly, and continued at it without any hesitation or losse, but with full scope, and all my reason free about me, as if it had been at my own table, from that time till past three in the afternoon.
>
> 5th March, 1668. *Ibid.*, vol. VII, p. 350.

Everyone congratulated him, including the King; and admired his capacity for argument and his great eloquence.

His home life was continually giving him trouble. There were lawsuits about an inheritance; there were the less reliable members of his family to be supported and admonished; there was constant difficulty in finding and keeping good servants, and not flirting with the pretty ones too openly; there were quarrels with his wife when she complained that he neglected her for his work, and refused to take her to plays, and threatened to have his father to live with them, or when he complained that she was a bad manager, or grew jealous because she took pleasure in other men's company. She was often careless:

> Myself somewhat vexed at my wife's neglect in leaving of her scarfe, waistcoate, and night-dressings in the coach today that brought us from Westminster; though, I confess, she did give them to me to look after, yet it was her fault not to see that I did take them out of the coach. I believe it might be as good as 25*s.* loss.
>
> 6th Jan., 1663. *Ibid.*, vol. III, p. 6.

Once when she was thoroughly provoked by his behaviour with one of the maids he woke to find her standing over him with a red-hot pair of tongs, ready to pinch him. But their quarrels were always being made up, for basically they were very fond of one another.

All his minor fears, annoyances and feelings of shame were recorded in the diary. He was so taken aback when a dog attacked him in the street that he quite forgot he was wearing a sword and could have defended himself. He was frightened by a late-night encounter with a man carrying a cudgel, however much the man assured him that he was a good subject of the King; he fully expected to be knocked on the head before he reached home. He was furious when he heard that his wife and father had buried his money in the garden at Brampton by daylight, when anyone could have seen them, and so shallow in the ground; and more furious when they could not remember exactly where they had buried it, and it was difficult to recover, and very dirty. He was cross when he spoiled a new pair of silk breeches, going to the office in the rain, and when he tore a new cloak on the latch of Sir George Carteret's door; it was mended by his tailor, 'but it troubled me'. He was piqued when no one asked him to stay to dinner at the house where the King was visiting. He was ashamed to think of his father wearing half a dozen pairs of his own old shoes, and that his wife was not sufficiently well dressed at the theatre, in comparison with other women. He indulged in pornographic literature, but did not want it to be known:

> Thence away to the Strand, to my bookseller's, and there staid an hour, and bought the idle, rogueish book, *L'escholle des filles*; which I have bought in plain binding, avoiding the buying of it better bound, because I resolve, as soon as I have read it, to burn it, that it may not stand in the list of books, nor among them, to disgrace them if it should be found. . . . I to my chamber, where I did read through *L'escholle des filles*, a lewd book, but what do no wrong once to read for information sake.

> 8th, 9th Feb., 1668. *Ibid.*, vol. VII, pp. 310–11.

He felt ashamed of cheering up so soon after his brother's death. After the funeral:

> I and my wife and Madam Turner and her family to my brother's, and by and by fell to a barrell of oysters, cake, and cheese, of Mr Honiwood's, with him, in his chamber and below, being too merry for so late a sad work. But, Lord! to see how the world makes nothing of the memory of a man, an houre after he is dead! And, indeed, I must blame myself; for,

though at the sight of him dead and dying, I had real grief for a while, yet presently after, and ever since, I have had very little grief indeed for him.

18th March, 1664. *Ibid.*, vol. IV, p. 81.

Most of all, he was ashamed of his casual affairs. It was not that he did not love his wife, but that he could never resist a pretty woman. He seldom committed adultery, partly because of his scruples, partly for fear of disease, but he went a very long way with a large number of women. Everyone who would respond was fair game, whether it was the wife of one of the naval captains, or a sempstress, or the pretty maid in his household, 'whom I love should be fiddling about me', combing his hair and helping him to undress, or the girl he stood by in church 'whom I did labour to take by the hand and the body; but she would not, but got further and further from me; and, at last, I could perceive her to take pins out of her pocket to prick me if I should touch her again—which seeing I did forbear, and was glad I did spy her design' (18th Aug., 1667). He had erotic dreams of Lady Castlemaine, one of the King's mistresses, and then

dreamt that it was only a dream, but that since it was a dream and that I took so much real pleasure in it, what a happy thing it would be if when we are in our graves (as Shakespeare resembles this) we could dream, and dream but such dreams as this, that then we should not need to be so fearful of death as we are in this plague time.

2nd Sept., 1665. Not in Wheatley's edition; quoted A. Bryant, *Pepys: the Man in the Making* (1933), p. 263.

He retained an odd sense of moral values throughout: he told his maid Deb, when she was leaving, that she must not let anyone else handle her as he had done, and he was shocked at the compliant Mrs. Martin:

Thence to Mrs Martin's, and there did take a little pleasure both with her and her sister. Here sat and talked, and it is a strange thing to see the impudence of the woman, that desires by all means to have her mari come home, only that she might be at liberty to have me para toker her, which is a thing I do not so much desire.

21st Aug., 1667. Pepys, *op. cit.*, vol. VII, pp. 74–5.

When Pepys felt particularly guilty, he gave his wife a present—a diamond ring, a pearl necklace, or a new petticoat.

All the time, his position in the world was improving. Nearly always when he cast up his accounts he found himself richer both in gold and in household goods: not only because of his official salary but because of the presents that accrued to him in his position. In 1663 Sir William Warren gave him

> a pair of plain white gloves for my hand, and a fair state dish of silver, and cup, with my arms, ready cut upon them.
>
> 10th Feb., 1663. *Ibid.*, vol. III, p. 37.

He calculated that these were worth eighteen pounds. On 3rd April he met Captain Grove in Whitehall, who handed him a letter which felt as if it might contain money:

> I broke it open, not looking into it till all the money was out, that I might say I saw no money in the paper, if ever I should be questioned about it. There was a piece in gold and £4 in silver.
>
> 3rd April, 1663. *Ibid.*, vol. III, p. 83.

On 1st May Captain Grove was less judicious in his choice:

> [he] sent me a side of pork, which was the oddest present, sure, that was ever made any man; and the next, I remember I told my wife, I believe would be a pound of candles, or a shoulder of mutton.
>
> 1st May, 1663. *Ibid.*, vol. III, p. 108.

However, the presents mounted up, and Pepys found himself able to make structural alterations to his house, building on another storey, stripping and re-plastering most of the rooms, and providing them with new hangings, buying elaborate chimney-pieces and costly pictures. He laid down a good and varied cellar of wine. His scale of entertainment rose rapidly. Even as early as January of 1663 he was able to put on a dinner that cost almost five pounds:

> I had for them, after oysters, at first course, a hash of rabbits, a lamb, and a rare chine of beef. Next a great dish of roasted fowl, cost me about

30s., and a tart, and then fruit and cheese. My dinner was noble and enough.

13th Jan., 1663. *Ibid.*, vol. III, p. 13.

This was provided for six guests, all friends of the family, round his fine new table. In January 1669 he was entertaining much more elevated company: Lord Sandwich, Peterborough, Sir Charles Harbord, Lord Hinchingbroke, Mr. Sidney Montagu and Sir William Godolphin. He put on six or eight dishes, in series, and a variety of good wines,

as noble as any man need to have, I think; at least, all was done in the noblest manner that ever I had any, and I have rarely seen in my life better anywhere else, even at the Court.

23rd Jan., 1669. *Ibid.*, vol. VIII, p. 208.

Perhaps the sign of social advancement that delighted him most was the acquisition of his own coach and horses, and a livery for his servant, who was to drive it. The coach was light and elegant, and had the new glass windows. He was always mentioning, after this, that he went to this or that place 'in our coach'.

He was a great playgoer, though he felt it was a vice, and was always making good resolutions to refrain from visiting the theatre. He found innumerable reasons for not keeping his vow; it did not, for instance, apply to a theatre that had not been opened when he made the vow; or he was being taken as a guest, and therefore it was not an extravagance. (This has a strong resemblance to his treatment of his vow not to drink wine; when the doctor who had suggested it died, he considered himself absolved from the vow.) He had very decided reactions to the plays he saw, thinking some very stupid, but enjoying *Macbeth, Hamlet, The Tempest, Volpone* and *Bartholomew Fair*. He also enjoyed the sight of the audience, but was disappointed if there were no pretty woman near him. Sometimes he went alone, and without his wife's knowledge; but on one such occasion he met Sir William Penn there, and decided it would be safer to tell his wife where he had been when he got home. Sometimes he took not only his wife but some of the family and friends; this was apt to be expensive in oranges, which cost sixpence each. He enjoyed sitting near Sir Charles Sedley one evening, and hearing his running commentary on a dull play. He was

particularly delighted by a remark he overheard when Lady Castlemaine was there in a box:

> It was pleasant to hear an ordinary lady hard by us, that it seems did
> not know her before, say, being told who she was, that 'she was well
> enough'.
>
> 7th March, 1664. *Ibid.*, vol. IV, p. 68.

And there was the lady at the performance of *Tu Quoque*:

> One of the best parts of our sport was a mighty pretty lady that sat behind
> us, that did laugh so heartily and constantly, that it did me good to hear
> her.
>
> 16th Sept., 1667. *Ibid.*, vol. VII, p. 115.

Pepys could find pleasure everywhere: in having a picnic in the
cowslip fields, or promenading in Hatfield Park; in listening to a
blackbird which began on many tunes very well, but then left off and
started another; in finding that he could easily shave himself, instead
of employing a barber—'I shall continue it, it saving me money and
time'; and in his relief that it was his uncle's horse and not his own that
had been stolen from the inn stables in the middle of the night. But he
was much more than a man with a genius for pleasure, even when his
services to the Navy are not taken into consideration. He was an
antiquary who made a large collection of naval manuscripts, a book-
lover who read widely among the serious literature of his day, and who
had his books uniformly bound and beautifully housed; a lover of art
who patronized the famous miniaturist, Cooper, and commissioned
Henry Dankers to paint the King's palaces on panels in his dining-
room; a thoroughly musical man who both played and composed; a
man of literary sensibility who admired Chaucer and suggested to
Dryden that he should try his hand at translating Chaucer; a man of
scientific curiosity who took an interest in the affairs of the Royal
Society and was made a Fellow shortly after its incorporation. Moreover, he painted the best picture of a man and his times that exists in
English literature.

Though Pepys's diary is unique in quality, his many-sidedness was
shared by not a few of his contemporaries. It was a versatile age. Sir

John Vanbrugh was both a competent dramatist and a good architect, Sir Christopher Wren an outstanding architect, a good scientist, and an inventor on a wide front, from a drill for sowing grain evenly, to a method of blood-transfusion. John Ray not only laid the foundations of modern botany and zoology, but made linguistic studies which recognized the importance of local dialects, and contributed to the new religious outlook. John Locke was a leader in the fields of epistemology, metaphysics, psychology, political theory, religion and education, and made contributions to medical and botanical knowledge in his spare time. John Evelyn was a thoroughly cultivated gentleman who wrote on a wide variety of topics, including copper engraving, forestry, navigation and commerce, medals, and the abatement of the nuisance of smoke in London. There were many great personalities, including the Marquis of Halifax, the Earl of Clarendon, John Bunyan, John Dryden, Jonathan Swift and Samuel Pepys himself. It was an age of culture, talent and intellectual curiosity, that deserves to be remembered for its serious achievements rather than for the ephemeral productions of its theatres.

II

THE ENTERTAINERS

THE Londoners who required entertainment in this period fall into two
main groups: the Wits and their satellites, and the lower middle classes.
The Wits were a well-known court circle,[1] favoured by the King, and
led by Buckingham, Dorset, Rochester, Sedley, Etherege and
Wycherley. All these were noblemen or gentlemen, and amateurs of the
arts; Dryden and Settle lived on the fringes of the group, by pen and
patronage. Their adherents and servants faithfully followed the pattern
of living and writing that they set. Their influence outlasted the circle
itself, which was virtually dissolved by the time Charles II died. The
lower middle class consisted of apprentices and indoor servants, who
did not have to spend their wages on living. There was a very large
number of domestic servants in London; Pepys, in 1669, normally kept
five for a household of two persons. There were also the poor, who
could not afford entertainment, and almost certainly could not read;
and the wealthier citizens, who were often too Puritan in outlook to
indulge in the lighter forms of recreation. City wives, however, formed a
section of the romance-reading public; they had far more leisure than
their predecessors, now that most necessaries could be bought in shops,
instead of having to be made or preserved in the home.

For rather different reasons, these groups encouraged the production of superficial literature of varying sorts. The Wits need not have
done so; they were intelligent men, many of them perfectly capable, in
later life, of working as useful Members of Parliament, responsible
court officials, diplomatists or governors of colonies. Many of them
had serious interests, even in the sixties: Buckingham tried on two
occasions to introduce a Toleration Act, and ran a factory in Lambeth;
Dorset and Savile were employed on a diplomatic mission; several of

[1] For details, J. H. Wilson's *The Court Wits of the Restoration* (Princeton,
1948) should be consulted.

them were elected to membership of the Royal Society. Dorset was a generous and constant patron of the arts. But few of the Wits seemed to have quite enough to do. Those who sat in Parliament had to do so as King's men at this time, and vote as he pleased. Their court appointments were mainly a matter of being in attendance, in rotation, as Gentlemen or Grooms of the Bedchamber. Many other posts, such as that of the Master of the Horse, were sinecures that brought more prestige than work or income. Their occupations were irksome rather than satisfying. The result was that the Wits made the most of their spare time. The town provided a variety of diversions: plays, operas, concerts, masquerades. There were coffee-houses where they could talk, and taverns where they could get drunk and wildly irresponsible. In this state Rochester smashed the sundial in the King's Privy Garden because its shape suggested a rape on Time, and Sedley and his friends shocked some citizens from the balcony of the Cock Tavern. The details of these escapades were probably invented by current gossip, but there is no doubt that the Wits were carefree and licentious in their behaviour. Much time was spent on the serious business of being fashionably dressed, and more on mistresses; it was decidedly old-fashioned not to 'keep', as Francis North discovered. Variety was added by affairs with anyone else who was willing—including citizens' wives.

Poetry and drama took their place amongst these diversions. One must write, because it was an elegant and witty occupation; the primary aim was to amuse, and to win approval from other Wits. Unfortunately, the same superficial level of mind was used for showing off in a tavern, winning a mistress, or writing a play. The gentlemen were having a refined fling which was imitated by the professionals. What depths they had found little outlet in the theatre or in social poetry. The Wits governed taste in the theatre, and in most kinds of poetry. They controlled the first partly by writing plays which set the standard, and partly by their loud criticisms of other men's plays. They controlled the second by making poetry a public affair. The Elizabethans had circulated their poems in manuscript amongst their private friends; the Wits had them read out in taverns and coffee-houses. They were often sent there anonymously and read by a waiter to the company, so that the author could gauge their critical reception. This practice made for a lack of subtlety; the daring, the clever and the 'easy' were cultivated. Translations were less affected by this practice than lyrics.

The lower middle classes controlled the standard of their own literary entertainment less directly. They did not, on the whole, write; they did not criticize. But when they did not buy, they had some influence on the kind of fiction that was published. They encouraged the production of short pieces. Full-scale romances, philosophical or sentimental, were too lengthy to be easily afforded; an unbound volume cost two and threepence, and most ran into several volumes. They were prepared to buy smaller works costing up to a shilling. That meant that they could buy chap-book abbreviations of the romances, lively tales of the length of Neville's *Isle of Pines* (1668), jest-books, the lives of famous criminals, or broadside ballads or newspapers, which were even cheaper. The material had to be exciting, and out of the rut of ordinary life; not, however, completely extravagant. A setting in foreign countries or in the underworld was an advantage. Apart from brevity and excitement, what was demanded was easy reading. No effort should have to be made to follow the story; everything must be capable of appreciation on first reading. These semi-educated readers created a demand for literature which was popular in the bad sense.

By the end of the century, the middle class began to demand respectable plays and stories. This meant that they wanted a sound moral attitude, and characters that reassured them of the essential goodness of the nature of man. The demand led to the dullness of sentimental comedy. It made Vanbrugh and Colley Cibber dilute their comedies of manners with moral material; women now had strength of mind and men were considerate. It also produced Mrs. Aphra Behn's only interesting work, *Oroonoko* (1688), which satisfied the craving for a noble and natural hero, while still preserving the exotic flavour of a New World setting.

All in all, these three groups gave rise to hardly any works that are of value when set beside the serious literature of the age. There were a handful of good lyrics, some worthwhile translations from the classics, an elegant parody of the romance (Congreve's *Incognita*, 1691), one good comedy (Etherege's *The Man of Mode*, 1676), and one serious attempt at tragedy (Otway's *Venice Preserv'd*, 1682). Some of the remainder is of historical or social interest: the rogue biography was the ancestor of Defoe's novels, and the failed comedies and heroic plays show what was wrong with Restoration court circles—moral uncertainty and a coarseness of sensibility that varied between fashionable cynicism and sentimentality.

THE DRAMATISTS

The theatre suffered from being a royal monopoly, patronized by a very limited audience. There were never more than two companies, the King's Men and the Duke's Men, and they performed not only in the public theatres but in the King's private theatre in Whitehall. The theatre managers were court officials, the actors were the King's servants. The public theatres were often poorly attended, and the main part of the audience consisted of courtiers, hangers-on and prostitutes. Because of the size of the playgoing community, long runs were impossible, and plays succeeded one another very quickly. Some of these were straightforward revivals of Jacobean plays, some were adaptations of them. Authors of original plays had to work fast; they often resorted to a series of stock devices. Throughout, the taste of the King and the Wits was the standard of reference. It did not lead to the writing of good plays.

Much of the audience's interest in the plays was sexual. It was now customary for women to act on the public stage, and the playwrights took full advantage of this, presenting passionate love-scenes and exciting situations. The language became more consciously voluptuous; the plays of Lee abounded in romantically pornographic descriptions of the heroine slumbering on a flowery bank in inadequate clothing. The women in the comedies were very frank in speech and behaviour. When the novelty of seeing women in women's parts had worn off, variations were tried. Killigrew's *The Parson's Wedding* (1663) was played by an all-female cast. In Vanbrugh's *The Relapse* (1697) Mrs. Kent played the part of Young Fashion, a rake who recouped his fortunes by marrying a rich country girl, with the assistance of the homosexual Coupler, whose attentions were part of the price for the service. Young children were sometimes employed to speak bawdy epilogues.

The sophisticated taste of the court also demanded elaborate scenery and stage effects. Scenery had, of course, been extensively used in the masque, and effects were not uncommon in the later Jacobean theatre, but it was not until Sir William D'Avenant introduced scenery painted in perspective that plays were adorned on such a magnificent scale. To the ghosts and spirits and witches of the earlier stage were added vast displays of natural phenomena, transformation scenes and heavenly hosts. In *The Rival Queens* (1677) Lee made use of a spectacular prelude to the second act:

> The Scene draws, and discovers a Battel of Crows or Ravens in the Air; an Eagle and a Dragon meet and fight; the Eagle drops down with all the rest of the Birds, and the Dragon flies away. Soldiers walk off, shaking their heads.
>
> Lee, *Works* (1722), vol. III, p. 230.

In his *Sophonisba* (1676) Hannibal has a premonitory vision of the death of Rosalinda, who

> rises in a Chair, pale, with a Wound on her Breast; two *Cupids* descend, and hang weeping over her. (Act IV.)
>
> *Ibid.*, vol. III, p. 52.

Dryden has a full-scale storm at the beginning of his version of *The Tempest* (1674), and in *The State of Innocence* (1677), his adaptation of *Paradise Lost*, he opened with a spectacle of

> Chaos, or a confus'd Mass of Matter . . . A Symphony of warlike Musick is heard for some time; then from the Heavens (which are open'd) fall the rebellious Angels wheeling in the Air, and seeming transfix'd with Thunderbolts . . . Angels discover'd above, brandishing their swords . . . the Scene shifts, and on a sudden represents Hell: Part of the Scene is a Lake of Brimstone or rowling Fire; the Earth of a burnt colour: The fall'n Angels appear on the Lake, lying prostrate.
>
> Dryden, *Dramatick Works* (1717), vol. IV, p. 29.

Later in the performance there was to be a sun moving orbicularly with the moon below it; Lucifer would arrive in the centre of a black cloud, and Uriel in a chariot drawn by white horses. Admittedly this was called an opera, but there was a strong tendency to turn plays into divertissements, in which scenery, costumes, dancing, singing and dramatic action were of about equal importance. This has certainly happened in Dryden's and Howard's *The Indian Queen* (1665) The audience was easily entertained by these devices. Even Shadwell complained:

> Then came machines, brought from a Neighbour Nation;
> Oh how we suffered under Decoration!
>
> > Prologue to *The Squire of Alsatia*, quoted
> > Beljame, *Men of Letters and the English
> > Public* (1948), p. 37.

The King and the Wits were also responsible for imposing some of the conventions of contemporary French drama on the English theatre. The unities of place and time were exalted. Dryden kept to these imposed unities in his *All for Love* (1678), rejecting the global scale of Shakespeare's *Antony and Cleopatra*; everything happened in the course of a day in Alexandria. The King liked rhymed verse, in imitation of French Alexandrines; therefore it was used for some time in serious plays instead of blank verse. The beat of the rhyme was always distracting in English drama; Dryden did not write a serious play of any worth until he turned back to blank verse.

The material of Restoration comedy was the life of gentlemen, fops and citizens of the time. Scenes were set in St. James's Park, Mulberry Gardens, Westminster Hall; current fashions in morals, manners, dress and conversation were displayed. The plots generally turned on love (licit and illicit) and money. But this material was handled with far more amusement than criticism. The spirit of Restoration comedy was very different from that which had informed *Volpone* or *The Alchemist*. As Horace Walpole said of Congreve's characters:

> We want breath or attention to follow their repartees; and are so charmed with what every body says, that we have not leisure to be interested in what any body does. We are so pleased with each person, that we wish success to all; and our approbation is so occupied, that our passions cannot be engaged . . . For these reasons, though they are something more, I can scarce allow Congreve's to be true comedies. No man

would be corrected, if sure that his wit would make his vices or ridicules overlooked.

Thoughts on Comedy, Works (1798), vol. II, pp. 316–17.

However much the individual dramatist protested in prologues and epilogues that he was castigating the vices and follies of the age, there was a general atmosphere of overlooking faults, and a confused moral attitude governing the structure of the play.

It is perhaps unfair to speak of the comedy of the period as if it were homogeneous. There were differences in artistic level. There was crude farce, where the humour depended on a series of dilemmas from which the characters had to extricate themselves (Dryden's *Mr. Limberham, or the Kind Keeper*, 1680); romantic and sentimental comedy, often composed in verse (Dryden's *The Rival Ladies*, 1664); there was elegant comedy of manners and intrigue (Etherege's *The Man of Mode*, 1676; Congreve's *The Way of the World*, 1700). The last kind is what is generally meant when Restoration comedy is discussed with any degree of seriousness.

In the main, modern critics agree on several issues. First, they have decided that the immorality of the subject-matter is of little consequence. What roused Jeremy Collier's indignation in his *Short View of the Immorality and Profaneness of the English Stage* (1698) (bawdry, blasphemy and satire on the clergy) does not trouble modern taste. The plays do not demoralize the reader or the spectator. As Macaulay put it in 1841:

> We find it difficult to believe that, in a world so full of temptation as this, any gentleman whose life would have been virtuous, had he not read Aristophanes and Juvenal will be made vicious by reading them.
>
> 'Leigh Hunt', *Essays* (1883), pp. 570–1.

Historically speaking, the choice of subject-matter was understandable. It was occasioned by a violent reaction against the Puritan attitude to sex, and the repressive measures of the Commonwealth, which had made fornication and adultery capital crimes. After the Restoration, wenching was almost a demonstration of loyalty to the new régime, and obvious material for comedy.

Secondly, the critics agree that most of the plays contain good humorous portrayals of a variety of types. The fop and the fine gentle-man are the ones most frequently cited, but these are only the beginning of a list that includes hoydens, sea-dogs, pert maids, astrological maniacs, zenophobes, puritans, *nouveaux-riches*, misanthropes, trollops, *femmes magistrales*, misers, gulls, charwomen. They are known almost entirely by their eccentricities, but as two-dimensional figures they are often vivid. Two of the best are Vanbrugh's Lord Foppington and Wycherley's Margery Pinchwife.

Lord Foppington, in *The Relapse* (1697), is ingeniously drawn. He has just bought himself a title, and has all the child's excitement about the possession of a new toy. He loves being called Your Lordship:

> Well, 'tis an unspeakable pleasure to be a Man of Quality—Strike me dumb—My Lord—Your Lordship—My Lord *Foppington—Ah, c'est quelque Chose de beau, que le Diable m'emporte* . . . Sure whilst I was but a Knight, I was a very nauseous Fellow. (Act I.)
>
> *Works* (ed. B. Dobrée, 1927), vol. I, p. 25.

Tailor and sempstress and hosier and perruquier dance attendance on him, and he tries to disguise his excitement beneath an assumption of *savoir-faire*; he is a man of the world and knows the fashions far better than they do. His manner is one of gentle condescension, unless their ignorance of fashion arouses his indignation:

> Death and Eternal Tartures! Sir, I say the Packet's too high by a Foot.
> *Tailor:* My Lord, if it had been an Inch lower, it would not have held your Lordship's Pocket-Handkerchief.
> *Lord F.:* Rat my Pocket-Handkerchief! Have not I a Page to carry it? You may make him a Packet up to his Chin a purpose for it: But I will not have mine come so near my Face . . . the Packet becomes no part of the Body but the Knee.
>
> *Ibid.*, pp. 26–7.

He stipulates that the padding in the calf of his new stockings should be the thickness of a crown-piece less:

> If the Town takes notice my Legs are fallen away, 'twill be attributed to the Violence of some new Intrigue.
>
> *Ibid.*, p. 27.

He has ordered a new wig, but it does not please him, for his face can be seen under it for the breadth of two inches:

> I'll wear it today, tho' it shew such a manstrous pair of Cheeks: Stap my Vitals, I shall be taken for a Trumpeter.
>
> *Ibid.*, p. 28.

He does not pretend to learning; gentlemen do not need it. He loves reading, passionately—'but I never think of what I read'. He has a neat library, ranged with gilded books and looking-glasses:

> It is the most entertaining thing in the World to walk and look upon 'em . . . Far to mind the inside of a Book, is to entertain ones self with the forc'd Product of another Man's Brain. Now I think a Man of Quality and Breeding may be much diverted with the Natural Sprauts of his own. (Act II, sc. 1.)
>
> *Ibid.*, pp. 36–7.

His vanity persuades him at the first meeting with the wife of a friend that she is longing to become his mistress; she boxes his ears, and her husband draws his sword and pinks the noble lord, who is sure that he has been run through. He thinks he is dying—'Love's the Devil indeed, *Ned.*' The surgeon plays on his credulity and extracts £500 for a cure. It is good round humour, and Vanbrugh has handled the absurdities with imagination.

Mrs. Pinchwife, in Wycherley's *The Country Wife* (1675), is more of a rounded character. She is represented as completely inexperienced and ingenuous, having been brought up in the country where she was unable to make comparisons between her old husband and the gallants of the town, between the dullness of home life and the perpetual round of gaiety in London. But she is quick to take hints, and when her jealous husband foolishly tries to warn her against the vices of London, he merely succeeds in rousing her interest:

> Ay, my Dear, you must love me only, and not be like the naughty Town Women, who only hate their Husbands, and love every Man else, love Plays, Visits, fine Coaches, fine Cloaths, Fiddles, Balls, Treats, and so lead a wicked Town-life.
>
> *Mrs. P.:* Nay, if to enjoy all these things be a Town life, *London* is not so bad a place, Dear . . . Pray, let me to go a Play, Dear.

Mr. P.: Hold your Peace, I wo'not . . .

Mrs. P.: Pray, why, Dear?

Mr. P.: First, you like the Actors, and the Gallants may like you.

Mrs. P.: What, a homely Country Girl? no Bud, no body will like me.

Mr. P.: I tell you, yes, they may.

Mrs. P.: No, no, you jest—I won't believe you, I will go.

Mr. P.: I tell you then, that one of the lewdest Fellows in Town, who saw
you there, told me he was in love with you.

Mrs. P.: Indeed! who, who, pray who was't? . . . Pray, Husband, is he a
pretty Gentleman, that loves me? (Act II.)

Works (ed. Summers, 1924), vol. II, pp. 23–4.

The idea has great attractions, particularly when she meets Mr. Horner,
who is posing as impotent in order to have unrestricted access to other
men's wives. For safety, her husband has disguised her as a boy,
and Horner takes advantage of the disguise to send kisses and
messages to the boy's supposed sister, Mrs. Pinchwife. When Pinchwife
later tries to make her send a scornful letter to Horner, discouraging
his advances, she substitutes a very loving one. Yet a great deal of the
original ingenuousness remains. When Horner becomes her lover, she
is inexperienced enough to think that she can live with him on a
permanent basis, and she tries every shift to make him let her stay.

I don't know the way home, so I don't . . . No, don't you believe, that
I'll go at all; what are you weary of me already? (Act V.)

Ibid., p. 82.

In the end she nearly ruins all Horner's carefully laid plans for easy
love-affairs, by betraying her personal knowledge of his sexual capacity.

Good characters were produced even by writers who hardly wrote
one good comedy; in the better writers they abound. They all had the
gift of inventing typical speech-patterns for each character. There was
Dryden's Melantha in *Mariage-à-la-Mode* (1672), run charmingly mad
after French manners and vocabulary, Congreve's bluff sailor Ben in
Love for Love (1695) who could not express himself except in nautical
metaphors, or his beautifully garrulous Tattle, or Etherege's finicking
Sir Fopling Flutter in *The Man of Mode*. They were all delightful
types, but no more than amusing.

Another point on which critics of Restoration comedy are agreed is

the mediocre handling of plot. The plots vary between the inconse-
quential assemblage of events in Vanbrugh's *The Provok'd Wife* (1697)
and the relatively tidy working out of plot and sub-plot in *The Country
Wife*. Plot, on the whole, was not important, though it could be highly
involved. The reader spends a good deal of time keeping clear in his
mind the various interwoven strands of such a play as Congreve's *The
Way of the World*. Normally, the right people were married off to one
another by the end of the play, and the wrong ones, after attempts to
foil this conclusion, were foiled themselves, and ended in exposure or
in a disappointing marriage. Alternatively, some husband who deserved
it was cuckolded. But the plot was purely a vehicle for the display of
the characters and modes of the time, and a peg for witty conversation.

The fourth point of critical agreement (Professor L. C. Knights
excepted) is on the wit displayed by a very high proportion of the
characters. The playwrights consciously aimed at this mark. Dryden,
in his preface to *An Evening's Love*, stated it explicitly:

> I would have more of the *urbana, venusta, salsa, faceta*, and the rest
> which Quintilian reckons up as the ornaments of wit . . . As for repartee
> in particular; as it is the very soul of conversation, so it is the greatest
> grace of Comedy, where it is proper to the characters.
>
> *Essays* (ed. W. P. Ker, 1900), vol. I, p. 139.

It was intended as an improvement on the earlier drama, which had
thought puns and word-play a sufficient source of wit. The new drama
was to be more courtly, gallant and refined than that of the Elizabethans. Few critics now pretend that this wit goes deep, or has much
subtlety or range of matter, but for stage purposes it has the asset of
neatness and momentary vitality, though it does not bear serious
examination. It is very much of a kind, relying on the surprising image
and the succinct antithesis. Two examples from Congreve, always
considered the most elegant of the playwrights, must serve as illustra-
tion:

> *Bellmour:* Why faith I think it will do well enough—If the Husband be
> out of the way, for the Wife to shew her fondness and impatience of
> his Absence, by choosing a Lover as like him as she can; and what is
> unlike she may help out with her own Fancy.
> *Vainlove:* But is it not an abuse to the Lover to be made a Blind of? For
> she only stalks under him to take aim at her Husband.

Bell.: As you say, the Abuse is to the Lover, not the Husband: for 'tis an Argument of her great Zeal towards him, that she will enjoy him in Effigie.

Vain.: It must be a very superstitious Country, where such Zeal passes for true Devotion. I doubt it will be damn'd by all our Protestant Husbands for flat Idolatry.

The Old Bachelor, Works (ed. Summers, 1923), vol. I, p. 170.

Mirabell: You are no longer handsome when you've lost your Lover; your Beauty dies upon the Instant: For Beauty is the Lover's Gift; 'tis he bestows your Charms—Your Glass is all a Cheat. The Ugly and the Old, whom the Looking-glass mortifies, yet after Commendation can be flatter'd by it, and discover Beauties in it: For that reflects our Praises, rather than your Face.

Millamant: O the Vanity of these Men? *Fainall,* d'ee hear him? If they did not commend us, we were not handsome? Now you must know they could not commend one, if one was not handsome. Beauty the Lover's Gift—Lord, what is a Lover, that it can give? Why one makes Lovers as fast as one pleases, and they live as long as one pleases, and they die as soon as one pleases: and then if one pleases one makes more.

Witwoud: Very pretty. Why you make no more of making of Lovers, Madam, than of making so many Card-matches.

Mill.: One no more owes one's Beauty to a Lover, than ones Wit to an Eccho: They can but reflect what we look and say; vain empty Things if we are silent or unseen, and want a being.

Mira.: Yet, to those two vain empty Things, you owe the two greatest Pleasures of your Life.

Mill.: How so?

Mira.: To your Lover you owe the Pleasure of hearing yourselves prais'd; and to an Eccho the Pleasure of hearing yourselves talk.

Witwoud: But I know a Lady that loves Talking so incessantly, she won't give an Eccho fair play; she has that everlasting Rotation of Tongue, that an Eccho must wait till she dies, before it can catch her last Words.

The Way of the World, ibid., vol. III, pp. 33-4.

There is refinement of language here, and a certain grace in the cadences, but the thoughts never rise above the level of ingenuity Moreover, Witwoud is supposed to represent false wit; in this passage at least his remarks do not differ in quality from those of the true wits.

Modern critics disagree to a considerable extent about the seriousness of these comedies: the degree to which they were written as critical comment on the situation they portrayed:

A defence of Restoration comedy must demonstrate that its sex jokes
have a serious social function. I think it can be shown that they have.
'L. C. Knights and Restoration Comedy', *Essays in Criticism*, vol. VII,
no. 1, p. 59.

Mr. Bateson's thesis is that the playwrights effected a compromise
between the Puritan and the Cavalier attitudes to sex, of which the
Augustan age had the benefit. This rationalization of sex was, he
thinks, achieved completely in the relationship of Mirabell and
Millamant in *The Way of the World*.

The rationalization of sex presumably means the establishment of a
situation in which sex is not limited to the process of seduction, but
seen as a normal part of life, and linked with respect for individuality,
affection, care and concern. In Restoration comedy, the concept of sex
resolves itself into statements about the sex-war; they are saying either,
'I must have you, though I don't care for you', or, very occasionally,
'I am in love with you, but I won't admit it for fear you take advantage
of it'; and—according to sex—'I want everyone to know' or 'I want no
one to know'. The assumptions mentioned by Professor Knights—that
wives and constancy are boring, and that the appetite always needs
fresh stimulus—serve to underline the narrow understanding of sex
presented in the plays. If the plays are to contribute, as critical comedies,
to the rationalization of sex, these conventional attitudes must be made
ridiculous or offensive by the authors. In the bulk of Restoration
comedy they have clearly not done this. Much as they protest that they
are satirizing the life of the town, what they normally do is to praise the
successful and to ridicule the unsuccessful in the particular way of life
endorsed by the town. It is necessary to examine the comedies generally
acknowledged as the best in the period to demonstrate this point of
view: Wycherley's *The Country Wife* and *The Plain Dealer*, Congreve's
Love for Love and *The Way of the World*, and Etherege's *The Man of
Mode*.

In *The Country Wife* the comedy is wholly concerned with sex. Its
wit is more sardonic and its characters more obviously unlikable than
those of any other play of the period. But are these unpleasant characters being satirized? Are their actions seen as wrong, and if so, what is
the emotional charge on the work—'interesting', or 'despicable'? The
hero, Horner, is ingenious, and single-minded in his determination to

seduce other men's wives; the pretence of impotency for this purpose
was a new device. But neither Horner's aims nor his methods are made
ridiculous; instead, his victims are ridiculed—both Sir Jasper Fidget,
who encourages him to go in to Lady Fidget in the bedroom, and
Pinchwife, who takes his own wife, masked, to Horner's lodgings,
thinking her to be his sister. People who believe in his impotence regard
him with pitying scorn or with disgust, according to their sex. The
women who know the truth label his pretence clever and generous; he is
accepting a shameful status for their mutual benefit. The direction of
the ridicule endorses the social code, and the total effect is not satiric.
Wycherley is not accusing the wrong-doers but inviting the audience to
come and see the wrong being done.

In *The Plain Dealer* Wycherley clearly meant to satirize the town,
but the result is not satire, because of his confused moral standards. He
wanted to use the hero, Manly, as the standard of honest virtue by
which to decry the wicked Olivia, his hypocritical former mistress, who
was unfaithful to him and stole his goods. Manly was a debased version
of Molière's Misanthrope; his character was surly, and the stand he
made for honesty did not preclude self-deception. When he had discovered Olivia's treachery, he still desired her. He tried to get his page
to pimp for him, rationalizing his motives, 'I will lie with her out of
revenge'. Wycherley underlined his 'virtue' by giving him Fidelia as his
page, an heiress of £2000 a year who had fallen in love with him and
dressed up as a boy. This pseudo-Viola soliloquized in thin and sentimental blank verse, the falsity of which was made apparent by the
vigorous prose spoken by the other characters. Manly, of course, was
married off to her at the end, and her income would be very useful in
reconciling him to the wicked world. His friend Freeman finally undermined the honesty of his former protests against the world:

> I think most of our quarrels to the World, are just such as we have to
> a handsome Woman: only because we cannot enjoy her, as we wou'd do.
> Wycherley, *op. cit.*, vol. II, p. 196.

Neither this play nor Congreve's *Love for Love* seem primarily concerned with the rationalization of sex. In both plays the hero's problems
are solved by money. Valentine is not satirized for his sexual adoles-
cence, but for his prodigality, as Congreve acknowledged in his reply to

Jeremy Collier. It is perfectly clear that Valentine's resolution to marry excuses his wild oats and his bastards. Neither the problems of his past nor the problems of his actual relationship with Angelica are seriously treated. Angelica's intentions remain unknown until the end of Act V, when she rather unconvincingly says she has been struggling throughout the play to conceal her love for Valentine. Valentine is in danger of being disinherited for his past extravagances; this would leave him too poor to marry Angelica. By the end of the play his father's machinations have been thwarted and his devotion is rewarded.

In *The Way of the World* Mirabell and Millamant have, it has been suggested, a saner view of sex. Mirabell is presented as a fine gentleman who has had love-affairs in the past, and who has disposed of his most recent mistress by marrying her off to a very unpleasant friend of his, in case she has become pregnant. He does, however, still protect her financial interests. He now wants to marry Millamant, a charming and witty woman with a great gift for teasing. His arguments with her are not the conventional flyting; they know one another, and are working towards an adjustment. Mirabell tends to be possessive, presumably because he feels insecure of her love; he tries irritably to prevent her from spending her time talking to fools. Millamant refuses to be managed by him; she will not have him until he has learned to respect her individuality. The famous scene where they come to terms about marriage is in the main an elaboration of this point: marriage does not give you complete rights over a woman, though there are things that you can reasonably ask her not to do. Millamant insists that they must not fall into a cat-and-dog relationship; they must continue to be well bred with one another, 'as if we were not marry'd at all'. Here there is some idea of marriage as a relationship between two adults who intend to retain their individuality and respect that of the other. There is a suggestion that their affection is of the kind that can come to terms with wit and humour. This is an improvement on the normal presentation of sex in Restoration comedy, but it is not complete enough to be termed a rationalization of sex. Too many aspects are still ignored, and the problem of Mirabell's past behaviour to Mrs. Fainall is not resolved; like Valentine's promiscuity, it appears to be wiped out by the decision to marry.

The comedy of the period which is most honest about the consequences of hedonism and sexual promiscuity is, as Mr. Wain suggested (in 'Restoration Comedy and its Modern Critics', *Essays in Criticism*, vol. VI, no. 4), Etherege's *The Man of Mode*. It was written from a viewpoint which differed from that of the hero, Dorimant. He was recognized as a mixed character, with great charm and serious faults. Sir Richard Steele, in the 65th issue of *The Spectator*, mistakenly complained that Dorimant was not what he understood by a fine gentleman, and was certainly unfit to be the hero. A fine gentleman meant to Steele a man who was honest in his actions and refined in his language (i.e. did not swear)—a preview of Sir Charles Grandison. John Dennis replied that the word 'genteel' surely meant only that a man was agreeable in his air, graceful in his motions and polite in his conversation. Clearly Dorimant was the type of a fine gentleman in the time of Charles II, when Etherege was writing. Moreover, said Dennis, the character of Dorimant kept the decorum of comedy. He was a young man, and therefore prone to certain standard faults: Horace had listed these in his *De Arte Poetica*. They were pride, carelessness, amorousness, inconstancy and extravagance:

> *Dorimont* [sic] is a young Courtier, haughty, vain, and prone to anger, amorous, false, and inconstant. He debauches *Loveit*, and betrays her; loves *Belinda*, and as soon as he enjoys her is false to her.
>
> *Critical Works* (ed. Hooker, Baltimore, 1939–43), vol. II, p. 247.

He is meant to show up badly, and he suffers for his behaviour in the course of the play. Dennis was saying, very justly, that within the best kind of comedy the central figure is within the comic pattern—as she is in Jane Austen's *Emma*.

Dorimant's behaviour is presented as unfeeling from the start. When the play opens he is plotting to discard Mrs. Loveit, whose first and only lover he has been. Belinda is to assist him by making her jealous of a new mistress (Belinda herself) seen with him at the play the day before. He acknowledges to one of his friends that what he enjoys most is his power over women:

> Next to the coming to a good understanding with a new Mistress, I love a quarrel with an old one; but the Devils in't, there has been such a

calm in my affairs of late, I have not had the pleasure of making a Woman so much as break her Fan, to be sullen, or forswear herself these three days.

Works (ed. Brett-Smith, 1927), vol. II. p. 195.

The friend comments on his treatment of Mrs. Loveit: 'She cou'd not have pick'd out a Devil upon Earth so proper to Torment her.' Mrs. Loveit herself is very well aware of his character, but is unable to stop loving him:

I know he is a Devil, but he has something of the Angel yet undefac'd in him, which makes him so charming and agreeable, that I must love him be he never so wicked.

Ibid., p. 210.

Dorimant treats her abominably. He visits her on purpose to quarrel with her, when she has just been primed by Belinda with information about his new mistress. He denies that he knows her name as yet:

Loveit: False in this as in your Vows to me, you do know!
Dorim.: The truth is, I did all I cou'd to know.
Lov.: And dare you own it to my Face? Hell and Furies!
Dorim.: Spare your Fan, Madam, you are growing hot, and will want it to cool you.
Lov.: Horrour and distraction seize you. Sorrow and remorse gnaw your Soul, and punish all your Perjuries to me—(*Weeps.*)
Dorim.: So Thunder breaks the Cloud in Twain,
          And makes a passage for the Rain.

Ibid., pp. 215–16.

She must not expect constancy from a man of his age. Love made him appear charming—'but soon the Gold wears off, and then again the native Brass appears'. He has the effrontery to put the blame for the decline of their liaison on her:

Dorim.: I cannot endure the torture of a lingring and consumptive passion.
Lov.: Can you think mine sickly?
Dorim.: Oh, 'tis desperately Ill! What worse symptomes are there than your being always uneasie when I visit you, your picking quarrels with me on slight occasions . . .

Ibid., p. 217.

All this takes place in the presence of Belinda. She is frightened by the display, and it takes him a little time and some expenditure of charm to make her agree to keep their rendezvous that night.

He is inordinately vain. When Mrs. Loveit appears to be getting on well with the fop, he is furious—'She cannot fall from loving me to that!'—and considers forcing her into a further display of her passion for him. Instead, it is he that is discomfited. Having promised Belinda to see Mrs. Loveit only in public, he calls on her immediately after making love to Belinda—only to find Belinda herself visiting Mrs. Loveit. Both women attack him, and Mrs. Loveit's maid joins in. He has little to say for himself:

> Here is fine work towards! I never was at such a loss before . . . 'Tis time to fly! I shall be scolded to death else.
>
> *Ibid.*, p. 273.

He rushes off, promising lamely that he will explain everything later. The life of pleasure can lead to awkward complications.

Mrs. Loveit is not the conventional deserted mistress, melodramatically or ridiculously presented. She is honest with herself about the continuance of her devotion to Dorimant. When her maid offers sympathy for his ill-treatment, she acknowledges that she still prefers him:

> *Pert.:* I wish Mr. Dorimant wou'd not make it his business to defame you.
> *Lov.:* Shou'd he, I had rather be made infamous by him, than owe my reputation to the dull discretion of those Fops you talk of.
>
> *Ibid.*, p. 211.

When she hears that she has been displaced, the worst fate that she can imagine for her rival is to feel as she herself does about Dorimant:

> Who e're she be, all the harm I wish her, is, may she love him as well as I do, and may he give her as much cause to hate him.
>
> *Ibid.*, p. 213.

When Dorimant himself comes to gloat over her ruined reputation, she flies out at him—anyone else has the right to reproach her, but it is an outrage that the man who seduced her should do so. Her violence of feeling is reprehensible, but Etherege presents her as a human being who has been wronged.

The country heiress Harriet, whom Dorimant meets in the course of the play, is a match for him. She is attracted by him, but she has too much sense to let him get the upper hand. She looks delicate, but she has an underlying toughness:

> *Medley:* Teeth white and even, and pretty pouting lips, with a little moisture ever hanging on them that look like the Province Rose fresh on the Bush, 'ere the Morning Sun has quite drawn up the dew.
> *Dorim.:* Has she Wit?
> *Med.:* More than is usual in her Sex, and as much Malice.
>
> *Ibid.*, p. 193.

She holds her ground successfully in bouts of fencing with Dorimant:

> *Dorim.:* Is the name of love so frightful that you dare not stand it?
> *Har.:* 'Twill do little execution out of your mouth on me, I am sure.
> *Dorim.:* It has been fatal——
> *Har.:* To some easy Women, but we are not all born to one destiny; I was inform'd you use to laugh at Love, and not make it . . . When your Love's grown strong enough to make you bear being laugh'd at, I'll give you leave to trouble me with it. Till when pray forbear, Sir.
>
> *Ibid.*, pp. 249–50.

She will make no promise; she will not even hear his suit in London. He must visit her in Hampshire, where there is no company but her mother and an elderly aunt,

> perch'd up on Chairs at a distance in a large parlour; sitting moping like three or four Melancholy Birds in a spacious vollary—Does this not stagger your Resolution?
>
> *Ibid.*, p. 287.

He is to be tested before he is accepted, and his acceptance is not certain. Harriet can be as ruthless as Dorimant himself, not only to him, but to Mrs. Loveit, whom she scorns as a defeated rival, lacking in the strategy to win Dorimant:

Mr. Dorimant has been your God Almighty long enough, 'tis time to think of another——

Ibid., p. 286.

The play shows critically the barbarity that underlies the urbane charm of the lady and gentleman of the period. Hedonism, however, does not ensure one's comfort; the war can go both ways. The standard of judgment on the main characters is a blend of moral and social; they qualify in elegance, but they are deficient in some of the moral values. These defects are not glossed over, and the result is a satirical comedy of some brilliance—almost the only serious treatment of Restoration sexual life within the period. Horace Walpole explained the general decline from the level of Jacobean comedy in terms of over-emphasis on good breeding; manners and fashions had superseded morality.

Most of Restoration comedy has amusement value, if the audience is prepared to jettison moral standards for the evening; there is a pleasant patter of epigrams, plus the spectacle of some judiciously exaggerated 'type characters'. Few of the dramatists, when they were being honest, thought they were offering more than entertainment. Dryden set out the contemporary theory of comedy in his preface to *An Evening's Love* (1671), 'The business of the poet is to make you laugh.' It is not surprising that the age did not produce great comedy.

The growing influence of the city created a demand for a different kind of comedy, in which good characters behaved morally after a variety of near-lapses. The tide was already turning when Collier launched his attack on the stage; Vanbrugh was introducing heroines like Amanda who could retreat from sin at the last moment, often in blank verse. George Farquhar followed suit, drawing soft-hearted young men and even models of virtue. Even his villains repented; poetic justice was meted out to all. Wild young men were tamed by innocent girls. Sentimentalism triumphed over laughter, and what was produced was a moral play devoid of the comic spirit. Steele's *The Conscious Lovers* (1723) was one of the worst examples of this tendency.

The audience which enjoyed itself at the comedies also liked to indulge in heroics. Most of the Wits of the inner circle scorned the absurdities of the heroic play, but Dryden made a great success of it for some years. It was essentially a Restoration invention: an extended

hyperbole, in which larger-than-life characters displayed the depth
of their passion and the height of their courage. The plays were made
up of a series of strong dramatic situations, in which the fortunes of the
characters suffered continual reverses. The plots were intricate, and the
main characters were always finding themselves impaled on the horns
of a succession of dilemmas to which they had to find an honourable
solution. The complications were usually caused by the desires of some
of the subsidiary characters for either the throne or the heart that could
only be deserved by the hero. Some of these minor characters died;
others were so impressed by the nobility of hero or heroine that they
were converted from their wicked designs. The virtue that finally
triumphed was far from pallid—it was vigorous and independent. even
in the heroines. The dialogue, constrained by the dilemmas to take the
form of passionate debates, was in energetic couplets, ranging from the
magnificent to the absurd. The most famous of these plays are Dryden's
The Conquest of Granada (1672) (in ten acts) and *Aureng-Zebe* (1676),
although *Tyrannick Love* (1670), *The Indian Queen* (1665) and *The
Indian Emperor* (1667) were admired in their day.

In spite of its concern with love and war, Dryden considered Sir
William D'Avenant's pre-Restoration *The Siege of Rhodes* (1656) an
imperfect example of the heroic play; it lacked greatness of design,
variety of characters and stirring images. He proposed to raise the
imaginative level of the genre by imitating the examples of Homer,
Virgil, Statius, Ariosto, Tasso and Spenser in introducing 'gods and
spirits, and those enthusiastic parts of poetry' in their epics. The introduction of these was not intended as a piece of spectacle and sensa-
tionalism. Dryden considered the epic, or heroic poem, to be 'the
highest pattern of human life', and he wanted to elevate the plays to
that level. The playwright had to enthrall the spectators with his soaring
imagination, and get an 'absolute dominion' over their minds. He
justified the use of extravagant images by the practice of Virgil and
Horace. It is difficult to tell how serious Dryden was being; but the
quality of the plays he wrote suggests that these prefaces were merely a
piece of good salesmanship.

The play he wrote with Sir Robert Howard, *The Indian Queen*, is the
least characteristic. There is more tenderness and self-sacrifice in it
than magnificence or nobility. In *The Indian Emperor*, which depicts

the struggles of the Indians against the invading Spaniards, the most memorable part is the portrayal of the New World as a kind of earthly paradise that enjoys perpetual spring, refreshing after the decay of Europe:

> Methinks we walk in Dreams on Fairy Land,
> Where golden Ore lyes mixt with common Sand;
> Each Downfal of a Flood the Mountains pour
> From their rich Bowels, rolls a Silver Shower.
> (Act I, sc. 1.)
> *Dramatick Works* (1717), vol. I, p. 250.

The conquered Indians retreat with dignity from this paradise, finding a worth in independence:

> Of all your Goodness leaves us to dispose,
> Our Liberty's the only gift we chuse . . .
> Northward, beyond the Mountains we will go,
> Where Rocks lie cover'd with eternal Snow,
> Thin herbage in the Plains and fruitless Fields,
> The Sand no Gold, the Mine no Silver yields:
> There Love and Freedom we'll in Peace enjoy:
> No Spaniards will that Colony destroy.
> (Act V, sc. 2.)
> *Ibid.*, vol. I, p. 311.

Tyrannick Love, published in 1670, presented a villain-hero, Maximin, the Emperor of Rome, tyrant and persecutor of the Christians. Unfortunately he fell in love with his Christian captive, Catherine, and gave her the choice of being his mistress or his martyr. She took the second alternative. Maximin gave vent to some splendid extravagances, declaring war on the Gods:

> And shoving back this Earth on which I sit,
> I'll mount—and scatter all the Gods I hit.
> (Act V, sc. 1.)
> *Ibid.*, vol. II, p. 442.

But the absurdities of the complicated plot must be set against the seriousness of some of the play's meditative passages:

4

Could we live always, Life were worth our Cost;
But now we keep with care what must be lost.
Here we stand shiv'ring on the Bank, and cry,
When we should plunge into Eternity.
One Moment ends our Pain:
And yet the shock of Death we dare not stand,
By Thought scarce measur'd, and too swift for Sand. . . .

(Act V, sc. 1.)

Ibid., vol. II, p. 431.

Not until *The Conquest of Granada* in 1672 did Dryden create his ideal hero, Almanzor, who combined the drive and energy of Maximin with virtue. The action takes place in southern Spain, in the final stages of the Moorish domination. Boabdil's kingdom is divided by the factions of the Zegrys and the Abencerrages. First one side triumphs, supported by Almanzor, then the other when he changes his allegiance. No ruler whom he supports is willing to fulfil the extravagant promises made to him before the battle; affronted, he changes sides, only to be treated in the same way again. He wants the virtuous Almahide, Boabdil's fiancée. Unlike Boabdil, he always believes in her virtue, however strong the evidence against it; his noble spirit recognizes the extent of her perfections. The vicious Lyndaraxa is perpetually complicating the issue of events by promising herself to whoever gets the crown in the end. This involves her in a large number of volte-faces, which gradually undeceive those who have been in love with her. The relationship of Almanzor and Almahide is noble throughout. Almanzor himself is supremely independent. When Boabdil gives orders for his execution, he says:

No Man has more Contempt than I of Breath,
But whence hast thou the Right to give me Death?
Obey'd as Sov'raign by thy Subjects be,
But know, that I alone am King of me.
I am as free as Nature first made Man,
E'er the base Laws of Servitude began,
When wild in Woods the noble Savage ran.

(Act I, sc. 1.)

Ibid., vol. III, p. 37.

Later in the play Boabdil once again threatens to have Almanzor executed, but Almahide says she will commit suicide if he does so. She secures his release by promising to marry Boabdil immediately, and then commands Almanzor to live. He replies:

> When Death, the last of Comforts, you refuse,
> Your Pow'r, like Heav'n upon the Damn'd, you use . . .
> I go—but if too heavily I move,
> I walk encumber'd with a Weight of Love . . .
> > (Act V, sc. 1.)
> > *Ibid.*, vol. III, p. 91.

In Part II Boabdil soon finds himself in need of Almanzor's help. He can only obtain this through Almahide. Though Almanzor receives no reward but Almahide's scarf, Boabdil becomes wildly jealous. Almanzor welcomes such a chance for magnanimity:

> You've given my Honour such an ample Field,
> That I may die, but that shall never yield.
> Spite of myself I'll Stay, Fight, Love, Despair,
> And I can do all this, because I dare.
> > (Part II, Act II, sc. 3.)
> > *Ibid.*, vol. III, p. 122.

Later, he tries to persuade Almahide to become his mistress:

> *Almah.:* Who dares to interrupt my private Walk?
> *Almanz.:* He who dares Love, and for that Love must die,
> > And knowing this, dares yet love on, am I . . .
> > Be you like me, dull Reason hence remove,
> > And tedious Forms, and give a Loose to Love.
> > Love eagerly; let us be Gods tonight;
> > And do not, with half yielding, dash Delight . . .
> > Live but to Night, and trust to Morrow's Mind:
> > E're that can come, there's a whole Life behind . . .
> > > (Part II, Act IV, sc. 3.)
> > > *Ibid.*, vol. III, pp. 151–3.

Only Almahide's threat to kill herself restrains him. In the end, Boabdil is conveniently killed in a battle in which Spain overcomes the divided Moors, and Almanzor is recognized by his previously unknown Spanish father. The Queen of Spain tells Almahide that she must marry Almanzor when her year of widowhood is up. It cannot be said that any of the ten acts lacks excitement or magnificent declamation. Nell

Gwynn was a great favourite as Almahide, and the whole performance probably created a willing suspension of disbelief in the audience.

The last of Dryden's heroic plays, *Aureng-Zebe*, was on a more human scale. The style was supremely competent, and lacking in the extravagances that brought the previous plays to the brink of absurdity. The play was full of passages which were not essentially dramatic in character; they lose little by being isolated from their setting:

> Dare to be Great, without a guilty Crown;
> View it, and lay the bright Temptation down:
> 'Tis base to seize on all, because you may:
> That's Empire, that which I can give away . . .
> 　　　　　　　　　　　　(Act V, sc. 1.)
> 　　　　　　　　　　　　*Ibid.*, vol. IV, p. 151.

> Oh had I courage but to meet my Fate;
> The short dark passage to a future State;
> That melancholy Riddle of a Breath,
> That something, or that nothing, after Death . . .
> 　　　　　　　　　　　　(Act V, sc. 1.)
> 　　　　　　　　　　　　*Ibid.*, vol. IV, p. 156.

Two speakers were concerned in the final passage, but its effect does not depend at all on who said it. The voice is Dryden's, in a variety of moods. He never flagged; he enjoyed himself in every play he wrote, even if he acknowledged its badness later on:

> I remember some verses of my own *Maximin* and *Almanzor*, which cry vengeance upon me for their extravagance . . . All I can say for those passages, which are, I hope, not many, is, that I knew they were bad enough to please, even when I writ them; but I repent of them amongst my sins . . .
> 　　　*Dedication of the Spanish Friar, Essays*, vol. I, p. 246.

The heroic plays did not, perhaps, satisfy his criterion of being worth study in print, but they must have been impressive on the stage. For a time, they satisfied feelings for the primitive and natural which were stifled by the sophistication of contemporary comedies.

The other writers of the period who made a success of the heroic play were the Earl of Orrery, whose *Mustapha* (1668) was probably his best, and Settle, whose *Empress of Morocco* (1673) was deliberately taken up by some of the Wits as an insult to Dryden. Buckingham's play *The Rehearsal* was adapted in 1671 as an attack on the heroic play. It gave an unfair picture of Dryden himself as the fussy and stupid Mr. Bayes, but it was a lively comment on the technical absurdities of the heroic play itself by someone who did not sympathize with the spirit informing Dryden's attempts.

Some of the dramatists tried to create more serious plays, which they called tragedies. Apart from a few portrayals of Cromwell and James II (after his abdication) as tyrants, they took their plots from private rather than public life. The audience seemed more interested in love than in problems of ambition and responsibility. Despite the frequent use of antique or distant settings, there was a domestic air about the plotting: too many women in love with one man, forced marriages, unintentional bigamy or incest, love versus friendship. Dryden's Antony was not torn between Cleopatra and Rome, but between two loving women. Ambition was the villain's problem; he upset everyone's domestic arrangements to attain his own ends. The characters may have been emperors, but this did not elevate them above the human scale. There was much play with feeling, and a pathetic atmosphere prevailed. Dryden, Otway and Lee were among the foremost writers of such plays.

It might be supposed that the human scale would have given the tragedies of this period a foundation of truth. In fact, the improbabilities of the plotting, combined with the guiltless nature of the heroes, made even the humanity slightly hysterical in appearance. It seems that what a Restoration audience wanted was not tragedy proper— a depiction of the worst that can be imagined for the time—but an opportunity for an interval of emotional self-indulgence. No one thought that the plays depicted an aspect of reality: the author was careful to show the audience, by means of cynical prologues and epilogues, that he knew the absurdity of the tragic attitudes:

> You've seen a Pair of faithful Lovers die:
> And much you care, for most of you will cry,
> 'Twas a just Judgment on their Constancy.
> For, Heaven be thank'd, we live in such an Age,
> When no man dies for Love, but on the Stage:
> And e'vn those Martyrs are but rare in Plays;
> A cursed sign how much true Faith decays:

> Love is no more a violent desire;
> 'Tis a meer Metaphor, a painted Fire.
>> Dryden, *Epilogue to Lee's Mithridates, Poems*
>> (ed. Sargeaunt, 1913), p. 230.

Such defensive techniques were also characteristic of the heroic play (*see*, in particular, Nell Gwynn's epilogue in *Tyrannick Love*).

The critical theories of the day endorsed this trend towards sentimentality. Dryden attributed tragic fear to a realization by the audience that no one was privileged from the turns of fortune, and tragic pity to the knowledge that the most virtuous were not exempt. This doctrine lifts responsibility from the tragic hero. He no longer suffers because he has acted, he merely suffers what fate ordains. If, in addition to being a victim, the hero is thoroughly virtuous, the play comes near to being the spectacle of innocent suffering condemned by Aristotle. The degree of suffering becomes the criterion of tragedy.

The innocent hero appeared frequently in the plays of the period: Ziphares in Lee's *Mithridates* (1678), the honourable brother in Otway's *The Orphan* (1680), Theodosius in Lee's play of that name (1680), the negro prince in Southerne's *Oroonoko* (1696). There was a tendency to exploit suffering by dwelling on it, and to miss no opportunity for pathos. *The Orphan* and *Mithridates* were two of the more dignified of the pathetic plays. Lee's verse could be moving. Monima, Mithridates's rejected bride, refrains from reproaching him:

> I am hush'd
> As a spent Wave, and all my fiery Powers
> Are quench'd, when I but look upon your Eyes,
> Where, like a Star in Water, I appear
> A pretty Sight, but of no Influence,
> And am at best now but a shining Sorrow . . .
>> (Act II, sc. 1.)
>> *Works* (1722), vol. II, p. 33.

There is a delicate plangency here, reminiscent of some of Ford's dramatic verse, but it lacks fibre and intensity.

The playwrights like to wring the heart with the agonies of hero and heroine who had lost their loved one, and then to turn away from the absolute worst with a happier solution, as in Congreve's *The Mourning Bride* (1697). This tendency was particularly noticeable in their adaptations of earlier plays. Apparently the audience could not bear the agony of some of Shakespeare's endings. It was in this period that Nahum Tate gave *King Lear* (1681) its 'happy ending' with Cordelia married to Edgar and Lear left alive and in power. Dryden made his Cressida innocent and misunderstood, and she and Troilus were romantically reconciled in death.

It is worth examining one or two of the adaptations more closely, for they show most clearly the altered demands of the audience. Dryden's *Troilus and Cressida* (1679) was a sentimentalization of Shakespeare's, which had shown the ignobilities of love and war. The war was empty bravery, declining to treachery and deceit. Cressida was an experienced wanton, well able to look after herself in the Greek camp. Troilus was adolescent, but disillusionment made him resolute and able to face the worst truths. Helen was stale and stupid, Paris effeminate, Achilles a bully and a coward. Dryden's adaptation was fundamental: he purged nearly every character of guilt and sin, and it was all a dreadful misunderstanding discovered too late for the lovers to survive it. The whole tenor of the play proved how wrong Thersites was when he wrote off the activities of Greeks and Trojans as nothing but brawls and lechery. There was no lechery, and war was presented as a glorious occupation. When human beings were faced with disaster, they would always rise to the occasion and demonstrate the inherent nobility of man. Cressida killed herself because she could not bear to live if Troilus thought her unfaithful; Troilus was saved from further remorse by a comfortably quick death in battle.

Troilus was refocussed. Shakespeare had satirized him slightly as the conventional lover. Dryden gave him a childlike innocence and an impeccably romantic career. Cressida was recast as a Pure Woman, in terms of the feminine virtues recommended by Richard Allestree: piety, modesty, meekness, compassion and affability. Shakespeare had made her a coquette, but Dryden altered her attitude to one of modest reserve:

> Long has my secret Soul lov'd Troilus . . .
> Why then, why said I not, I love this Prince?
> How could my Tongue conspire against my Heart
> To say I lov'd him not?
>
> (Act I, sc. 2.)
>
> *Dramatick Works* (1717), vol. V, p. 51.

She was full of feminine compassion for Troilus—'What think you of a hurt Bird, that flutters about with a broken wing?' Before she lets Troilus approach her, she asks piously:

> And will you promise that the holy Priest
> Shall make us one for ever?
>
> (Act III, sc. 2.)
>
> *Ibid.*, vol. V, p. 76.

In the Grecian camp she made good use of her time by converting her father Calchas to his ancient allegiance. She is broken by the thought that Troilus suspects her fidelity, and kills herself to re-establish it, vindicated by Troilus's 'O thou purest, whitest Innocence'. This portrayal of virtuous womanhood obviously pleased the audiences.

Dryden's version of *Antony and Cleopatra*, entitled *All for Love* (1678), involved a radical change in the concept of the story. The power of Shakespeare's play depends to a great extent on two things: Antony's greatness and Cleopatra's splendour as an entirely unpredictable courtesan, and the fire of their love for one another, regardless of each other's faults. If Cleopatra were to become a normal woman with domestic virtues and ambitions, Antony's behaviour would look absurd. Why Cleopatra instead of Octavia? And why this consuming passion?—what such a Cleopatra would want was affection and support.

In fact, Dryden removed most of the qualities that had given greatness to Shakespeare's play. His Antony was on a smaller scale, a man content with memories and trifles, of whom it could never be said that 'crowns and empires were as plates dropped from his pocket'. And his Cleopatra is really a wife manquée, as she says herself—very like Octavia in her make-up:

> Nature meant me
> A Wife, a silly harmless houshold Dove,
> Fond without Art; and kind without Deceit;
> But Fortune, that has made a Mistress of me,
> Has thrust me out to the wide World, unfurnish'd
> Of Falshood to be happy.
>
> (Act IV, sc. 1.)
>
> *Ibid.*, vol. IV, p. 240.

She would rather darn Antony's socks than practise wiles on him. She is essentially submissive, keeps nothing back, and shows him the full extent of her devotion:

> I have refus'd a Kingdom,
> That's a Trifle:
> For I could part with Life: with any thing
> But only you. O let me die but with you!
> (Act II, sc. 1.)
> *Ibid.*, vol. IV, p. 221.

She is constant when Antony is false; she cannot bring herself to hate him. She is sincerely pathetic, not striking an attitude, when she says to Antony:

> What Place have I to go to? my own Kingdom?
> That I have lost for you: Or to the *Romans*?
> They hate me for your sake: Or must I wander
> The wide World o'er, a helpless, banish'd Woman,
> Banish'd for love of you; banish'd from you,
> Aye, there's the Banishment!
> (Act IV, sc. 1.)
> *Ibid.*, vol. IV, p. 254.

For such a woman, Antony's words would be a suitable epitaph—'Then art thou innocent, my poor dear love?' She is conceived as a woman who merits pity and very little else; certainly not the kind of woman of whom it could be said:

> Age cannot wither her, nor custom stale
> Her infinite variety: other women cloy
> The appetites they feed, but she makes hungry
> Where most she satisfies . . .
> (Act II, sc. 2.)
> *Antony and Cleopatra.*

Still, at times, Dryden succeeds in making the reader forget the character of his Cleopatra, and remember only the intensity of the moment. Such a moment comes in the second act, when Antony is asserting that he never wanted to leave her:

How I lov'd
Witness ye Days and Nights, and all ye Hours,
That danc'd away with Down upon your Feet,
As all your Bus'ness were to count my Passion.
One Day past by, and nothing saw but Love;
Another came, and still 'twas only Love:
The Suns were wearied out with looking on,
And I untir'd with loving . . .

His mood becomes more bitter:

While within your Arms I lay,
The World fell mouldring from my Hands each Hour,
And left me scarce a grasp (I thank your Love for't).
(Act II, sc. 1.)
Op. cit., vol. IV, p. 218.

That has a careless magnificence that can be compared with Shake-speare's dramatic poetry. Or, of Octavius:

Ay, there's his Choice.
He would live, like a Lamp, to the last wink,
And crawl upon the utmost verge of life.
(Act II, sc. 1.)
Ibid., vol. IV, p. 213.

When Dryden invented in the spirit of Shakespeare, he could write great poetry.

Otway, in *Venice Preserv'd*, rose above most of the limitations of his age. He created a grim dilemma for his hero which did not admit of an easy emotional solution; he was completely honest about the conse-quences of the hero's actions and left him to die without any sense of exaltation or expiation of his guilt. Otway's moral standards here were absolute. Within the play, the corruption and violence of public life destroy the *hortus conclusus* of private relationships. Although the play was set in Venice, the audience could not have kept the events at a comfortable distance; the conspiracy was too close a reminder of the continual rumours of Catholic and Whig plots that had disturbed the country over the past few years, and one of the Whig leaders, Shaftesbury, was caricatured as a Venetian senator.

Otway did not present a sentimentalized black-and-white picture of noble conspirators and villainous government, or the reverse. The two senators who typify the vices of the government are not melodramatic villains, but one is inhumane and the other irresponsible and perverted. Priuli's daughter has married in defiance of his wishes; he takes pleasure in seeing her and her husband descending into poverty, and prays that her future will be barren and unhappy. Antonio is a masochist who uses his wealth and his senatorial privileges to corrupt honest women. In this decadent city

> All agree to spoil the Publick Good,
> And Villains fatten with the brave man's Labours . . .
> The Laws (corrupted to their ends that make 'em)
> Serve but for Instruments of some new Tyranny,
> That every day starts up t'enslave us deeper . . .
> (Act I, sc. 1.)

Works (ed. Summers, 1926), vol. III, p. 18.

But their discontented subjects are no better. They say they want to restore liberty to Venice, but it is clear that they are not disinterested; they want to ruin Venice in order to establish their own government. Their leader incites them to

> Let loose the murmuring Army on their Masters
> To pay themselves with Plunder . . .
> Turn out their droning Senate, and possess
> That Seat of Empire which our Souls were fram'd for.
> (Act. II, sc. 3.)

Ibid., vol. III, p. 31.

They gloat over the prospect of indiscriminate bloodshed and fire. They are not even personally reliable: Renault, their leader, tries to seduce the hero's wife when she is left with him as proof of the hero's good faith.

The hero Jaffeir works himself into a position where he must either betray his friends or betray Venice. His impulsiveness has led him to join the conspiracy in a mood of false exaltation:

> How rich and beauteous will the face
> Of Ruin look, when these wide streets run Blood.
> (Act III, sc. 2.

Ibid., vol. III, p. 42.

His wife Belvidera, Priuli's daughter, shows him the appalling responsibilities of his situation; he must be guilty either of failing to prevent the destruction of the city, or of betraying his fellow conspirators, including his friend Pierre, to a peculiarly horrible form of punishment. He betrays the conspiracy to the Senate, and abases himself in front of Pierre. He has to bear the full weight of the consequences: the knowledge that he is despised and despicable, that because of him the conspirators will suffer an agonizing death, and that his relationship with Belvidera can never be happy again. The only mitigation Otway allowed was that Jaffeir should have an opportunity of stabbing Pierre on the scaffold and saving him from the shame of public torture, and of committing suicide. He dies cursing the Senate, unreconciled and unsatisfied. Jaffeir's weakness makes him an entirely credible character, and, although some of the episodes are stagily presented (the conspirators are the epitome of all their Jacobean ancestors), the basic situation is true to life.

Moral standards are not abrogated for pathetic effects. Jaffeir is far from being the virtuous hero struck down by fortune. His weakness makes him forfeit nearly all the admiration due to a hero; in his abasement he is an almost disgusting figure. It is his fault that he is far too easily swayed, not his misfortune. But he is shown facing the worst that he can imagine, and being defeated by it. He tries continually to do what is right, first conspiring for what he thinks is a worthy purpose, then betraying the conspirators to save the citizens. He discovers that each effort has been an ignoble one, and comes to a full realization of his degradation. There is no way out; in that sense the play is perfectly serious. He tries desperately to insulate himself from the effect of his actions by taking refuge in his wife's devotion:

> Oh *Belvidera*! I'm the wretched'st creature
> E'r crawl'd on earth: now if thou'st Vertue, help me,
> Take me into thy Armes, and speak the words of peace
> To my divided soul, that wars within me . . .
>
> (Act IV.)
>
> *Ibid.*, vol. III, p. 62.

But his actions have made it impossible for their happy relationship to continue. Belvidera may deceive herself, and prophesy a shared old age of comfort, but he cannot. He is a failure, but, in the end, a failure who knows himself. The sordid nature of events and the weakness of the principal characters is underlined by Otway's avoidance of heroic diction which might give them a better appearance.

This play came as near to tragedy as was possible in the period. Jaffeir is not a tragic hero, but his inadequacy is almost tragic. The dilemma, and the impossibility of finding a solution to it, evoke the requisite feelings of pity and fear, though there is no sense of exaltation in the play. The moral issues are clearly seen: Jaffeir is guilty because he tries to remedy evils by evil means, and he must suffer. There is no attempt to make the best of it, nor any enjoyment of the worst. The play has faults, but it is really disturbing in a way which was uncommon at the time.

It seems clear, however, that Restoration drama as a whole has little literary value. It is interesting as a phenomenon, because it reveals the needs, taste and moral uncertainties of the theatre-going section of the London public. But it does not merit the lengthy critical works that have been devoted to it.

THE POETS

Lyric and translation were the most popular forms of poetic entertainment in this period. There were, of course, exceptions. Neither a topographical poem like Cotton's *The Wonders of the Peak* (1681) (enshrined by Thomas Hobbes in the dignity of Latin) nor a mock-heroic one like Garth's *The Dispensary* (1699) belongs in either category. Both poems are read more as forerunners than as achievements in their own right. The main output of lyrics and translations belonged to London and the Wits, but outside the circle two poets at least deserve consideration: Charles Cotton, the country gentleman, and John Oldham, the Croydon usher whose work some of the Wits admired, and whose early death was lamented in Dryden's most moving elegy.

The lyrical poetry of the period owed much to the traditions of the earlier seventeenth-century lyric, but the richness and delicacy of the earlier period had, in the main, disappeared. The love-songs of the Wits were descended from the fluent songs of the Cavalier poets; the nature poetry owed something to the Elizabethan pastoral, and to Herrick. Suckling's tones could be felt behind the lyrics of Sedley, Dorset, Dryden and Etherege. Sometimes the lyric was neat, polished and polite in form and style, but superficial in sentiment. Sedley's address to Celia is accomplished, but it fails to move:

> Not *Celia*, that I juster am
>   Or better than the rest,
> For I would change each Hour like them,
>   Were not my Heart at rest.
>
> But I am ty'd to very thee,
>   By every Thought I have,
> Thy Face I only care to see,
>   Thy Heart I only crave.
>
> All that in Woman is ador'd,
>   In thy dear Self I find,
> For the whole Sex can but afford,
>   The Handsome and the Kind.
>
> Why then should I seek farther Store,
>   And still make Love a-new;
> When change itself can give no more,
>   'Tis easie to be true.

> *Works* (ed. de S. Pinto, 1928), vol. I, pp. 6–7.

This is technically unexceptionable, but tiresomely clever in its reasons for constancy; moreover, the tone of the second stanza is belied by the conclusion. A somewhat pornographic modification of this kind of lyric was popular in the plays of the period. It was a 'slick' song, set to a straightforward melody, lacking the rhythmic subtlety and delicate repetitions of the Elizabethan lute-songs. Sometimes the wording was completely outspoken; more often the actions were conveyed by suggestive hints. Rochester and Sedley had a fondness for writing poems in which harmless phrases like 'et cetera' acted as a substitute in the refrain for words which the listener could supply. At their best, these lyrics have a certain force, but it is not a poetic intensity; they act directly on the feelings by crude means. Their rhythms are insistent and their vocabulary stereotyped; 'dying' is one of the most overworked of their euphemisms. These stanzas from Dryden's *An Evening's Love* are typical of the genre:

> When the denial comes fainter and fainter,
>   And her Eyes give what her tongue does deny,
> Ah what a trembling I feel when I venture,
>   Ah what a Trembling does usher my joy!
>
> When, with a Sigh, she accords me the blessing,
>   And her Eyes twinkle 'twixt pleasure and pain;
> Ah what a joy 'tis, beyond all Expressing,
>   Ah what a joy to hear, shall we again!

Poems (ed. Sargeaunt, 1913), p. 373.

Desire was as forcefully and far more poetically expressed by Rochester in a lyric such as *The Insensible*, but he had to move away from this sing-song form to achieve it.

When Rochester wanted to express deeper feelings, he found an impressive use for the original of the form that had been debased by the playwrights. He wrote lyrics which were fundamentally evocative, not merely neat or fluent. They imply that there is a meaning in life; emotions cannot be cynically dismissed, or written off as lust and pique. They have overtones; more is implied than can be delineated by the language of statement. Their simplicity is the result of a refining of feeling to the bone. Intensity of feeling is presented in a framework of apparent calm.

The first lyric is on the theme of mutability. In a world which exists in time, the present is the only sure reality for love. Rochester is not being flippant about the necessity of snatching pleasures before they disappear, but lamenting human limitations, of which the most restricting is Time :

> All my past Life is mine no more,
>   The flying Hours are gone:
> Like transitory Dreams giv'n o'er,
> Whose images are kept in store,
>   By Memory alone.

The Time that is to come is not;
  How can it then be mine?
The present Moment's all my Lot:
And that, as fast as it is got,
  Phillis, is only thine.

Then talk not of Inconstancy,
  False Hearts, and broken Vows;
If I, by Miracle, can be
This live-long Minute true to thee,
  'Tis all that Heav'n allows.

Poems (ed. Q. Johns, 1933), p. 28.

In the second poem, Rochester is asking for leave to prove to himself that only this one woman can hold his love and give him the fixed centre that will be his salvation. He hopes that his life will end before he is unfaithful to her:

Absent from thee I languish still:
  Then ask me not, When I return?
The straying Fool 'twill plainly kill,
  To wish all Day, all Night to mourn.

Dear: from thine Arms then let me flie,
  That my fantastick Mind may prove,
The torments it deserves to try,
  That tears my fixt Heart from my Love.

When wearied with a world of Woe,
  To thy safe Bosom I retire,
Where Love and Peace and Truth does flow;
  May I contented there expire.

Lest once more wand'ring from that Heav'n,
  I fall on some base Heart unblest;
Faithless to thee, false, unforgiven,
  And lose my everlasting rest.

Ibid., p. 20.

Here there is a tenderness of feeling and a delicacy of movement that recalls the achievement of the earlier metaphysical poets. The lines have the assured tranquillity that comes from artistry, instead of the current bounce of self-satisfaction. The complex feelings have been perfectly distilled into words.

The pastoral was still a popular form for love-poems. Sometimes the poet straightforwardly re-created Elizabethan attitudes, reciting the beauties of the mistress in terms of nature. Rochester wrote a charming one called *A Pastoral Courtship*, in which he gave simple and unqualified praise:

> Now let me sit, and fix my Eyes
> On thee, that art my Paradise.
> Thou art my all; the spring remains
> In the fair violets of thy Vains:
> And that it is a Summers day,
> Ripe Cherries in thy Lips display . . .
>
> *Ibid.*, pp. 204–5.

More often, Rochester used the convention with a witty difference, and with full consciousness of what had gone before. His *Dialogue between Strephon and Daphne* has the traditional form, but its theme and imagery are not Elizabethan. The theme is the rejection of the shepherdess by a surfeited shepherd, who asserts that change has greater charms than she has, and discovers that she knew this before he did:

> Silly *Swain*, I'll have you know,
> 'Twas my practice long ago:
> Whilst you vainly thought me true,
> I was false in scorn of you . . .
>
> *Ibid.*, p. 6.

The sentiments of Restoration comedy have been accommodated in the pastoral dialogue, and the nature images have changed their function. They are no longer an idealized setting, but a polite outline of events, in which the lightning of attraction gives way to the thunder of embracing and the relief of showers.

Charles Cotton, who was unaffected by the standards of the Wits, kept far more to the spirit of the original pastoral, though his offers were on a more realistic level than those of Marlowe or Herrick. His Phyllis will not live in Arcadia, but in a world where winter happens:

> But when the sapless season brings
> Cold Winter, on her shivering wings,
> Freezing the river's liquid face,
> Into a crystal looking glass,

> And that the trees their naked bones
> Together knock, like skeletons,
> Then, with the softest, whitest locks,
> Spun with the tribute of thy flocks,
> We will o'ercast thy whiter skin,
> Winter without, a Spring within.

Poems (ed. J. Beresford, 1923), p. 100.

This is delightful in itself, as a picture of winter, and witty in its variation on the earlier tradition. The whole poem is firmly based in the Peak district; it is the River Dove in which they will bathe, and Cotton will go wildfowling to provide her with food.

The pastoral was used for elegiac laments as well as for love-poems. John Oldham turned to it, just as Milton had done more than forty years earlier. He mourned Rochester's untimely death in a poem that imitated the Greek of Moschus. It was often gracefully and melodiously phrased:

> Mourn ye sweet Nightingales in the thick Woods,
> Tell the sad news to all the *British* Floods . . .
> How *Bion's* dead, how the lov'd Swain is gon,
> And with him all the Art of graceful Song . . .
> Nothing is heard upon the Mountains now,
> But pensive Herds that for their Master low . . .
> Ne'r did the Dolphins on the lonely Shore
> In such loud plaints utter their grief before:
> Never in such sad Notes did *Philomel*
> To the relenting Rocks her sorrow tell . . .
> Such was the force of thy enchanting tongue,
> That she for ever could have heard thy song,
> And chid the hours, that did so swiftly run,
> And thought the Sun too hasty to go down,
> Now does that lovely *Nereid* for thy sake
> The Sea, and all her fellow Nymphs forsake:
> Pensive upon the beach, she sits alone,
> And kindly tends the Flocks from which thou'rt gone.

Works (1684), pp. 74–80.

This has the plangent simplicity of an earlier period, and some of Milton's skill in re-echoing a phrase. This was not the language of Oldham's time, but it is a most successful pastiche.

Even the nature-poetry of the period was not entirely free of imitation and conscious variation on the tradition of the past. Cotton in his Morning, Noon, Evening and Night quatrains played with the Spenserian set-piece describing place or time. In Spenser's poetry the sun does not rise; Phoebus's fiery car climbs up the eastern hill, full envious that night so long his room did fill. Nature and myth are married to produce a sense of the urgency of daybreak. Cotton, describing evening, had as much fresh delight in nature as Spenser himself, but his use of classical images was sophisticated and deliberately fantastic. He saw the chariot of Phoebus making its way down the sky, but for Cotton it was not a godlike progress. It was the struggle home of some weary farm-horses:

> The day's grown old, the fainting sun
> Has but a little way to run,
> And yet his steeds, with all his skill,
> Scarce lug the chariot down the hill.

Op. cit., p. 53.

Yet he combines this delight in the fantastic with an accurate picture of natural phenomena. He goes on to describe the curious effects made by the sun when it is almost on the horizon, creating absurd shadows:

> The shadows now so long do grow,
> That brambles like tall cedars show,
> Mole-hills seem mountains, and the ant
> Appears a monstrous elephant.
>
> A very little, little flock
> Shades thrice the ground that it would stock;
> Whilst the small stripling following them,
> Appears a mighty Polypheme . . .

Ibid., p. 54.

The villainous giant loses his threatening associations and becomes merely the sheep-boy's shadow. This is delicately handled in Cotton; but later on, in the verses of Swift, the technique degenerated into mere parody of the legends, in vulgar terms. At this time there was much to be said for these variations on a theme.

The poetic translations of the Restoration period were one of its notable achievements. Writers succeeded in producing versions of the classics which made them completely alive for the contemporary reader. The fact that Mr. Day Lewis's translation of the *Georgics* is preferred by the twentieth-century reader is no criticism of the adequacy of Dryden's for his own time. Dryden himself translated enormous tracts of classical authors—Theocritus, Lucretius, Horace, Homer, Ovid, Virgil, Juvenal, Persius. He was at his best when translating certain parts of Virgil, Horace and Ovid.

The English tradition had always tended towards free rather than literal translation, and Denham had reminded authors that they were not translating mere language, but poetry. Dryden himself, in his *Preface to the Translation of Ovid's Epistles*, advocated paraphrase, midway between the literal pedantry of metaphrase and the new creation that was falsely labelled 'imitation'. He realized that the concentrated idiom of Latin would sound ungraceful if it were put directly into English. Poetry needed freedom to move. He reminded his reader that the translator himself must be a critic who could appreciate the distinctive beauties of each work and a poet who could communicate them to the public.

Dryden translated Virgil's *Eclogues*, his *Georgics* and his *Aeneid*. His couplets were consistently vigorous, and his vocabulary elevated enough to suit the taste of the time. There were some effects that lay beyond his reach; he substituted for sublimity the somewhat rhetorical language of his own heroic plays. The pathos of the descent to Avernus and the passion of Dido's end eluded him; the couplets were too conscious.

> Dear Pledges of my Love, while Heav'n so pleas'd,
> Receive a Soul, of Mortal Anguish eas'd:
> My fatal Course is finish'd; and I go
> A glorious Name, among the Ghosts below.
> A lofty City by my Hands is rais'd;
> *Pygmalion* punish'd, and my Lord appeas'd. . . .
> Yet ev'n this Death with Pleasure I receive;
> On any Terms, 'tis better than to live.

> *The Works of Virgil translated into English*
> *Verse by Mr Dryden* (1697), p. 234, ll. 937–
> 42, 947–8.

This misses the intensity of Virgil's *Sed moriamur, ait. Sic, sic juvat ire sub umbras*. Yet his narrative passages were often felicitous. This description is taken from the third book of the *Aeneid*:

> The Night proceeding on with silent pace,
> Stood in her noon, and view'd with equal Face,
> Her sleepy rise, and her declining Race.
> Then wakeful *Palinurus* rose, to spie
> The face of Heav'n, and the Nocturnal Skie;
> And listen'd ev'ry breath of Air to try:
> Observes the Stars, and notes their sliding Course,
> The *Pleiads*, *Hyads*, and their wat'ry force;
> And both the Bears is careful to behold;
> And bright *Orion* arm'd with burnish'd Gold.
> Then when he saw no threat'ning Tempest Nigh,
> But a sure promise of a settled Skie;
> He gave the Sign to weigh; we break our sleep;
> Forsake the pleasing Shore, and plow the deep.
> And now the rising Morn, with rosie light,
> Adorns the Skies, and puts the Stars to flight:
> When we from far, like bluish Mists, descry
> The Hills, and then the Plains of *Italy*.

> *Ibid.*, p. 287, ll. 668–85.

He showed a lyrical richness and ease in his translations of the *Eclogues*. The fourth (taken to prophesy the birth of Christ) foreshadowed a golden age, where

> Unlabour'd Harvests shall the Fields adorn,
> And cluster'd Grapes shall blush on every Thorn.
> The knotted Oaks shall show'rs of Honey weep,
> And through the Matted Grass the liquid Gold shall creep.

> *Ibid.*, p. 18, ll. 33–6.

In the fifth, Menalcas is offering consolation for the death of Daphnis:

> *Daphnis*, the Guest of Heav'n, with wondring Eyes,
> Views in the Milky Way, the starry Skyes:
> And far beneath him, from the shining Sphere,
> Beholds the moving Clouds, and rolling Year.

> *Ibid.*, p. 23, ll. 86–9.

This is an imaginative rendering of the lines:

> Candidus insuetum miratur limen Olympi,
> Sub pedibusque videt nubes et sidera Daphnis.

Dryden has caught the spacious detachment of Daphnis's situation. When he handles the *Georgics*, he writes sympathetically of the labours of the bees:

> Plains, Meads, and Orchards all the day he plies,
> The gleans of yellow Thime distend his Thighs:
> He spoils the Saffron Flow'rs, he sips the blues
> Of Vi'lets, wilding Blooms, and Willow Dews . . .
> Then having spent the last remains of Light,
> They give thir Bodies due repose at Night:
> When hollow Murmurs of their Ev'ning Bells,
> Dismiss the sleepy Swains, and toll 'em to their Cells.

Ibid., p. 130, bk. IV, ll. 266–9, 274–7.

Yet Dryden's translation of the fourth book of the *Georgics* is less good than that of Sedley, who was far less experienced as a translator. Sedley had a sensitive awareness of natural beauty, and a feeling for diction that was unusual in this period. He wrote of the summer sun that 'expands the sky' after winter's departure. He was lyrical about the Pleiades; the bees have two broods a year:

> Once when the lovely *Pleiades* appear,
> And their new Light above the Ocean show;
> The other when those Stars feel Winters blow,
> And to moist Northern *Pisces* leave their Place,
> Hiding in stormy Seas their sullen Face.

Sedley, *op. cit.*, vol. I, ll. 260–4.

His lines suggest sense effects. He was not content with the poetry of statement, but tried to make the reader feel the events. Orpheus was being warned of the difficulty of wrestling with Proteus, god of shapes: he will

> crackle like a kindling Flame, or slide
> Out of thy Chains like a declining Tide . . .

Ibid., ll. 449–50.

In the second line with its delaying assonance on 'i' there is a suggestion of slow subsidence and dissolution. In his rendering of the sorrows of Orpheus when he has lost Eurydice for the second and irrevocable time, he shows a feeling for the wild and strange:

> Alone he wanders, where the Northern Wind
> Beats upon snowy *Tanais* chilling Shoar,
> Where Ice ne're fails, and ceasless Tempests roar;
> There his lost Wife he mourns . . .
>
> *Ibid.*, ll. 575–8.

He could make the domestic descriptions charming, when he was explaining what sort of garden should be created near the hives:

> For I under *Tarentums* lofty Towers,
> On yellow Fields, where slow *Galasus* pours
> Her fruitful Stream, remember to have known
> A good old Man; some Acres of his own
> He did possess . . .
> In the new Spring he cropt the earliest Rose,
> And the first Apples ripen'd on his Boughs;
> When even Rocks with cold fierce Winter cleaves,
> And every Stream his icy Chain receives,
> He the soft Sprigs of yielding Bearsfoot binds,
> Chides the late Summer, and slow Western Winds . . .
>
> *Ibid.*, ll. 136–40, 148–53.

Sedley achieved this one satisfying translation, but in range Dryden could always surpass him. Dryden's rendering of the twenty-ninth Ode of the Third Book of Horace was deservedly singled out by Professor Nichol Smith as one of his great translations, with its trumpeting proclamation of triumph over time:

> The joys I have possest, in spight of fate, are mine.
> Not Heav'n it self upon the past has pow'r;
> But what has been, has been, and I have had my hour.
>
> *Poems* (ed. Sargeaunt, 1913), p. 405, ll. 70–2.

He showed an equally sure touch in translating Ovid, particularly when dealing with his *Epistles* and his *Ars Amoris*. The lively machiavellianism of the attitude suited him perfectly, and he had scope for vivid colloquial phrasing. This is his rendering of the passage about the avarice of women who find they can take advantage of their lovers:

> To chuse for her she craves thy kind Advice;
> Then begs again, to bargain for the Price:
> But when she has her Purchase in her Eye,
> She hugs thee close, and kisses thee to buy.
> 'Tis what I want, and 'tis a Pennorth too:
> In many years I will not trouble you.
> If you complain you have no ready Coin:
> No matter, 'tis but Writing of a Line,
> A little Bill, not to be paid at Sight;
> (Now curse the Time when thou wert taught to Write)
> She keeps her Birth-day; you must send the Chear;
> And she'll be Born a hundred times a year.

Ibid., p. 527, ll. 480–91.

Dryden was clearly enjoying himself. His versatility was remarkable, and his energy never flagged; his translations from Ovid alone add up to more than seven thousand lines.

THE WRITERS OF FICTION

The seventeenth century used to be considered a blank period for the novel. There had been a burst of immature glory in the Elizabethan age, with the didactic polish of Lyly, the vigour of Nashe, the 'realism' of Deloney and the noble adventures of Sidney's heroes; then the novel disappeared for nearly a century, to reappear in the time of Defoe. This is an improbable theory; literary forms are not given to behaving like Rip Van Winkle. More recently it has been shown that the development of prose fiction was continuous through the century. It is true to say that no good novel was produced between 1660 and 1700, but the period contains one elegant romance and several stories which are of interest in showing the growth of both the romantic and the realistic novel.

The romance proper still dragged on. The Earl of Orrery's *Parthenissa*, in six volumes, began to appear in 1654 and was completed by 1665. It had little vitality; the values which had informed Sidney's *Arcadia* now sounded completely unreal. For the lower middle class who wanted their romances on a smaller scale, there was the long short story, often crammed with the plot of a full-dress novel. The most popular writer of these was Mrs. Aphra Behn. Her titles show the kind of story: *The Nun, or the Perjur'd Beauty, The Fair Jilt, The Lucky Mistake*. *The Perjur'd Beauty* is a revealing specimen of the type; it has all the action and passion Mrs. Behn could compress within twenty-one pages. It concerns the very entangled love-affairs of five young Spaniards: three men, two of whom are friends and the third their implacable enemy, on account of a wrong done to his sister, now in a convent; the second woman is the beautiful and entirely inconstant Ardelia. Ardelia falls in love, in series, with all three young men, and causes the death of all five characters. It is arrant melodrama, and the heroine's violent changes of heart are merely recorded instead of being made psychologically plausible. After all of them have behaved with the utmost lack of both nobility and common sense they are pitied for their hard fate, which is put down to the malicious influence of the stars. The story is entirely lacking in both wit and human interest.

Travellers, travel-books and the setting of some of the heroic plays of the period encouraged novelists to make use of exotic backgrounds for their romances. The public was beginning to like 'romantic true stories'. A transatlantic background enabled the writer to pass off an invented tale as an up-to-date happening, since there was no one to discredit the facts. A judicious use of detail concerning the flora, fauna and customs of the area added both verisimilitude and glamour to the story. The middle classes were also demanding morality rather than wit. Mrs. Behn had the sense to provide the public with exactly what was wanted when she wrote *Oroonoko, or the Royal Slave* (1688). She claimed to have known her hero personally when she was staying in Surinam, of which her father had been appointed Governor; he went with them on a tour up-country when he was a slave in that province. It now seems clear that her biography was as fictitious as her novels. If she did set foot in the New World, it was as the mistress of Scott, the regicide's son. Her information was obtained from George Warren's *An Impartial Description of Surinam*, published in 1667. She told a pathetic story of nobility betrayed, in an inflated style that made the most of heroic and tender feelings. Her hero was the negro prince Oroonoko of Coromantien, a gentleman educated by a French tutor, who combined the morals of real Christianity with the innocence of Nature, and who was wickedly sold into slavery. His bride-to-be was the lovely Imoinda, daughter of a General. Misfortune dogged their paths, but never made them less than noble; they came to tragic ends.

The events were well plotted and described, and the background was vividly sketched. Mrs. Behn's treatment of her characters' feelings was relatively full in this story, and she worked hard to involve the reader's sympathies. She created figures to admire, but they were not human characters, however deep their emotional reactions to events. The account of Oroonoko's reunion with Imoinda in Surinam gives a just idea of the quality of the writing:

> [Oroonoko] swore he disdained the Empire of the World, while he could behold his *Imoinda*; and she despised Grandeur and Pomp, those Vanities of her Sex, when she could gaze on *Oroonoko*. He ador'd the very Cottage where she resided, and said, That little Inch of the World would give him more Happiness than all the Universe cou'd do; and she vow'd, it was a Palace, while adorned with the Presence of *Oroonoko*.
>
> *Shorter Novels* (Everyman's Library, 1930), vol. II. p. 190.

Mrs. Behn had produced a romance that had a respectable colouring of realism, and she had shown a humanitarian attitude to slavery that was far in advance of her age. She had some devoted imitators at the end of the century and in the first half of the eighteenth century—Mrs. Manley and Mrs. Haywood were the most prolific of these.

It is only against the background of such romances that Congreve's mock-romance, *Incognita*, can be appreciated. He wrote it in 1691, at the age of nineteen. In his preface he commented on the incredibility of the average romance, and the way in which it left its readers vexed at the 'giddy delight' they had had. He took romance material and shifted the emphasis from wonder to delight, making the characters and incidents more familiar, more like those in a comedy. He provided a plot peopled by characters who had romantic tendencies and were ready to fall in love, thereby getting the best of both worlds. But he handled his romantic material so delicately that the reader at once believes in it and sees it as a charming commentary on the romances. Congreve regarded his lovers with a mixture of sympathy and amusement. His idea of the novel was closer to that of Fielding; the author was present in the story *qua* author, commenting on it and making cheerful asides to the reader.

The friends Aurelian and Hippolito are two accomplished young gentlemen. Aurelian is returning to Florence after an absence of two years. There in Florence they find a fiesta about to begin, and Aurelian decides not to go home until the festivities are over. There is to be a ball that night, and they must have new clothes for it. They find difficulty in obtaining them at such short notice, but in the end Hippolito is fitted out with the new suit of a gentleman who has been seriously wounded in a duel since he ordered it. Congreve gave them a suitable send-off for the ball:

> You must know, that about the fall of the Evening, and at that time when the *aequilibrium* of Day and Night, for some time, holds the Air in a gloomy suspence between an unwillingness to leave the light, and a natural impulse into the Dominion of darkness, about this time our Hero's, shall I say, sally'd or slunk out of their Lodgings, and steer'd toward the great Palace, whither, before they were arrived, such a prodigious number of Torches were on fire, that the day, by help of these Auxiliary Forces, seem'd to continue its Dominion; the Owls and Bats apprehending their mistake, in counting the hours, retir'd again to a convenient darkness; for Madam Night was no more to be seen than she was to be heard; and the Chymists were of Opinion, That her fuliginous Damps, rarefy'd by the abundance of Flame, were evaporated.
>
> *Works* (ed. Summers, 1923), vol. I, p. 116.

As Fine Writing, this deserves several stars in the margin to mark the magnificence of the conceits. It is much more elegantly handled than the later excursions into the mock-heroic made by Fielding.

At the ball, Aurelian succeeds in making himself agreeable to an unknown lady, and engages in a witty passage of compliment, where the lady proves more expert at raillery than he. The conversation moves crisply on a social level, and it is the politenesses rather than the raptures of falling in love that are stressed. They dance, and Congreve remarks:

> I should by right now describe her Dress, which was extreamly agreeable and rich, but 'tis possible I might err in some material Pin or other, in the sticking of which may be the whole grace of the Drapery depended.
>
> *Ibid.*, vol. I, p. 119.

Hippolito meanwhile is drawn aside by a lady who has mistaken him for her cousin on account of his costume, and caught up in an adventure. In the course of it he learns that Aurelian's father is planning to marry him to the beautiful Juliana when he returns to Florence. When Aurelian's unknown lady asks him his name, he gives that of Hippolito, not wishing his father to know that he has returned. In exchange, he is offered either her name or the sight of her face :

> *Aurelian* who was really in love, and in whom Consideration would have been a Crime, greedily embrac'd the latter . . . Aurelian (from whom I had every tittle of her Description) fancy'd he saw a little Nest of Cupids break from the Tresses of her Hair, and every one officiously betake himself to his task. Some fann'd with their downy Wings, her glowing Cheeks; while others brush'd the balmy Dew from off her Face, leaving alone a heavenly Moisture blubbing on her Lips, on which they drank and revell'd for their pains; Nay, so particular were their allotments in her service, that *Aurelian* was very positive a young Cupid who was but just Penfeather'd employ'd his naked Quills to pick her Teeth. And a thousand other things his transport represented to him, which none but Lovers who have experience of such Visions will believe.
>
> *Ibid.*, vol. I, p. 126.

Of course, after many complications and vicissitudes it is discovered that Aurelian's unknown lady is the Juliana to whom his father means to marry him, and love and duty are reconciled. Hippolito also wins his lady.

Congreve's characters are recognizably human, instead of being mouthpieces for noble or tender sentiments. He had an adult outlook, in spite of his youth; the story is the product of genuine poise. It is also tightly plotted. In an age when fiction tended to wander from incident to incident, agglomerating material, Congreve's plot stands out as dramatic and well contrived. All the threads are drawn together, and the whole action is simply the working out of the first incident—the arrival of the young men in Florence. It is a thoroughly elegant and controlled performance.

Besides the romances, stories of rogues and criminals sold well in this period. Sometimes these were mere copies of the earlier jest-books, collections of second-hand tricks and cheats; such were *The Tales and Jests of Hugh Peters* (1660), Head's *Nugae Venales* (third edition,

1686) and Crouch's *English Jests Refin'd* (1687). Occasionally there was an attempt to compose something more original. Head and Kirkman meant to emulate the example of Aleman, writing the adventures of the English instead of the Spanish rogue. The first part of *The English Rogue* (1665) was amusing, and was centred on the adventures of Meriton Latroon, a picaro who ends up in Newgate but is reprieved, and has further adventures abroad. The criminal biography, which was equally popular, also had its roots in the earlier part of the century. The best of the Jacobean biographies had been the lively account of the thief Gamaliel Ratsey. In 1665 *The Highwaywoman* described the crimes of Marcy Clay, who made a habit of decamping with goods obtained on approval, leaving a chest full of stones as security. *The Cheating Sollicitor Cheated* described Richard Farr, who made a living by forging deeds and running a band of thieves. There were accounts of the horrifying criminal as well as the amusing one: *Murther upon Murther*, published in 1684, gave gruesome descriptions of a series of six. At the end of the century, compilations began to be made of the Lives of Highwaymen and the Newgate Calendar.

None of the stories mentioned has any literary merit, but they did provide an alternative to a monotonous diet of romance. They certainly helped to foster a taste for realism, in that they were pseudo-real biographies of genuine low-life characters. Biography is rather a misleading term for them: they were no more truthful than Defoe's elaborated accounts of the careers of Moll Flanders and Roxana, their direct descendants. Their methods at this stage were catchpenny, and their sales depended on the immediate notoriety of the hero.

From time to time, however, these fictional biographies showed some artistry in the handling of their material. Professor Bernbaum has shown some of the differences in quality in the pamphlets which took for their subject the life of Mary Carleton, a bigamist who passed herself off as a German princess. Most of these pamphlets used the current mixture of fact and falsification unimaginatively, with little attempt to integrate the incidents into a pattern, or to examine the motives and reactions of the heroine. Such were: *Memories of the Life of Madam Mary Charlton, Life and Character of Mrs. Mary Moders, The Memories of Mary Carleton*. But Kirkman's *The Counterfeit Lady* was a different kind of production, though it was published in 1673, at the same time as the others. In verisimilitude, in plotting, in characterization and in tone it represented a measurable advance in the art of low-life story-telling.

Kirkman took pains to make his story sound authentic. He claimed personal knowledge of the affair through his acquaintance with her associates and her husband Mr. Carlton, and others of her victims. He tried to make an impression of caution by admitting that there were some details of her life which he did not know. Sometimes he refused to invent conversations 'that I may not seem to romance by telling you all their private discourses' (quoted Bernbaum, *The Mary Carleton Narratives*, Cambridge, Mass., 1914, p. 56). He described her appearance as a condemned prisoner:

> I am sure she was much dejected and very humble when I was with her . . . She was as clouded in her spirit as she was in her face, for her hood was still over it down to her mouth, and she very rarely turned it up; and her speech was very low and faint, broken and interrupted with deep and often sighing.
>
> *Ibid.*, p. 67.

He made causal connections between the various incidents in her life, so that they appeared to follow in an organic sequence. He showed why, at any given moment, she committed the specific crime attributed to her. Out of small incidents he made fully clothed dramatic scenes. Where the original narrative seemed to him implausible, he forestalled objections by inventing circumstantial details. Where the heroine seemed to effect her deceptions too easily, he invented further obstacles for her to surmount; her victims were made more reluctant and wary, and she had to locate their weak points. In a variety of ways he added suspense to the narrative, and made it altogether more lively. The level of improvement can be seen by juxtaposing two of the passages quoted by Bernbaum, one from the Appendix of the *Life and Character of Mrs. Mary Moders* (her 'dying confession') and one from *The Counterfeit Lady*. They concern the story of her theft from the man who was keeping her at the time. When he came home drunk and incapable, she rifled his letter-case and found a goldsmith's bill. In the morning she sent him off on a fool's errand to see a friend at Brentford, who, she said, wanted to see him urgently:

This Horton having a great many effects of the old gentleman's in his hands, wherefore he judging something more than ordinary, made all possible speed to Brentford.

The coast being now clear, she was resolved to march off and leave her old friend.

She breaks open the locks of a trunk and box, and rifles them both, where she finds twenty pieces of old gold, a golden seal, an old watch, and some pieces of plate. These, together with the rings, pendents, and necklaces, the old gentleman had presented her with, made a tolerable booty. And now she trips off to a new lodging towards West Smithfield, and there lies close.

(Appendix.)

'Now,' said she, 'I thought fit to call you thus early, that you may have time enough to go and return again before night; for you know I cannot be content without your company.'

He, hearing her discourse, and not having any occasion to hinder him, soon rises, and taking leave of her begins his journey. No sooner was he gone, but she made ready for hers; and, being dressed, she takes coach for the goldsmith's. When she was almost come thither, she drew out the bill to look at it. And it was well she did so, or else all her project would have been spoiled, for she intended to demand a just hundred pound, when, looking on the backside of the bill, she found that twenty pound of the hundred had been received. This startled her, and troubled her to think that she was twenty pound worse than she thought for. But she was glad she saw it before she came to the goldsmith's, who might else have distrusted her, had she asked him for the full hundred pound.

She, being now come to the goldsmith's shop, told him that she came from such a gentleman, who had such a day left a hundred pound, but had received twenty pound; and he, being sick had sent her for the eighty remaining. There was no distrust, nor no cause for it, wherefore the money was paid and the bill delivered up.

She, being now the mistress of this rich cargo of eighty pound in money, the jewel of fifty pound which he had given her, and several other rings, pendants and necklaces to a good value, was resolved to march off, leave her old friend, and seek a new, or at leastwise new quarters. But she was much disturbed and vexed that she was disappointed twenty pound in her expectation, and thought how she might make that good. And being now resolved to leave her old lover, and therefore to make the most of him, and knowing she had enough time by reason of his being out of town, she therefore returned to her lodging, and, not having the keys, breaks open the locks of a trunk and box, and rifles them both, where she finds twenty pieces of old gold, a golden seal, an old watch, and some odd pieces of plate. These, and all things of any worth, she takes. And then, without taking any leave of her landlady, she again takes coach, and marches off to a new lodging at another end of the town, where for some days she keeps close.

The Counterfeit Lady, quoted Bernbaum, *ibid.*, pp. 72–3.

Kirkman characterized even the minor figures in the story. He showed why the heroine took to a life of crime: her head was stuffed with romances, and she was tired of being poor. Her character altered in the course of the story; by the end of it she was thoroughly depraved. Previous accounts had gloated over her punishment and been sardonic about her exploits. Kirkman took a moral attitude that anticipated that of Defoe; he told the story as a warning to sinners, in serious tones. The opening paragraph and the peroration were particularly solemn.

Although Kirkman himself did not produce a work of lasting value, he developed a technique of realistic narration which could be easily employed by the genius of Defoe in the next generation. The eighteenth-century novel owed far more to this school of writing than it did to the romances produced by Kirkman's contemporaries.

THE SATIRISTS

SATIRE was an increasingly popular form of art in the period between the Restoration and the mid-eighteenth century. An age of change turns naturally to satire: the past provides the standards and the present the material. Where writers such as Clarendon merely lamented the breakdown of morals since the beginning of the civil wars, others like Dryden or Swift took it upon themselves to castigate and ridicule modern behaviour, which undoubtedly deserved the greater part of their criticism. There was some comfort in satire also: for some men the satirists took the place of a private conscience. They were a public scourge which acknowledged the presence of evil, and which could be observed falling on the rest of the community. Men who were half aware of the aimlessness of life now that the deeper levels had been prudently excluded felt a certain satisfaction in watching the scourge in operation, since it assured them that higher standards still existed, even if the majority did not trouble to aspire to them. Even if the Wits and their adherents were highly immoral, still there were men even outside the ministry who were not afraid to denounce such behaviour. Someone at least was fighting on behalf of virtue.

The cult of reason was a contributory factor in the rise of satire—which became, in the age of Pope, the most important genre of poetry. In art, the cult led to a revival of classicism, a mode in which satire had flourished: for the satirist was essentially a classic when he attacked excess and attempted to establish the norm or the golden mean. Restoration critics and men of letters developed a great admiration for the fathers of satire. Juvenal, Persius, Horace were translated or 'imitated' by a great variety of writers. Two main kinds of satire were recognized, both with Roman originals: that which railed at vice with the virulent ferocity of Juvenal and that which made it petty and

5   113

ridiculous with the urbanity of Horace. The relative merits of these ancestors were debated with vigour in contemporary critical writing. A fair case was made out for all of them, in spite of the very different tones in which they wrote.

Dryden gave the most just account of their value, though it was not a view shared by his contemporaries. He clearly admired Juvenal the most:

> I must confess, that the delight which Horace gives me is but languishing . . . His urbanity, that is, his good manners, are to be commended, but his wit is faint; and his salt, if I may dare to say so, almost insipid. Juvenal is of a more vigorous and masculine wit; he gives me as much pleasure as I can bear; he fully satisfies my expectation; he treats his subject home: his spleen is raised, and he raises mine: I have the pleasure of concernment in all he says; he drives his reader along with him. . . . His expressions are sonorous and more noble; his verse more numerous, and his words are suitable to his thoughts, sublime and lofty.
>
> *A Discourse concerning the Original and Progress of Satire, Essays* (1900), vol. II, pp. 84–5.

The average reader preferred urbane raillery to invective, and the sentiments expressed in Mulgrave's versified *Essay upon Poetry* (1682) are probably more representative of contemporary opinion than Dryden's are. The poem was soundly praised by Bishop Burnet, by Addison and Pope, as a salutary return to Augustanism. Mulgrave first praised satire as the surest reformer of the age, then gave advice on tone and style:

> Of well-chose words some take not care enough,
> And think they may be, as the Subject, rough.
> This great work must be more exactly made,
> And sharpest thoughts in smoothest words convey'd.
> Some think if sharp enough, they cannot fail,
> As if their only business was to rail:
> But 'tis mens Foibles nicely to unfold,
> Which makes a Satyr different from a Scold.
> Rage you must hide, and prejudice lay down;
> A Satyr's Smile is sharper than his Frown.
>
> *An Essay upon Poetry*, ed. Spingarn, *op. cit.*, vol. II, p. 290.

When Dryden turned from the discussion of high satire to low satire, he expressed his approval of the Horatian mode in terms that correspond with Mulgrave's:

> The nicest and most delicate touches of satire consist in fine raillery. ... How easy it is to call rogue and villain, and that wittily. But how hard to make a man appear a fool, a blockhead, or a knave, without using any of those opprobrious terms! ... There is still a vast difference betwixt the slovenly butchering of a man, and the fineness of a stroke that separates the head from the body, and leaves it standing in its place.
>
> Dryden, *op. cit.*, vol. II, pp. 92-3.

There had been a striking change in what men expected of a satirist; the roughness and sharpness cultivated by Marston and Donne in their vocabulary and versification were out of favour, and urbanity was now required as well as vigour.

It is impossible to generalize about the scope of satire in the period. It ranged from limited attacks on particular contemporary abuses in morals, politics, literature, religion, to more comprehensive attacks on the condition of man. It is not profitable to draw neat dividing lines. Most of Marvell's satire is political, directed against the kind of authoritarianism advocated by Hobbes; Dryden's most famous satires are either political or literary, though there is much satire also in his *Religio Laici* and *The Hind and the Panther*; Oldham writes mainly against the Jesuits; Eachard is primarily concerned with contemporary styles of preaching. But Rochester, Butler and Swift had wider aims, and do not fit into any one category. Moreover, many smaller men wrote the occasional satire in imitation of the classics: Duke, Stepney, Pomfret. It is only possible to examine the excellencies of some particular works within the period; there is no room for an assessment of each satirist as a whole.

The impulse to write satire is more easily accounted for than is the pleasure gained from reading it. In life, anger is an unattractive emotion; in art, the satirist's anger can cause an upsurge of righteous moral indignation as the reader identifies himself with the writer. Some pleasure comes from his admiration of the satirist's wisdom, experience of the world, honesty and sincerity. But the pleasure is never complete unless the satirist is also remarkable for his imagination, his powers of invention, his command of language. Satire which is to give pleasure must provoke more than the comment 'How true'—the reader must also feel how superbly the author said it. The satirist must have transmuted his feelings of rage into poetic energy.

The technique of suggestion used by satire is fundamentally an intellectual one. It has little scope for the vibrant overtones and subtle sense-impressions of lyrical or dramatic writing. Its suggestions are effected by such devices as incongruous juxtapositions, omissions, irony, judicious exaggeration or understatement, apparent magnanimities that slay in retrospect. This technique was perfected by Dryden in *Absalom and Achitophel* (1681–2). It can be seen in little in the following passage where his ridicule is directed against the court and the vicars of the Church of England. (In this allegory the Jews stand for the English.) Dryden is describing the activities of the Roman Catholic missionaries sent into England:

> Their busie Teachers mingled with the *Jews*
> And rak'd for Converts even the Court and Stews:
> Which *Hebrew* priests the more unkindly took,
> Because the Fleece accompanies the Flock.
>
> *Poems* (ed. Sargeaunt, 1913), p. 51, ll. 126–9.

The juxtaposition of court and stews (brothels) as the lowest imaginable forms of life, fit only to be raked as one rakes a dunghill, was a speedy method of indicating his opinion of both. There was both sting and urbanity in the next taunt about the avarice of the Anglican vicars who resented the desertion of their congregation to Rome mainly because their financial contributions departed with them—the fleece accompanying the flock. They should have been tending shepherds, but they were shearers only, wanting to exploit their flocks. This passage is closely packed with meaning, but its suggestive value is primarily intellectual; the feelings are stimulated only when the mind has grasped the implications of the statement. The technique represents the norm of good Restoration satire.

Oldham, the young poet of whom Dryden had such high hopes before his death at the age of twenty-nine, made the mistake of thinking that ingenious invective was enough for satire. He had a great deal of vigour, but he lacked imagination and constructive power. Probably the best of his satires is the third of the series written against the Jesuits in 1681. They had become even more unpopular because of the Popish plot; they were suspected of being the ringleaders of a plot to kill Charles II and install his Catholic brother James on the throne. This satire is in dramatic form. Oldham depicts Loyola on his death-bed, giving last instructions to his followers for their future bad behaviour. Since he has grown ripe for hell, the Roman Church is sure to canonize him. He requires absolute obedience to the Pope:

> To the unerring Chair all Homage Swear,
> Altho a Punk, a Witch, a Fiend sit there. . . .
> Tho he be Atheist, Heathen, *Turk* or *Jew*,
> Blasphemer, Sacrilegious, Perjur'd too:
> Tho Pander, Bawd, Pimp, Pathick, Buggerer,
> What e're old Sodom's Nest of Lechers were. . . .
> What e're he says, esteem for Holy Writ,
> And text Apocryphal, if he think fit . . .
> Again, if he Ordain't in his Decrees,
> Let every Gospel for meer Fable pass:
> Let Right be Wrong, Black White, and Vertue Vice,
> No Sun, no Moon nor no Antipodes:
> Forswear your Reason, Conscience and your Creed,
> Your very Sense, and *Euclid*, if he bid.

Oldham, *Works* (1684), pp. 43–5.

This is a method based on the simple accumulation of indignation and abhorrence. Oldham never tires of adding another layer. Loyola incites his followers to bloodshed and inquisition. All recruits must be educated out of their scruples. The brotherhood must arm itself with stories of fantastic miracles to deceive the elderly. The confessional provides opportunities both for blackmail and for seduction. The Bible

117

must be kept out of reach; it is absurd that laymen should think themselves entitled to interpret it:

> Pray that kind Heav'n would on their hearts dispense
> A bounteous, and abundant Ignorance,
> That they may never swerve, nor turn awry
> From sound, and Orthodox Stupidity.
>
> *Ibid.*, p. 66.

Any Jesuit suspected of disloyalty should be killed at once. But this is
Loyola's last commandment. He has come to the end of his powers. He
has hardly time to give the crowd his blessing before demons seize his
soul for hell. Oldham ends with a flourish, but there is little artistry
here. The irony is heavy and long-drawn-out; there is no relief from the
deadly seriousness of the tone. The reader is good and the Jesuits are
bad—that is the whole story. The energy of Oldham's fury is remarkable; he is single-minded and quite remorseless. Loyola is made to
damn himself. His speech to his followers occupies the whole of the
poem; what he extravagantly praises is wrong, what he despises is
right. The variety of the poem lies only in the variety of the actual
crimes described; the method remains the same. The language is not
distinguished; it has punch, but no concentration and no polish.
Oldham's energy is beyond doubt, but the work is hardly a poem—
more of a canalization of popular feeling. Oldham could, however, be
more urbane; in the *Satire Addressed to a Friend that is about to leave
the University* he had a lighter and more delicate touch.

SAMUEL BUTLER (1612–80)

The most large-scale satire of the period, Samuel Butler's *Hudibras*,
began to appear in 1662, before the cause of smoothness had been won.
Its basic purpose was to satirize the nature of man, a foolish enthusiast
and a hypocrite, impossibly proud of himself. This purpose was
complicated by subsidiary ones. In basing the plot (slight as it was)
on that of *Don Quixote*, Butler was mocking the contemporary taste for

elaborate long romances, such as Dorothy Osborne confessed she read. In making Hudibras and his squire Ralph Presbyterian and Independent respectively, he was hitting at unpopular sects, now safely out of power. There were hits at the Civil Wars, at the inconclusiveness of the Rump Parliament, at the rites of the Rosicrucians, at 'sympathetic powder' that was supposed to heal at a distance, at echo poems. If Butler had not given up writing the poem, almost anything could have put in an appearance: architectonically it resembles a rag-bag. The minor butts were not the only distraction from the main theme. Butler became so fascinated with the technique of low satire, with the way in which he was introducing his diminishing comparisons, his trite proverbs, his absurd images and ludicrous rhymes, that he often lost sight of the goal in enjoying his own performance.

Butler despised man for his hypocrisy, his lack of common sense and proportion, his petty desire to dictate, his readiness to solve problems by violence, his assumption that he is always right, his acquisitive and predatory tendencies which he cloaks with the names of chivalry and devotion. Man was, for Butler, an undignified creature who deserved to be exposed. In his first few lines he undermined the worth of man's most recent 'heroic' enterprise, the Civil Wars which formed the background of the poem:

> When *civil* fury first grew high,
> And men fell out they knew not why,
> When hard *Words*, *Jealousies*, and *Fears*,
> Set Folks together by the Ears,
> And made them fight, like mad or drunk,
> For Dame *Religion* as for Punk,
> Whose honesty they all durst swear for,
> Though not a man of them knew wherefore . . .
>
>   *Hudibras* (ed. A. R. Waller, 1905), Bk. I, canto 1, ll. 1–8.

He wrote off the Cause as nothing more than a worthless drab fought over by a set of drunks. He ranged over the whole field of human activity and learning: man's martial virtues, his 'chivalry', his wooing, his pedantry which fails to disguise ignorance. Hudibras himself, as philosopher and logician, was

> Profound in all the Nominal
> And real ways beyond them all;
> And with as delicate a Hand,
> Could twist as tough a Rope of Sand.
> And weave fine Cobwebs, fit for Skull
> That's empty when the Moon is full;
> Such as take Lodgings in a Head
> That's to be lett unfurnished.
>
> *Ibid.*, Bk. I, canto 1, ll. 155–62.

Hudibras was an expert in many fields. He spoke a Babylonish dialect of patched and piebald languages; he was a marvellous rhetorician, who could find a profound reason for an accidental cough. Nothing was difficult for him, not even the profoundest divinity; he understood it by implicit faith:

> He knew *what's what*, and that's as high
> As *Metaphysick Wit* can fly.
>
> *Ibid.*, Bk. 1, canto 1, ll. 151–2.

As for his squire Ralph, he could penetrate through all the Aristotelian causes to the primal stuff of the universe:

> (as he profest)
> He had *First Matter* seen undrest:
> He took her naked all alone
> Before one Rag of *Form* was on.
>
> *Ibid.*, Bk. I, canto 1, ll. 559–62.

These are the main characters, but the rest do nothing to elevate the status of humanity.

The plot which sets these characters in motion is very simple. The framework is that of Cervantes's *Don Quixote*: an anachronistic errant knight who sets out to right wrongs and win the hand of his lady, but merely makes an arrant fool of himself. The action itself would take up about four of Cervantes's hundred and thirty-odd chapters. Butler's Hudibras was a Presbyterian knight, accompanied by an Independent squire called Ralph. Together they sallied forth to rid the world of evil. The knight hoped to get enough fame by his exploits and his sufferings to win a rich widow for his wife. In the first book they attacked a crowd who were engaged in bear-baiting, and succeeded in imprisoning the fiddler that led the rout. The crowd rallied, released the fiddler from the stocks, and put Hudibras there instead. In the second book Hudibras was visited by the widow, who released him from the stocks in return for a promise that he would scourge himself for love of her. Hudibras and Ralph then quarrelled, and were prevented from coming to blows only by the arrival of a ludicrous procession, the Skimmington, whose purpose was to deride henpecked husbands. They joined forces to attack the cavalcade, and were worsted by unsavoury ammunition. The knight then went off to consult a Rosicrucian about his chances of winning the widow, quarrelled with him, and defeated him, leaving him for dead on the floor. He returned to the widow and tried to pretend that his injuries came from carrying out his vow to scourge himself. Ralph undeceived her, and she arranged for the knight to be punished by an interrogation and a beating. There was then an interlude presenting the endless debates of the Rump Parliament. The last canto that Butler wrote returned to the knight, who was plotting to sue the widow for breach of promise. Dr Johnson voiced the criticism of the ordinary man:

> I believe every reader regrets the paucity of events, and complains that in the poem of Hudibras, as in the history of Thucydides, there is more said than done. The scenes are too seldom changed, and the attention is tired with long conversation.
>
> Johnson, *Works* (1796), vol. IX, p. 193.

These are the incidents. In themselves they are not worth much, but Butler succeeded in making them all highly ludicrous by caricature, by burlesque of Romance conventions, and by studied extravagance of phrase, image and rhyme. There is, for instance, a great deal of diverting material in the account of the fight with the bearward and his friends: Hudibras and Ralph are on horseback, and Ralph's horse is upset by the application of a thistle:

> He gave the Champions Steed a thump,
> That stagger'd him. The *Knight* did stoop
> And sate on further side aslope,
> This *Talgol* viewing, who had now
> By flight escap'd the fatal blow,

He rally'd, and again fell to't;
For catching him by nearer foot,
He lifted with such might and strength,
As would have hurl'd him twice his length,
And dash'd his brains (if any) out.
But *Mars* that still protects the stout,
In Pudding-time came to his aid,
And under him the *Bear* convey'd;
The *Bear*, upon whose soft Fur-Gown
The *Knight* with all his weight fell down.
The friendly Rug preserv'd the ground,
And headlong *Knight* from bruise or wound,
Like Feather-Bed betwixt a Wall,
And heavy brunt of Cannon-ball. . . .
The *Bear* was in a greater fright,
Beat down and worsted by the *Knight*.
He roar'd, and rag'd, and flung about,
To shake off bondage from his snout.
His wrath enflam'd boil'd o'er, and from
His jaws of Death he threw the fome,
Fury in stranger postures threw him,
And more, than ever Herald drew him,
He tore the Earth, which he had sav'd
From squelch of *Knight*, and storm'd and rav'd
And vext the more, because the harms
He felt were 'gainst the *Law of Arms*:
For Men he always took to be
His friends, and Dogs the Enemy:
Who never so much hurt had done him,
As his own side did falling on him.

Ibid., Bk. I, canto 2, ll. 854–72, 877–92.

The whole incident is a mixture of high-flown heroics and homely anti-climax. Mars and the laws of chivalry are mixed up with the rugs and feather-beds, with the feather-bed masquerading as a heroic simile. The tone seems solemn at times, but the solemnity is always destroyed by a turn or a parenthesis 'and dash'd his brains (if any) out' which denies that the event was in the least important. Mars, too, is protecting the literally stout on this occasion, not the stout-hearted. There is a constant reversal of the normal; one would expect the bear to have protected the knight in his fall, but in fact he protected the ground from the impact of the knight. There is a general bounce and jocularity about the movement that makes the account into an enjoyable burlesque. There are comparable scenes that parody heroic and romantic conventions in a similar way: Orsin in search of his bear is inveigled into a colloquial echo-scene, where echo's replies are uninterested and rude; Hudibras in the stocks discourses on the power of love to the widow; the widow and the knight exchange heroical epistles.

Most of the time, the reader's amusement at Butler's burlesques, his wit and ingenuity more than half obscures the original satirical purpose. He cannot help being distracted by the way Butler has made free with the language, punning, splitting words, inventing classical mouthfuls like 'cynarctomachy' (fight between dogs and bears), tagging Latin, dashing between the pedantic and the slang phrase, discovering fantastic rhymes—brief as, preface; flambeau, damned blow. The poem becomes irresponsible. Butler runs after incredible extravagances, spins out long-winded excuses, turns short with a shrewd aphorism. The purpose has been forgotten in the frivolling, although the decline in seriousness is never accompanied by any sympathy for the objects satirized. All that has happened is that Butler has taken his eye off the object for the moment—a thing that can easily happen in a poem as loosely constructed as this.

Often, however, his shrewdness and his satirical wit are apparent, particularly if he is read in small doses. His style at its best is terse and sharp, colloquial and vigorous. It shows up very well in the character sketches, with their succession of pithy epigrams. His account of Hudibras's religion is one of the most memorable passages:

> For his *Religion* it was fit
> To match his Learning and his Wit:
> 'Twas *Presbyterian* true blew,
> For he was of that stubborn Crew
> Of Errant Saints, whom all men grant
> To be the true Church *Militant*:
> Such as do build their Faith upon
> The holy Text of *Pike* and *Gun*;
> Decide all Controversies by
> Infallible *Artillery*;
> And prove their Doctrine Orthodox
> By Apostolick *Blows* and *Knocks*;
> Call Fire and Sword and Desolation,
> A *godly-thorough-Reformation*,

Which always must be carry'd on,
And still be doing, never done:
As if Religion were intended
For nothing else but to be mended.

Ibid., Bk. I, canto 1, ll. 189–206.

Here Butler is on one of his favourite topics: the narrow-mindedness
of creatures who insist on imposing their worthless opinions on others
by force. There is irony throughout the passage. The author appears
to be accepting violence as a valid proof of the orthodoxy of any
doctrine, approving of the artillery; but by the end of the passage he
is openly sardonic. They merely call their methods a godly-thorough-
reformation; no sensible man will agree, or feel anything but indignation at their perpetual patching and tinkering with faith and ritual. This
is not what was meant by becoming soldiers of Christ. The saints
are certainly errant. There is a neatness about each couplet, and a
pertness of tone, which reinforce the impression that the author is
entirely right; he proceeds with such assurance and command of
epigram. If Butler's verse had always been of this quality, and if he had
grappled better with the structure of the poem as a whole, all three
books of *Hudibras* might have been read with consistent pleasure.
Coleridge criticized the central defect:

> The great thing in poetry is, *quocunque modo*, to effect a unity of im-
> pression upon the whole; and a too great fulness and profusion of point
> in the parts will prevent this. Who can read with pleasure more than a
> hundred lines or so of Hudibras at one time? Each couplet or quatrain
> is so whole in itself, that you can't connect them. There is no fusion.

> *Coleridge on the Seventeenth Century* (ed. R. F. Brinkley, Durham,
> N.C., 1955), pp. 616–17.

Butler's contemporaries also had their reservations about *Hudibras* as
a poem. Dryden complained of being pleased against his will:

> We thank him not for giving us that unseasonable delight, when we
> know he could have given us a better, and more solid.

> *Essays* (ed. Ker, 1900), vol. II, p. 105.

Pepys bought a copy of the first part, did not enjoy it, sold it to a friend, and six weeks later bought another copy to see if he could discover why so many people thought it witty.

Butler did provide the better and more solid delight in other places. As a whole, the satire on virtuosi in general and the Royal Society in particular, *The Elephant in the Moon* (occasioned by a mouse trapped in the telescope), is much more artistically and decorously handled. In his prose characters, where there was less temptation to indulge in verbal horseplay, Butler was consistently impressive. There his wit was used to underline the seriousness, instead of obliterating it. Within these separate studies of men, his imagination could penetrate more deeply into their essential natures. At times, he wrote with an unexpectedly Baconian weight of significance, using images that carried a strong emotional charge. His language could be sonorous—something impossible within the scope of his octosyllabics. Two extracts must serve to illustrate this quality. The first comes from the character of a degenerate noble, or one that is proud of his birth:

> He is like a Turnep, there is nothing good of him, but that which is under-ground, or Rhubarb a contemptible Shrub, that springs from a noble Root. He has no more Title to the Worth and Virtue of his Ancestors, than the Worms that were engendred in their dead Bodies, and yet he believes he has enough to exempt himself and his Posterity from all Things of that Nature for ever. This makes him glory in the Antiquity of his Family, as if his Nobility were the better, the further off it is in Time, as well as Desert, from that of his Predecessors. . . . He is like a *Fanatic*, that contents himself with the mere Title of a Saint, and makes that his Privilege to act all manner of Wickedness; or the Ruins of a noble Structure, of which there is nothing left but the Foundation, and that obscured and buried under the Rubbish of the Superstructure. The living Honour of his Ancestors is long ago departed, dead and gone, and his is but the Ghost and Shadow of it, that haunts the House with Horror and Disquiet, where once it lived.

> *Characters* (ed. A. R. Waller, 1908), pp. 34–5.

The second describes a Squire of Dames:

> He is Esquire to a Knight-Errant, Donzel to the Damzels, and Gentleman Usher daily waiter on the Ladies, that rubs out his Time in making Legs and Love to them. He is a Gamester, that throws all Ladies that are

set to him, but is always out, and never winds but when he throws at the Candlestick, that is for nothing; a general Lover, that addresses unto all but never gains any, as Universals produce nothing. . . . One of his prime Qualifications is to convey their Persons in and out of Coaches, as tenderly as a Cook sets his Custards in the Oven and draws them out again, without the least Discomposure or Offence to their inward or outward Woman, that is, their Persons and Dresses.

Ibid., pp. 160–1.

These passages cannot match the surface brilliance of some parts of *Hudibras*, but they have a wisdom and a pregnancy of expression which were equally out of Butler's reach in the poem. Here is his genuine satire on the nature of man, unencumbered with his consciousness of his personal ingenuity.

JOHN DRYDEN (1631–1700)

Dryden is clearly the major poetic satirist of his period. If his *Absalom and Achitophel* is compared with Butler's *Hudibras*, Dryden's sense of responsibility as a satirist becomes clear. He never forgot the end he had in view. He managed to make his opponents look both ridiculous and pernicious, without having recourse to gymnastic antics himself. He had more sense of structure: instead of choosing a rambling story which had little reason for ever coming to an end, he chose the form of allegory, and kept strictly to the point. His wit, vigour and polish made an essential contribution to the satiric purpose, instead of distracting attention from it.

The story of Absalom and Achitophel, based on a considerably simplified version of the second Book of Samuel, made a useful parallel for the contemporary political situation. Absalom, assisted by Achitophel, was attempting to unseat his father King David and seize the throne of Israel. In England in 1681 the Earl of Shaftesbury was urging the Duke of Monmouth, Charles's favourite illegitimate son, to force his father's hand by a show of support in the country. He wanted to be declared his father's heir instead of Charles's Catholic brother James, the heir presumptive. If the machinations of the Whigs had been successful, he might well have succeeded Charles immediately.

Dryden wrote the satire in the hope of bringing Absalom to a better frame of mind, and of furthering a reconciliation between the King and the son he loved. Dryden stood for balance, moderation, adherence to established law and order. After his experience of the Civil Wars and the Commonwealth, he was only too well aware of the unpleasant results of violent change, however much it might be called reform. He wanted stability and a continuing central authority; he was anxious to avoid any political move which would once again divide the country into opposing camps:

> All other Errors but disturb a State,
> But Innovation is the Blow of Fate.
> If ancient Fabricks nod, and threat to fall,
> To Patch the Flaws, and Buttress up the Wall,
> Thus far 'tis Duty; but here fix the Mark:
> For all beyond it is to touch our Ark.
> To change Foundations, cast the Frame anew,
> Is work for Rebels who base Ends pursue:
> At once Divine and Humane Laws controul,
> And mend the Parts by ruine of the Whole.
>
> *Absalom and Achitophel, Poems* (ed. Sargeaunt,
> 1913), p. 59, ll. 799–808.

Part I of the poem gave Dryden opportunities for some of his best writing. He made the incidents, the people and the arguments vividly alive. He managed to make his highly finished verse sound entirely spontaneous, like brilliant impromptu. It appeared to be the language of conversation, raised to a higher pitch of intensity. He had enough force and pungency to make clowning unnecessary. Moreover, his handling of the allegory was firm and assured; he was as ruthless with the Bible original as Shakespeare was with history.

The Bible story was considerably more complex than Dryden's version of it. It made a suitable comparison in that Absalom was an illegitimate son of David, became very dear to him, and finally conspired against him. But in the Bible his reasons for the initial estrangement with David were not political; he kept away from his father because he had killed his brother Amnon in revenge for the rape of his sister Tamar. After three years there was a reconciliation. Then Absalom began to curry popular favour. Finally, with Achitophel's help, he went into Hebron with his followers and had himself proclaimed King. His conspiracy to kill David failed; Achitophel hanged himself, and there was a pitched battle between the armies of David and Absalom in which Absalom was killed. The King deeply lamented his death. When Dryden took over the story, he discarded the Amnon incident, and hinted that the reconciliation that historically followed it was about to put an end to Monmouth's disloyal moves, which had not yet reached the point of putting an army in the field against the King. Moreover, he enlarged Achitophel's responsibility so that he became much more of a Satan tempting an innocent Adam than a shrewd counsellor whose executive advice had not been taken. There were several advantages in using this story, even in an altered form. First, the identification of Charles with David was a good move. It linked the King with his father, who had often been cast as David in Royalist pamphleteering; it made his amours respectably patriarchal; and it emphasized his tenderness of nature, his affection for his son, which would make a reconciliation possible. Secondly, a sympathetic light was cast on Monmouth himself, since what is chiefly remembered of the Bible story is David's lament for his son, rather than that son's treachery. In addition, the known Bible ending cast the threat of impending tragedy over an unresolved situation, and acted almost as a *memento mori*.

Absalom and Achitophel is 'heroic' satire, on an entirely different plane from Butler's burlesque. But it is not heroic in the sense that Dryden's plays were; it is far from extravagant. Dryden made an impression of sanity by his treatment of the characters and his apportioning of blame. The heaviest attack fell on Shaftesbury as Achitophel, but Dryden did not spare the rest of those who worked against the government or established religion, whether they were the heads of the faction or merely an acquiescent rabble. He blamed the instigators of the 'Popish Plot' for giving a loose to faction; before this, it had slept, but now

> several Factions from this first Ferment
> Work up to Foam, and threat the Government.
>
> *Ibid.*, p. 51, ll. 140–1.

In this atmosphere of unrest, Achitophel made a bid for power which was more dangerous to the commonwealth. He was assisted by a set of well-meaning malcontents: some who thought the power of monarchy too much, some who thought kings too expensive a luxury, some who hoped for preferment, some who were 'dreaming saints' with anarchistic outlooks, some who merely feared Roman Catholicism but did not understand the political issues at all. Dryden gave brilliant character-sketches of all the leaders: Achitophel himself, Zimri (Duke of Buckingham), who hoped to recover what he had squandered, Shimei (Sheriff Bethel), the meanest man in London, and Corah (Titus Oates).

The poem is far from being a collection of character-sketches. After having set the stage, Dryden created a formal debate in which Monmouth was persuaded by Shaftesbury to conspire against his father. Shaftesbury attacked subtly, depicting Monmouth as the potential saviour of his country, on whom all men's hopes were pinned:

> The Peoples Pray'r, the glad Diviners Theam,
> The Young mens Vision and the Old mens Dream!
>
> *Ibid.*, p. 52, ll. 238–9.

Shaftesbury reproached him for refusing to make use of his virtues:

> Content ingloriously to pass thy days,
> Like one of Vertues Fools that Feeds on Praise.
>
> *Ibid.*, p. 52, ll. 246–7.

Unused, virtues tarnished; opportunities had to be seized. Fortune had a glorious prize in store for Monmouth, if he had the courage to grasp it, as his father in his own youth grasped the opportunity of returning to the throne of England. Monmouth had to imitate Charles's youthful vigour, not the sad decline of his age, when now he was 'naked of Friends, and round beset with Foes'. The nation was howling for liberty. If Monmouth became their chief, they would gain a leader of royal blood. From his own point of view, the people's love was a nobler title to power than hereditary right:

a Successive Title, Long, and Dark,
Drawn from the Mouldy Rolls of *Noah's* Ark.
Ibid., p. 53, ll. 301–2.

Monmouth was greatly attracted, but tried to resist the appeal. His
father was not a tyrant; he would have no excuse for leading a popular
rebellion. Yet he wished he had not been cursed with an ambitious
nature. He praised his uncle, for whose worthier head the crown was
destined; but he had said enough to show Shaftesbury how to proceed.
Shaftesbury stressed the King's weakness. James had become obnoxious
to the people; there was a chance that Charles might proclaim Monmouth his successor after all:

If not; the People have a Right Supreme
To make their Kings; for Kings are made for them.

Better one suffer, than a Nation grieve.
Ibid., p. 54, ll. 409–10, 416.

Let Charles give real proof of his love for Monmouth by not alienating
the crown from him (Shaftesbury is here presenting it as Monmouth's
right):

God said he loved your Father; could he bring
A better Proof than to anoint him King?
Ibid., p. 54, ll. 429–30.

Moreover, James was already jealous of Monmouth's popularity. If he
were allowed to come to the throne, Monmouth's life would be in
danger. Monmouth must defend himself:

And, that your Arms may have a fair Pretence,
Proclaim, you take them in the King's Defence.
Ibid., p. 55, ll. 463–4.

The irony of this suggestion lies in the fact that this was the parlia-
mentary excuse for having taken up arms against the King in the
Civil Wars. Monmouth allowed himself to be convinced that he
should 'commit a pleasing rape upon the Crown'. He left the court and

made a progress through the west country, explaining to the people
how much he sympathized with their hard lot :

> Youth, Beauty, Graceful Action seldom fail:
> But Common Interest always will prevail. . . .
>
> *Ibid.*, p. 58, ll. 723–4.

Monmouth glided into their hearts.

Dryden interrupted the narrative here to discuss Shaftesbury's
most dangerous argument—the theory that the people had the right
to choose their own kings. He asserted that people were bound to
accept the hereditary rulers; covenants must be kept, or the laws of
property would break down. If the choice were left to the people, that
was no guarantee of good selection: 'the Most may err as grosly as the
Few'. This principle would in any case lead to anarchy.

Many of Charles's supporters shared Dryden's views. He sketched
their portraits briefly, and stressed their virtues. Then the narrative
continued. These men warned Charles of Monmouth's intentions.
Reluctantly he was compelled to invoke the power of the law against
the offenders. He did so in a magnanimous speech from the throne
which summed up the situation neatly:

> My Pious Subjects for my Safety pray,
> Which to Secure, they take my Pow'r away.
>
> *Ibid.*, p. 61, ll. 983–4.

Dryden prophesied that a new series of times would follow, in which
willing nations recognized their lawful lord. There could not be a
climax of action in this satire; the whole aim was to prevent the action
from reaching its climax, and to cause it to fizzle out. The supporters
of the crown regained confidence as Dryden's satire made its impact on
the public. Monmouth was arrested as a disturber of the peace. The
'Rye House Plot'—as imaginary as the Popish Plot—enabled the
Tories to eliminate the leading Whigs. Until James II came to the
throne, Monmouth gave no more trouble.

Dryden's success may well have been due in part to the tone of
his satire. Most satirists write as epitomes of hatred and indignation;

he appeared to write as a whole and complete man. He had a very wide range of feeling; because of this width, the feelings seemed to be based on judgment. When satirists expend their whole ene⁻gy on one emotion, the judgment seems to be based merely on the feeling. Dryden wrote as a human being about men, not about effigies or caricatures; he allowed for good qualities even in people he loathed. His usual attitude was one of magnanimity. He was generous to Monmouth, whom he pictured as a noble youth, full of genuine charm:

> Whate'er he did was done with so much ease,
> In him alone, 'twas Natural to please.
>
> *Ibid.*, p. 49, ll. 27–8.

His nature was mild, and his only fault ambition, that 'spark of too much heavenly fire'. Dryden's final verdict was ' 'Tis juster to lament him, than accuse'. He was just even to Shaftesbury, praising him unreservedly for his uprightness as a judge. (Such magnanimity, of course, was politic in Dryden; it gained him the trust of his readers.) Dryden often called on his reader's better feelings; he was to feel admiration for the loyalty of someone like Ormond, pity for Charles, whose leniency had been abused. Interspersed with this came good reasons for deprecating the instability of the English nation:

> These *Adam*-wits, too fortunately free,
> Began to dream they wanted liberty.
>
> *Ibid.*, p. 50, ll. 51–2.

and for despising the meanness of Sheriff Bethel, who

> Did wisely from Expensive Sins refrain,
> And never broke the Sabbath, but for Gain.
>
> *Ibid.*, p. 56, ll. 587–8.

Because of this wide range of feeling, the reader is left with the impression of the wrong-headedness of the rebels, rather than with the taste of Dryden's scorn. It is completely persuasive.

The brilliance of Dryden's style can be demonstrated most easily

from one of the character-studies. This description of the poet Shadwell
comes from the two hundred or so lines that Dryden contributed to
Part II, mainly written by Nahum Tate. Og had a Falstaffian figure,
and Dryden saw him as a wine-barrel:

> Now stop your noses, Readers, all and some,
> For here's a tun of Midnight work to come,
> *Og* from a Treason Tavern rowling home.
> Round as a Globe, and Liquor'd ev'ry chink,
> Goodly and Great he Sayls behind his Link;
> With all this Bulk there's nothing lost in *Og*,
> For ev'ry inch that is not Fool is Rogue:
> A Monstrous mass of foul corrupted matter,
> As all the Devils had spew'd to make the batter.
> When wine has given him courage to Blaspheme,
> He curses God, but God before Curst him;
> And if man cou'd have reason, none has more,
> That made his Paunch so rich and him so poor. . . .
> But though Heaven made him poor, (with rev'rence speaking,)
> He never was a Poet of God's making;
> The Midwife laid her hand on his Thick Skull,
> With this Prophetick blessing—*Be thou Dull.* . . .
> A Double Noose thou on thy Neck dost pull
> For Writing Treason and for Writing dull;
> To die for Faction is a common Evil,
> But to be hang'd for Non-sense is the Devil.
> Hadst thou the Glories of thy King exprest,
> Thy praises had been Satyr at the best;
> But thou in Clumsy verse, unlickt, unpointed,
> Hast Shamefully defi'd the Lord's Anointed:
> I will not rake the Dunghill of thy Crimes,
> For who would reade thy Life that reads thy rhimes?

> *Ibid.*, p. 70, ll. 457–69, 474–7, 496–505.

The picture of Og making his way home from the pub is superb.
'Liquor'd ev'ry chink' conveys that he is full to bursting, and in the line
'Goodly and Great he Sayls behind his Link' Dryden has caught the
ridiculous assumed dignity of the really drunk—he sails as a nobleman
would, complete with his retinue. It is solid and dramatic, and the
effect is not achieved by any tricks of vocabulary or rhythm. The
construction is normally colloquial, little phrases being added to the
sentence as if it were being invented as Dryden progressed; not polish

but spontaneity was the effect he wanted. The loose constructions never make the sense less perspicuous; in fact the meaning is often most succinctly expressed. Dryden moved easily from the amplifying mode of the barrel image to the brief antithesis of 'He curses God, but God before Curst him', and 'For who would read thy Life that reads thy rhimes?' There is an unusual immediacy of detail, and a Shakespearean zest for humanity; the picture is richly comic as well as satirical. Though it is built up within the pattern of the couplet the reader is not conscious of a limiting form, except when Dryden meant him to notice the end of a line; it is a flow, not a string of beads. But of course Dryden could accelerate or retard the flow as he pleased—slow it up with the monosyllabic majesty of '*Be thou Dull*', or hurtle along with 'As all the Devils had spew'd to make the batter'. He pointed his thrusts with alliteration—'a Monstrous mass of foul corrupted matter', or with the rocking pause that gave a satisfying balance to the end of the line:

> And if man cou'd have reason, none has more,
> That made his Paunch so rich and him so poor.

The whole passage has a delightful assurance—the kind that comes from knowing that the writer is at the top of his form. There is a very real pleasure to be gained from Dryden's confidence, wit and natural ease. Eliot called it a 'satisfying completeness of statement'.

Dryden's satirical output was relatively small. He translated some of the satires of Juvenal and Persius. Besides *Absalom and Achitophel* he wrote one other political satire, *The Medall*, mainly an attack on Shaftesbury, and rather more solemn in tone than the other. Many of his *Prologues* and *Epilogues* were satirical. His remaining satire, *Mac Flecknoe*, was a mock-heroic encomium of Shadwell, splendidly serious in its opening. Flecknoe, who had long ruled the realms of Nonsense unopposed, was looking for an heir fit to succeed him. He found that Shadwell fitted the requirements perfectly:

> *Sh*—— alone my perfect image bears,
> Mature in dullness from his tender years;
> *Sh*—— alone of all my Sons is he
> Who stands confirm'd in full stupidity.

The rest to some faint meaning make pretence,
But *Sh*—— never deviates into sense.
Some Beams of Wit on other souls may fall,
Strike through and make a lucid intervall;
But *Sh*——'s genuine night admits no ray,
His rising Fogs prevail upon the Day. . . .

Ibid., p. 90, ll. 15–24.

Such brilliant inflation needs no comment upon the text.

JOHN WILMOT, EARL OF ROCHESTER (1648–80)

The Earl of Rochester had a very different background from the remainder of the satirists discussed here. He was the son of Wilmot, a devoted Cavalier who died well before the date of the Restoration. Rochester went to Oxford before he was twelve, left early for foreign travel, and came back to the court, precocious, witty and spirited, at the age of eighteen. He became a leader in court pleasures; he was very intelligent and generous, his conversation was unusually charming, and in an age which feared boredom he delighted the company by being entirely unpredictable and thoroughly mischievous. His elaborate frolics became notorious. He was the epitome of the Restoration Rake, and is said to have served as the model for Dorimant in Etherege's *The Man of Mode*. The history of his life makes the kind and quality of his satire all the more surprising. At his best he was a thoughtful moralist, pronouncing with wit and dignity on the foolishness of mankind. There was a serious side to him, which came out when his health broke down at the age of thirty, forcing him to retire from the court. He made a sincere repentance for his past life, under the guidance of Bishop Burnet, and soon afterwards died. At Rochester's request, the Bishop wrote an account of his conversion, in which he commented:

And I am apt to think that the Divine Goodness took pity on him, and seeing the sincerity of his Repentance, would try and venture him no more in Circumstances of Temptation, perhaps too hard for Humane Frailty.

An Account of the Life and Death of John Wilmot, Earl of Rochester (1680), p. 160.

Rochester's witty lampoons on the King and his mistresses are not relevant here. He wrote several genuinely satirical poems: *A Letter from Artemisia, A Satyr Against Mankind, Horace's Tenth Satire, An Imitation of Juvenal, Tunbridge-Wells, A Satire Against Marriage, The Rehearsal: A Satire, Upon Nothing, Rochester's Farewell.* Some of these were directed merely against the abuses and follies of the time, some, more seriously, against the nature of man. Of these the *Satyr Against Mankind* is undoubtedly the best. Here, he was examining man's essential limitations. He was writing from the Epicurean standpoint, deprecating the worship of human reason as a faculty capable of solving all the problems of man. This worship became a characteristic of the Augustan Age, and led to complacency. What made Locke comfortable—'The candle, that is set up in us, shines bright enough for all our purposes'—made Rochester uneasy. He was regretfully pessimistic about man, refusing to deceive himself. He spoke with an inescapable weight of experience, as seriously as could Dr. Johnson. He used his lively imagination and his wit to make his pronouncements more precise and pregnant.

The satire began with a lament that he had been born a man rather than an animal. Man, so proud of being rational, neglected his sure instincts and followed reason, a faculty far more likely to err:

> Reason, an *Ignis fatuus* of the Mind,
> Which leaves the Light of Nature, Sense behind.
> Pathless, and dangerous, wand'ring ways, it takes,
> Through Errours fenny Bogs, and thorny Brakes:
> Whilst the misguided Follower climbs with pain,
> Mountains of Whimseys, heapt in his own Brain;
> Stumbling from thought to thought, falls headlong down
> Into Doubts boundless Sea, where like to drown,
> Books bear him up a while, and make him try.
> To swim with Bladders of Philosophy:
> In hopes still to o'ertake the skipping Light,
> The Vapour dances, in his dazzled sight,
> Till spent, it leaves him to eternal night.

Poems (ed. Q. Johns, 1933), p. 59.

He was taking the common allegorical device of the journey (compare Herbert's *The Pilgrimage*, Vaughan's *Regeneration, The Search*) and enlivening it with realistic detail. The spectacle of the misguided traveller struggling up a range of mountains which he has manufactured for himself without realizing what he is doing was an image with the right emotional charge for Rochester's purpose; it acknowledged the genuine effort involved but at the same time made it inescapably ridiculous because it was unnecessary. In the same way, the learn-to-swim bladders of philosophy, which were all that man had to support him in the boundless sea of doubt, were both pathetically inadequate and intellectually absurd.

> His Wisdom did his Happiness destroy,
> Aiming to know the World he should enjoy.
>> *Ibid.*, p. 60.

Rochester was not writing a poem in praise of sensuous delight; he was merely pointing out that men who spent the whole of their energies trying to find a rational explanation for everything in the universe were very much beside the point, since reason was only a small part of that universe.

He then imagined that an opponent was arguing with him, a man for whom reason was God's best gift:

> What Rage ferments in your degen'rate Mind,
> To make you rail at Reason and Mankind? . . .
> Reason, by whose aspiring Influence,
> We take a flight beyond material Sense,
> Dive into Mysteries, then soaring pierce
> The flaming limits of the Universe,
> Search Heav'n and Hell, find out what's acted there,
> And give the World true grounds of hope and fear.
>> *Ibid.*, p. 61.

Rochester retorted that this was the stock view of reason. His opponent's cause for admiring it was his own for disliking it. It made man incredibly arrogant:

> This supernat'ral Gift, that makes a Mite
> Think he's the Image of the Infinite;
> Comparing his short Life, void of all rest,
> To the eternal and the ever Blest. . . .

> Filling with frantick Crouds of thinking Fools,
> The reverend Bedlams, Colleges and Schools,
> Born on whose Wings, each heavy Sot can pierce
> The Limits of the boundless Universe:
> So charming Ointments make an old Witch fly,
> And bear a cripled Carkass through the Sky.
>
> *Ibid.*, pp. 61–2.

The modern tendency was to spend time unprofitably speculating about the nature of things, and getting nowhere. Rochester, however, had a place for Reason in life—right reason, which distinguished by sense, and gave rules for conduct on that basis, not on the basis of inaccurate abstract speculation:

> My Reason is my Friend, yours is a Cheat:
> Hunger calls out, my Reason bids me eat;
> Perversly yours, your Appetite does mock;
> This asks for food, that answers what's a Clock.
>
> *Ibid.*, p. 62.

Rochester vindicated true reason, but he would not vindicate man. On every level, animals were to be preferred. If skill in necessary functions were compared, a hound was more efficient as a hunter than man was as chairman of a committee. If morals were compared, animals were more generous, just and trustworthy:

> Man with Smiles, Embraces, Friendships, Praise,
> Inhumanely, his Fellows Life betrays,
> With voluntary Pains, works his Distress;
> Not through Necessity, but Wantonness.
> For Hunger, or for Love *They* bite or tear,
> Whilst wretched Man is still in Arms for Fear:
> For Fear he arms, and is of Arms afraid;
> From Fear, to Fear, successively betray'd.
>
> *Ibid.*, pp. 63–4.

The austerity and penetration of the final couplet in this passage are genuinely impressive. It sums up succinctly the reasons for war and violence, and it stresses the uselessness of the remedy; you succeed only in meeting what you hoped to avoid, and start a series of betrayals whose end is never in sight. Rochester's talent for epigram was equalled by his liveliness in selecting images; for instance, there is the scornful picture of the fundamentally stupid man borne by the 'reason' of colleges and schools to the end of the universe, as he thinks:

> So charming Ointments make an old Witch fly,
> And bear a cripled Carkass through the Sky.

His satire was not always on this level. Much of his invective against the King and his mistresses was almost unprintable in its frankness. His more generalized satire is often little more than neat and sardonic. His norm is the language of *An Epistolary Essay*, where he is speaking of the meanness of Providence:

> In *Wit*, alone 't has been Magnificent,
> Of which so just a share to each is sent,
> That the most Avaricious are content.
> For none e'er thought (the due Division's such)
> His own too little, or his Friends too much.
>
> *Ibid.*, p. 57.

JONATHAN SWIFT (1667–1745)

The most considerable satiric achievement of the period was Swift's *A Tale of a Tub*. This was not published until 1704, but by far the greater part of it was written in 1696 and 1697 (*see* Guthkelch and Nichol Smith's edition, 1920, pp. xl–xlv). It is much more typical of the Restoration period than of the Augustan age. Swift's own attitude and technique changed considerably between the writing of his two large-scale satires, *A Tale of a Tub* and *Gulliver's Travels*. At the earlier stage he was indignant with the defects of man, rather than obsessed by his incurable depravities, and he enjoyed not only the invention of his material but the actual process of writing it out. The result was high-spirited and highly coloured, very different from the precise, deliberate tone of *Gulliver's Travels*, where Swift's invention was still vigorous and immediate, but his style controlled by a lucid despair.

Swift's complaint against man at this stage was simply that, being

a 'reasonable animal', he neglected to use this reason. Foolish en-
thusiasms were driving him to dethrone Reason completely and
subject himself to the operation of vapours. Self-conceit was making
man feel that he and his contemporaries, however ignorant, were
capable of anything, and a great advance on their predecessors. Hypocrisy led him to take up a variety of sycophantic and deceitful attitudes
to attain material ends—and all the while he pretended to morality.
Swift was championing the cause of Christianity and humanism against
modern values and the theory of Progress.

The main spheres in which Swift showed these defects in operation
were those of religion and learning. For Swift, anything which departed
from his norms of the Church of England and humanistic learning
smacked of excess and debasement. Both Nonconformity and the new
learning seemed to tend towards atheism, one being subversive of
authority and the other inclined to demote God to a mere Prime Mover
unable to intervene in the fixed laws of Nature. In *A Tale of a Tub* the
satire on abuses in religion formed the narrative nucleus. About a
third of the book was given up to the allegorical history of three
brothers, Peter, Martin and Jack, who represented the Roman Catholic
Church, the Anglican Church on its Lutheran basis, and the Calvinists.
The satire on learning occupied the greater part of the book. It was
contained in introductions, prefaces and digressions, and in the course
of it Swift covered all the abuses of learning in his day: the conceit and
hypocrisy of Grub Street hacks, the foolishness of Cartesian mechan-
istic theories, the pseudo-happiness of neo-Epicureanism, the insanity
of modern occultism with its 'universal systems', the pride of the
scientists in the unravelling of and control of the mysteries of the
universe, the arrogance of critics who decried the geniuses of the past
and the pedantry which the new bourgeois generation of scholars
substituted for wit.

The satire on religious abuses was the more simply handled. Nearly
all of it was contained in the allegory of the three brothers who were
left by their father a new coat each, together with instructions in his
will for their wearing and management. The coat represented the
Christian faith, and the will the New Testament. The brothers kept to
the terms of the will for some time, but when the world was distracted
by sartorism, or clothes-worship, they began to fall away and alter

their coats. First shoulder-knots were added, by dint of finding in the will the separate letters that made up the words and therefore justified them; then gold lace was justified by oral tradition, and flame-coloured satin linings by a newly added codicil. Silver fringes (which had been expressly forbidden in the will) were allowed because the word could also mean broomstick; it must have been broomsticks that were actually prohibited by their father as trimmings to their coats. And so on. Swift was attacking the actual perversions introduced after the first centuries: pageantry, images, the concept of purgatory, expensive ornaments and vestments. At the same time he was showing up the subterfuges by which these alterations were reconciled with the terms of primitive Christianity, by forcing or over-riding the sense of Scripture.

The brothers at length agreed to lock up the will in a strong-box (Latin) so that it was not accessible to the common people. Lord Peter then proceeded to introduce yet more 'reforms': a remedy for the worms (easy penances), a universal pickle or preservative (holy water), passing off bread as mutton (the doctrine of transubstantiation). Martin and Jack became tired of being ill-used by Peter, and broke with him, recovering a copy of their father's will. Martin unpicked his coat very slowly and carefully, removing nothing that would damage the fabric in the process, but Jack ripped his to pieces in a passion of zeal. He became the founder of the Aeolists, and set great store by doing nothing at all without express warrant from his father's will. He turned into a foolish predestinarian, a canting hypocrite, a persecutor who courted persecution.

Throughout the narrative, Swift's genius for fantastic invention had full play. Taking the great chain of the universe with its correspondences, and the 'accident' of Aristotelian logic, Swift decided that the universe was a modification of clothes, and man was not man clothed but clothes manned; clothes had become the soul:

> They held the Universe to be a large *Suit of Cloaths*, which *invests* every Thing: That the Earth is *invested* by the Air; the Air is *invested* by the Stars; and the Stars are *invested* by the *Primum Mobile*. Look on this Globe of Earth, you will find it to be a very compleat and fashionable *Dress*. What is that which some call *Land*, but a fine Coat faced with Green? or the Sea, but a Wastcoat of Water-Tabby? Proceed to the particular Works of the Creation, you will find how curious Journey-man

Nature hath been, to trim up the *vegetable* Beaux: Observe how sparkish a Perewig adorns the Head of a *Beech*, and what a fine Doublet of white Satin is worn by the *Birch*. To conclude from all, what is Man himself but a *Micro-Coat*, or rather a compleat Suit of Cloaths with all its Trimmings? As to his Body, there can be no dispute; but examine even the Acquirements of his Mind, you will find them all contribute in their Order, towards furnishing out an exact Dress: To instance no more; Is not Religion a *Cloak*, Honesty a *Pair of Shoes*, worn out in the Dirt, Self-love a *Surtout*, Vanity a *Shirt*, and Conscience a *Pair of Breeches*, which, tho' a Cover for Lewdness as well as Nastiness, is easily slipt down for the Service of both . . .

OTHERS of these Professors, though agreeing in the main System, were yet more refined upon certain Branches of it; and held that Man was an Animal compounded of two *Dresses*, the *Natural* and the *Celestial Suit*, which were the Body and the Soul; That the Soul was the outward, and the Body the inward Cloathing; that the latter was *ex traduce*; but the former of daily Creation and Circumfusion. This last they proved by *Scripture*, because, *in Them we Live, and Move, and have our Being*.

A Tale of a Tub (1920), pp. 77–80.

The hierarchy of investiture from macrocosm to microcosm is gaily developed in terms of modern fashions. Man at his worst may well be no more than a galvanized suit of clothes. The mental faculties which Swift instances are not edified by the comparisons: there is hard hitting and acuteness in his selection of correspondences and his description of the uses to which each faculty is put. Swift is playing wittily with the heresy of traducianism (the theory that the soul was transmitted directly by the parents), pointing out that the body must be inferior to clothes, since it was merely handed on, whereas the clothes were a new creation each day. The quotation from the Acts that concludes the passage is a reminder that anyone who makes such a god out of clothes is living blasphemously. Swift's learning is always lightly handled, adding zest and wit to an essentially serious attack. He makes an excellent exposure of learning subjugated to the will, when the three brothers are engaged in justifying their departures from their dead father's injunctions. Gold lace is the problem:

What should our three Knights do in this momentous Affair? They had sufficiently strained a Point already, in the Affair of *Shoulder-Knots*: Upon Recourse to the Will, nothing appeared there but *altum silentium*.

That of the *Shoulder-Knots* was a loose, flying, circumstantial Point; but this of *Gold Lace*, seemed too considerable an Alteration without better Warrant; it did *aliquo modo essentiæ adhærere*, and therefore required a positive Precept. But about this time it fell out, that the Learned Brother aforesaid, had read *Aristotelis Dialectica*, and especially that wonderful Piece *de Interpretatione*, which has the Faculty of teaching its Readers to find out a Meaning in every Thing but it self; like Commentators on the *Revelations*, who proceed Prophets without understanding a Syllable of the Text. *Brothers*, said he, *You are to be informed that, of Wills*, duo sunt genera, *Nuncupatory and scriptory*: *that in the Scriptory Will here before us, there is no Precept or Mention about Gold Lace*, conceditur: *But*, si idem affirmetur de nuncupatorio, negatur, *For Brothers, if you remember, we heard a Fellow say when we were Boys, that he heard my Father's Man say, that he heard my Father say, that he would advise his Sons to get* Gold Lace *on their Coats, as soon as ever they could procure Money to buy it. By G—— that is very true*, cries the other; *I remember it perfectly well*, says the third. And so without more ado they got the largest *Gold Lace* in the Parish.

Ibid., pp. 85–6.

The pomposity of the garbled logic adds point to the chain of tradition and report, and to the laborious method of self-justification. In such passages Swift succeeds admirably in making man ridiculous, and in delighting the reader with the mechanics while not distracting him from the main purpose of the satire.

The religious satire is cocooned and interspersed with satire on aspects of modern learning. The Tale itself is reached only after several preliminary layers have been unwound. These involutions are a parody of those writers who have followed the fashion of dedication, preface, introduction and diversions from the main theme. First comes the *Dedication to Lord Somers*, by the publisher, then a statement by the publisher to the reader; then the author's dedication to Prince Posterity, and the author's preface, explaining his intentions and his qualifications. Still the actual narrative is preceded by an introduction in which Swift discourses on oratorical machines and the products of Grub Street. There is never more than a chapter of the story at once; one or more digressions are inserted between each section of it, on critics, on digressions, on madness. The digressions often provide parallel instances of what is being satirized in the tale; the *Digression on Madness* comes close to the account of Jack's fanatical aeolism.

Within the separate sections, Swift used a diversity of techniques for his satiric purposes. One of the most obvious is that of the *persona*. Swift adopted the mask of a character that enabled him to parody the particular vice or folly with which he was dealing at any given moment. The ingenuous publisher, the experienced man of the world, the poor martyred writer, the up-to-date virtuoso, the pedantic critic—these were only a few of his poses. His publisher (called the bookseller) enabled him to ridicule the habit of grovelling before a patron which was apparently normal practice in an age where writers still found it difficult to live by the pen. The man is an innocent, ingenuously stupid, trying hard to say all the right things to Lord Somers:

> I should now, in right of a Dedicator, give your Lordship a List of your own Virtues, and at the same time, be very unwilling to offend your Modesty; But, chiefly, I should celebrate your Liberality towards Men of great Parts and small Fortunes, and give you broad Hints, that I mean my self. And, I was just going on in the usual Method, to peruse a hundred or two Dedications, and transcribe an Abstract, to be applied to your Lordship. . . .
>
> *Ibid.*, p. 23.

The praise is all intended to raise more money, rather than to give honour where honour is due, but this fact is not normally avowed so openly. When Swift wants to ridicule writers who boast of all they have done and suffered for the public good, he apes the aged Dryden, writing his postscript to the reader as part of the apparatus to his Virgil. He talks of 'the poor Remains of an unfortunate Life', reminds the public of the way in which he has worn his quill to the pith in the service of the State, in matters such as the Popish Plot, the Exclusion Bill, and so on, and instances his head broken in a hundred places by men of opposing factions. Finding the State has no more use for him, he is thankfully retiring into private life, to philosophize, 'having, to my unspeakable Comfort, passed a long Life, with a Conscience void of Offence' (*ibid*, p. 71). Later, Swift becomes a Modern Critic, full of his own virtues and assured that the present day will always overtop its predecessors. He explains, in *A Digression in the Modern Kind*, why he takes pains to point out to his readers the beauties of his own writings. He admires Dryden's success in this vein:

He has often said to me in Confidence, that the World would never have suspected him to be so great a Poet, if he had not assured them so frequently in his Prefaces, that it was impossible they could either doubt or forget it.

Ibid., p. 131.

Swift himself, in this guise, feels he ought to have put these details into a preface, but surely breaking a convention does not matter:

I here think fit to lay hold on that great and honourable Privilege of being the *Last Writer*; I claim an absolute Authority in Right, as the *freshest Modern*, which gives me a Despotick Power over all Authors before me.

Ibid., p. 130.

Or he can exchange the bluff assurance of this kind of critic for the elephantine gait of Bentley plodding through his abstruse authors by way of minute details, absurdities and digressions. *A Digression concerning Critics* contains several paragraphs where Swift talks precisely in Bentley's style, describing the true Modern Critic via Pausanius's allegory on pruning and Herodotus on horned asses (*ibid.*, pp. 98–9). Or he can outdo the cabalists in pretending to knowledge of the arcanum, alchemy, elixirs—and on this basis reproach Homer, as many modern critics had done, for his lack of knowledge of really important matters:

His Account of the *Opus Magnum* is extremely poor and deficient; he seems to have read but very superficially, either *Sendivogius*, *Behmen*, or *Anthroposophia Theomagica*. He is also quite mistaken about the *Sphaera Pyroplastica*, a neglect not to be attoned for; and (if the Reader will admit so severe a Censure) *Vix crederem Autorem hunc, unquam audivisse ignis vocem.*

Ibid., pp. 127–8.

Swift greatly enjoyed his series of poses, linked by the common factor of Modernism. They served as a kind of *reductio ad absurdum*, the force of which could be missed by none of his contemporaries.

His control of irony is remarkable. The serious tone in which Swift proclaims what he clearly does not believe constantly recurs. He makes play with the happy fate of the hack-writer who gets all his material from commonplace books, and is in a few weeks capable of handling the profoundest subjects:

> He will desire no more Ingredients towards fitting up a Treatise, that shall make a very comely Figure on a Bookseller's Shelf, there to be preserved neat and clean, for a long Eternity, adorn'd with the Heraldry of its Title, fairly inscribed on a Label; never to be thumb'd or greas'd by Students, nor bound to everlasting Chains of Darkness in a Library: But when the Fulness of time is come, it shall happily undergo the Tryal of Purgatory, in order *to ascend the Sky*.
>
> *Ibid.*, p. 148.

He writes with affected disgust of the officious behaviour of Reason when it demonstrated that the outside of things was not representative of what was within. By a process of cutting and opening and mangling and piercing, it unfortunately showed the wretchedness of the contents. You would hardly believe how much the process of flaying altered a woman for the worse. Swift pretends to approve the wisdom of the Epicureans, who know where to stop:

> He that can with *Epicurus* content his Ideas with the *Films* and *Images* that fly off upon his Senses from the *Superficies* of Things; Such a Man truly wise, creams off Nature, leaving the Sower and the Dregs, for Philosophy and Reason to lap up. This is the sublime and refined Point of Felicity, called, *the Possession of being well deceived*; The Serene Peaceful State of being a Fool among Knaves.
>
> *Ibid.*, p. 174.

Reason may shock men by showing them horrifying truths they would rather avoid, but at least it is the activity of intelligent and honest men.

Swift also delighted in the mock-heroic vein. It pleased him to create the figures of Posterity and Time, and to give elegant speeches to them, diversified by figures such as anthypophora (reasoning with oneself) and pysma (the asking of a string of sharp questions). Prince Posterity is to ask Time what he has done with the productions of Grub Street:

> To which he will answer. . . . by asking *Your Highness*, where they are? and what is become of them? and pretend it a Demonstration that there

never were any, because they are not then to be found: Not to be found!
Who has mislaid them? Are they sunk in the Abyss of Things? 'Tis certain,
that in their own Nature they were *light* enough to swim upon the Surface
for all Eternity. Therefore the Fault is in Him, who tied Weights so heavy
to their Heels, as to depress them to the Center. Is their very Essence
destroyed? Who has annihilated them? Were they drowned by *Purges* or
martyred by *Pipes*? Who administered them to the Posteriors of——?

Ibid., p. 32.

The vividness of his imagery contributed greatly to his satirical
effects. He was a persistent visualizer. His mad politician, his occultist
and his fanatical preacher were linked by the common factor of vapours
or wind, which he imagined as a bodily disturbance issuing at one end or
the other. They may have called it soul, spirit, inspiration, but it had
a grosser explanation. Swift described graphically the kind of con-
tortions produced in the face of the sufferer whose struggle was not
yet resolved. Again, he explained the recalcitrance of Fame in a series
of pictures: was she a fruit grafted on the body that could not grow
until its stock was in the earth, or a bird of prey eager for a carcase,
or had she simply discovered that

her Trumpet sounds best and farthest, when she stands on a *Tomb*, by the
Advantage of a rising Ground, and the Echo of a hollow Vault.

Ibid., p. 186.

He thought in images, even if the passage left him insufficient time to
develop and dwell on the separate images, piling them up with speed
and vigour. This gives the reader the impression that Swift has taken
all experience to be his province, and has strong contact with the
visible and tangible world. However potentially abstract the subject,
Swift netted it in his images and held it down to earth. In the *Digression
in Praise of Digressions*, he was talking of short cuts to knowledge
practised in his day. Some men served books

as some Men do *Lords*, learn their *Titles* exactly, and then brag of their
Acquaintance. Or Secondly, which is indeed the choicer, the profounder,
and politer Method, to get a thorough Insight into the *Index*, by which the
whole Book is governed and turned, like *Fishes* by the *Tail*. For, to enter
the Palace of Learning at the *great Gate*, requires an Expence of Time and

Forms; therefore Men of much Haste and little Ceremony, are content to get in by the *Back-Door*. For, the Arts are all in a *flying* March, and therefore more easily subdued by attacking them in the *Rear*. Thus Physicians discover the State of the whole Body, by consulting only what comes from Behind. Thus Men catch Knowledge by throwing their *Wit* on the *Posteriors* of a Book, as Boys do Sparrows with flinging salt upon their *Tails*. Thus Human Life is best understood by the wise man's Rule of *Regarding the End*. Thus are the Sciences found like *Hercules's* Oxen, by *tracing them backwards*. Thus are *old Sciences* unravelled like old Stockings, by beginning at the *Foot*.

Ibid., p. 145.

However wide Swift's range, the reader is conscious of the fundamental unity of the attack, and of the same acute mind at work through all its disguises. The apparent formlessness of the Tale was a deliberate part of the satire—a comment on the confused state of modern writing. Swift outdid all his contemporaries in this and their other defects, as Nashe had done in his *Unfortunate Traveller*; but Swift did so by ostensibly pleading their cause. He was both an aristocratic moralist and a lively writer, but he kept the second quality for the service of the first. The liveliness was not muted; it was merely harnessed to best advantage. He did not succeed in turning men against the Idea of Progress, but he wrote a satiric work of art. Even Dr. Johnson, who at one moment called the Tale a wild work, confessed that it showed a genius unequalled by Swift again:

It exhibits a vehemence and rapidity of mind, a copiousness of images, and vivacity of diction, such as he afterwards never possessed, or never exerted.

Johnson, *Works* (1796), vol. XI, p. 37.

IV

THE ENTHUSIASTS

What pestilential influences the genius for enthusiasm or opinionative zeal hath upon the public peace, is so evident from experience, that it needs not be proved from reason.

Archdeacon Parker, *A Free and Impartial Censure* (1666).

THE majority of men in this period reacted against fanaticism, and made calm and common sense an end in themselves. The safe middle way was cultivated. The law was kept, but emotional involvement was avoided. Tillotson, South and Allestree preached on the decorum of morality; what they conveyed of religious experience was muted and dull. *The Whole Duty of Man* (1659) and *The Ladies Calling* (1675), probably written by Allestree, are serious, proper and rather commonplace dissertations on the duty of a Christian; unexceptionable, highly popular, but uninspiring. South preached on the mysteries of religion in metaphors strongly reminiscent of Thomas Hobbes's. Hobbes had warned men that there were some doctrinal mysteries which must not be intellectually examined, but must simply be accepted as dictates of the Commonwealth:

For it is with the mysteries of our Religion, as with wholesome pills for the sick, which swallowed whole, have the vertue to cure; but chewed, are for the most part cast up again without effect.

Hobbes, *Leviathan*, chap. XXXII.

In Hobbes, who subordinated personal religion to the needs of the State, this attitude comes as no surprise, but when an Anglican divine makes a similar remark, and uses the same image, it is indicative of a startling change of emphasis within the Church. South was preaching on the doctrine of the Trinity:

149

And now, if there be any, whose Reason is so unruly and over-curious, as to be still inquisitive and unsatisfied, such must remember, that when we have made the utmost Explications of this Article, we pretend not thereby, to have altered the Nature of the subject we have been treating of; which, after all, is still a Mystery; and they must know moreover, that when the sacred Mysteries of Religion are discoursed of, the Business of a Christian is Sobriety and Submission, and his Duty to be satisfied, even though he were not convinced. The Trinity is a fundamental Article of the Christian Religion; and as he that denies it, may lose his soul, so he that too much strives to understand it, may lose his Wits. Knowledge is nice, intricate, and tedious, but Faith is easy; and what is more, it is safe. And why should I then unhinge my Brains, ruin my Mind, and pursue Distraction in the Disquisition of that which a little Study would sufficiently convince me to be not intelligible? Or why should I by chewing a Pill make it useless, which swallowed whole might be Curing and Restaurative? A Christian, in these matters, has nothing to do but believe; and since I cannot scientifically comprehend this Mystery, I shall worship it with the Religion of Submission and Wonder, and casting down my Reason before it, receive it with the Devotions of Silence, and the humble Distances of Adoration.

South, *Sermons* (1715), vol. IV., p. 305.

It is true that he concludes with references to submission and wonder, but the trend and tone of the discussion that led up to these words has made them little more than perfunctory gestures. If the mysteries are pills, and faith is recommended as the easy way, a prudential investment in a primrose path, the religion advocated is lacking in seriousness and depth. It has degenerated considerably from Tertullian's '*Certum est, quia impossibile est*'.

Against this Laodicean background several more imaginative men stand out, by virtue of their deep convictions and their power to move the reader. Their responses to life were individual and courageous. They worked out for themselves their views of the universe. Amongst the scientists the most prominent of these were Isaac Newton, Robert Boyle, John Ray, Thomas Burnet. There were many Dissenters of great distinction: John Milton, Richard Baxter, George Fox, John Bunyan—and many Anglicans: Benjamin Whichcote, Thomas Traherne, Henry More, Jeremy Taylor. All these men could have been accused by their age of 'enthusiasm', of living more by imagination and depth of feeling than by common sense. They explored the universe with a real sense of wonder. They were predominantly individuals.

Even within each group they differed in striking ways: Newton, the physicist, an outstandingly original mind, who believed in an omnipresent God, not in a detached First Mover of a mechanical universe; Thomas Burnet, Master of the Charterhouse, a Deist in some matters, but chiefly anxious to provide scientific explanations for the problems of the creation of the world, the action of the Flood, and the conflagration that was to destroy it. There was little in common to be found in the devout meditations of Baxter, the angry proselytism of Fox and the passionate arguments of Milton. The music and colour of Taylor's piety and charity may resemble those of Traherne, but Taylor was a man who took an active part in public affairs, whereas Traherne lived a secluded and private life; both differed from the Cambridge Platonists whose immediate sphere of influence was their university. What they have in common is simply the reality of their religious experience.

In the space available, it is impossible to give a fair account of all these men. Instead, one man from each group will be discussed in detail: John Bunyan, Thomas Traherne and Thomas Burnet. Bunyan is the preacher, concerned with the world of man, Traherne the contemplative, concerned with the inner world, and Burnet the speculative mind concerned with the world of nature.

JOHN BUNYAN (1628–88)

The most active of these three men, John Bunyan, was thirty-two at the time of the Restoration, and spent most of the first twelve years after 1660 in prison. He reacted violently against the world in which he lived. He hated both the sins of his own youth, and the sins of those who persecuted the Nonconformists. His trials and imprisonment made him very conscious of the suffering that had to be undergone in an earthly life. Relentless watchfulness, single-mindedness, the rigid casting aside of all obstacles in the straight and narrow path to heaven —these were the essentials of his attitude. The world was a City of Destruction; life was not to be enjoyed, but endured as a preparation for eternity. Bunyan's form of Puritanism, together with a certain innate neurotic tendency, made him feel that he was compassed about by adversaries, that he might unknowingly commit an unforgivable sin that would send him to an eternal and physical hell; only as he was dying could his life be illuminated by the sweetness and glories of heaven. Heaven offered a crown that was worth winning; death was not merely a welcome release from life, but something that called for positive rejoicing.

The attitude to death is shown most clearly at the end of the second part of *The Pilgrim's Progress*, where Christian's wife, children and friends follow him to the Holy City. The whole band of pilgrims were waiting in the country of Beulah to be summoned to heaven. Their mood was one of calmness and hope:

> Now the Day drew on that *Christiana* must be gone. So the Road was full of People to see her take her Journey. But behold all the Banks beyond the River were full of Horses and Chariots, which were come down from above to accompany her to the City-Gate. So she came forth and entered the River with a Beck'n of Fare well to those that followed her to the River side. The last words that she was heard to say here was, *I come Lord, to be with thee and bless thee.*
>
> *The Pilgrim's Progress* (ed. J. Brown, 1907), p. 416.

Even those who were weak gained strength at the moment of the summons. Mr. Dispondency and his daughter Much-afraid were more confident than they had ever been, and knew they would leave their doubts behind on this side of the river:

> When the time was come for them to depart, they went to the Brink of the *River*. The last words of Mr Dispondency were, *Farewel Night, welcome Day*. His Daughter went thorow the River singing, but none could understand what she said.
>
> *Ibid.*, p. 418.

When Mr. Valiant-for-Truth was summoned, he called for his friends, and made his will:

> *My Sword*, I give to him that shall succeed me in my Pilgrimage, and my *Courage* and *Skill*, to him that can get it. My *Marks* and *scarrs* I carry with me, to be a witness for me, that I have fought his Battels, who now will be my Rewarder. . . . So he passed over, and the Trumpets sounded for him on the other side.
>
> *Ibid.*, p. 419.

It is a triumphal last movement after conflict and suffering and des-
pondency. This is Bunyan at his most imaginative, convincing the
reader of his transcendental values and of the depth of his feeling both
for God and man. He was able to convey this intensity of religious joy
in his direct writing as well as in his allegories. At times, in *Grace
Abounding*, he recorded his despair and agony, but he also described
the moments when his fears were swallowed up in the love of God :

> I lived, for some time, very sweetly at peace with God through Christ;
> Oh, me thought, Christ! Christ! there was nothing but Christ that was
> before my Eyes, I was not now (only) for looking upon this and the other
> benefits of Christ apart, as of his Blood, Burial or Resurrection, but con-
> sidered him as a whole Christ!
>
> *Grace Abounding* (ed. J. Brown, 1907), par. 232.

> That night was a good night to me, I never had but few better; I longed
> for the company of some of God's People, that I might have imparted
> unto them what God had shewed me; Christ was a precious Christ to my
> Soul that Night; I could scarce lie in my Bed for Joy, and Peace, and
> Triumph, through Christ. . . .
>
> *Ibid.*, par. 264.

The depth and immediacy of Bunyan's religious experience stand out
strongly against the complacency and common sense of many of his
orthodox contemporaries.

He is, however, often accused of serious failures of the imagination.
It is said that he enjoyed the idea of a physical hell in which the damned
would suffer for ever; that his God was a tyrant who created multi-
tudes of souls predestined to damnation, and then encouraged them
on the downward path; and that his own emotional reactions to
religious torments were often childishly hysterical. There is some truth
in all of these charges, but they need to be seen in the context of
Puritanism at this time.

The general tendency in the Restoration period was to play down
the idea of a physical and eternal hell. Religion was 'a cheerful thing';
God was fundamentally magnanimous, 'Almighty, to forgive'. To
Puritans this attitude seemed frivolous and profane. God was a jealous
God, and sin against him could not escape everlasting punishment.

Bunyan, however, did not in fact gloat over the spectacle of the suffering of the damned. He did prefer that the confirmed sinner should be
damned rather than saved, which seems to us a failure in humanity.
But when Bunyan gave a vivid picture of hell, it was not inspired by
Schadenfreude; it was intended as a terrible warning, both to those as
yet unaware of religion and to those who were almost confirmed in
sin. The idea of hell was intended to set in motion the flight from the
City of Destruction.

The second charge against Bunyan is based on the form taken by
Bunyan's anthropomorphic and incomplete version of the doctrine of
predestination. In *The Life and Death of Mr. Badman*, God decides that
Mr. Badman is to be damned, and therefore sends him three companions to confirm him in his evil courses. At the end God ensures that
he dies peacefully, so that no deathbed repentance should frustrate
God's decree. This God who leads sinners into temptation sounds less
moral than man. He is immoral because Bunyan has seen only a part
of the doctrine. His religion was allegorically rather than intellectually
apprehended. He treated God purely as a person, and omitted to
consider the questions of God's foreknowledge and man's freewill.
If man had freewill, it was obvious that he could choose to sin. Foreknowledge made God able to foresee which men would sin; he could
therefore decree them to damnation, but his foreknowledge did not
constrain them to sin. Bunyan's God certainly does his best to induce
the damned to sin, and is repugnant to the imagination in this respect.
Still, Bunyan hoped—disregarding the logic of predestination—that
men would take this distasteful picture as a solemn warning, and
exercise what little freewill they had left. No predestinarian has ever
believed that warnings were entirely useless.

While it is hardly just to call his attitude hysterical, there is no
doubt that he gave undue importance to the part played by emotional
vacillations in the process of conversion. In *Grace Abounding* he gave a
painful account of his tug-of-war with the devil. Again and again his
feelings betrayed him and sided with the devil, leaving him with an
unbearable sense of reprobation. He thought he was lost for ever
because he once 'felt this thought of Christ pass through my heart,
Let him go if he will'. This was as much a betrayal of Christ as Judas's
bargain; Bunyan thought, for years, that he was irretrievably damned.

He was totally unable to see that these emotional disturbances were unimportant, provided that meanwhile the will was firm in its adherence to God. Puritanism had lost sight of the sound understanding of human psychology that was part of the Catholic tradition. Bunyan spent much time blaming himself for inevitable emotional failures, when he might have been spared agonies by the knowledge that his will was steadfast throughout. He said himself that

> my mind was now so turned, that it lay like an Horse-leach at the Vein, still crying out, *Give, give* (Prov. xxx, 15). Yea, it was so fixed on Eternity, and on the things about the Kingdom of Heaven.... that neither pleasures, nor profits, nor perswasions, nor threats could loose it, or make it let go its hold.

Ibid., par. 42.

While this state lasted, Bunyan had no real cause to reproach himself. His difficulties were caused less by a failure of imagination than by a gap in knowledge.

These defects are small beside his qualities. In his greatest works he can still hold the reader's imagination by his intensity and his peculiar honesty. He wrote a good deal, partly because of his lengthy periods of imprisonment. The first well-known book, *Grace Abounding to the Chief of Sinners*, was published in 1666; the first and second parts of *The Pilgrim's Progress* in 1678 and 1684; *The Life and Death of Mr. Badman* in 1680, and *The Holy War* in 1682.

Grace Abounding was a straightforward narrative of his own spiritual experiences, told in the first person. It was written during his imprisonment at Bedford, occasioned by his refusal to promise that he would not preach. Since he was cut off from preaching, he wrote this treatise to encourage his followers, showing the terrible trials of spirit which he had endured and from which he was now delivered. He wrote it as simply as he could, because of the desperately serious nature of the subject:

> I could also have stepped into a Stile much higher than this, in which I have here discoursed, and could have adorned all things more than here I have seemed to do; but I dare not: God did not play in tempting of me; neither did I play, when I sunk as into a bottomless Pit, when *the pangs of*

hell caught hold upon me; wherefore I may not play in relating of them, but be plain and simple, and lay down the thing as it was.

Ibid., p. 6.

It is precisely the honesty and vividness of Bunyan's writing that gives the book its strength. He was candid about his doubts and difficulties, without exhibitionism. His aim was not to show his own steadfastness and devotion to the faith, but his weaknesses, his torments of uncertainty, his youthful indifference to sin and entire lack of a sense of guilt. And at all times and in all places the mercy of God was at hand to help and preserve him. The stress was always on the mercy of God and the ridiculousness of his own doubts when he feared that God was unable to save him. Bunyan used the word ridiculous himself:

These things may seem ridiculous to others, even as ridiculous as they were in themselves, but to me they were most tormenting cogitations.

Ibid., par. 185.

He did not try to dignify the process of his conversion. He recorded literally the most fantastic misgivings put into his head by the devil. He gave the exact situation in which a warning from heaven would suddenly come to him. He told how he first became conscious of the burden of his sins one evening after a good sermon, when he thought he had succeeded in forgetting it by means of a good dinner and some gaming:

But the same day, as I was in the midst of a game at Cat, and having struck it one blow from the hole, just as I was about to strike it the second time, a voice did suddainly dart from Heaven, into my Soul, which said, Wilt thou leave thy sins, and go to Heaven; or have thy sins, and go to Hell?

Ibid., par. 22.

Admittedly by Puritan standards gaming was a sin, but Bunyan had committed more spectacular ones, in the course of which he could have been far more impressively reproved by the voice. But the fact is that it did happen then, and it was the fact that mattered to Bunyan. The voice is convincing to the reader precisely because it has not been put in an elaborate setting.

His fears are conveyed with similar immediacy and honesty. He described the time when he was forced to give up bell-ringing, and even to give up listening to it, because he kept on calculating the possibilities of the bells falling on him, wherever he stood. There was the time when he was terrified of speaking blasphemies:

> And in so strong a measure was this temptation upon me, that often I have been ready to clap my hand under my chin, to hold my mouth from opening.
>
> *Ibid.*, par. 104.

Equally convincing is his account of the struggle he had when he was threatened with imprisonment:

> The parting with my Wife and poor children hath oft been to me in this place, as the pulling the Flesh from my Bones, and that not only because I am somewhat too too fond of these great Mercies, but also because I should have often brought to my mind the many hardships, miseries and wants that my poor Family was like to meet with, should I be taken from them, *especially my poor blind Child*, who lay nearer my heart then all I had besides; O the thoughts of the hardship I thought my blind one might go under, would break my heart to pieces.
> Poor Child! thought I, what sorrow art thou like to have for thy Portion in this World? Thou must be beaten, must beg, suffer hunger, cold, nakedness and a thousand Calamities, though I cannot now endure the Wind should blow upon thee: But yet recalling my self, thought I, I must venture you all with God, though it goeth to the quick to leave you.
>
> *Ibid.*, pars. 328, 329.

Such passages as these make the reader trust Bunyan completely when he is describing both the depths of his despair, when he longed to die and yet was afraid to die for fear of hell, and the heights of his joy when he knew the mercies of God:

> My understanding was so enlightened, that I was as though I had seen the Lord Jesus look down from Heaven, through the tiles, upon me, and direct these words unto me. This sent me mourning home, it broke my heart, and filled me full of joy, and laid me low as the dust.
>
> *Ibid.*, par. 207.

Perhaps the most moving quality in *Grace Abounding* is the method of its construction. Bunyan did not present it as a record of steady progress and growth in faith, but as a journey where the setbacks seemed far greater than the advances, where he constantly escaped a little way from his fear that he had committed the sin against the Holy Ghost, only to be dragged back into a more unshakable feeling that he could not possibly be pardoned. Always, just as he was 'pretty well and savoury in my spirit', there would come 'a great cloud of darkness'. The genuineness of the experience comes home in every paragraph.

The Pilgrim's Progress had a larger audience in mind. It was intended to convert the indifferent, as well as to encourage those who had already started on their pilgrimage. Allegory was a form which came naturally to Bunyan. He was for ever interpreting his dreams as if they were allegories, and visualizing his beliefs in allegorical form. 'Visualizing' is an inadequate word, for Bunyan heard, felt and moved in these allegories. His symbols had for him a vivid physical reality. This tendency can be seen in the dream he had about his exclusion from the blessed, which he recounted in *Grace Abounding*. He saw the poor people of Bedford sitting in sunshine on a high mountain: he was cut off from them by a wall through which he had to squeeze himself with great difficulty. Throughout *The Pilgrim's Progress* the reader is made similarly conscious of the reality of the landscape; it is a real hill that towers over Christian's head and nearly falls on him, and he descends perceptibly into the mist and mire of the Valley of the Shadow of Death.

It is a satisfying allegory. Readers who treat it as a novel are bound to be disappointed by the interspersion of moral debates and sermons, and of emblematic set-pieces, even if they are not discouraged by such things as the foolishness of Christian who forgets, when imprisoned in Doubting Castle, that he has a key with him to open all its locks. Bunyan never meant to write a novel. He chose the central concept of the pilgrimage very well. It was particularly suited to his religious views in that it put the emphasis on the goal all the time. All through life the pilgrim was to struggle against the forces of evil, making his way towards heaven without much hope of enjoying life on earth. Courage and perseverance were as necessary to the pilgrim as they were to the Nonconformist of Bunyan's day, contending with persecution and ridicule as well as all the normal temptations of Vanity

Fair. The symbols of temptation were equally telling. Incidents which appeared disappointing if they were read as literal adventure made good allegorical symbols, once their meaning was understood. The Slough of Despond was not the exciting kind of bog that closed over a Victorian villain, but it had its own importance. It was made up of the 'scum and filth that attends conviction for sin'—that is, as soon as a man had realized the enormity of his sins, the first step towards salvation, he suffered from fears and doubts, and his past clung to him like mire. That is why Christian fell in and was soiled by the slough, but not overwhelmed by it. It could not swallow him up, because his own conviction of sin made up the firm ground under the slough itself, on which he touched bottom and could stand. Similarly, Doubting Castle was the symbol of the prison that could be created by losing sight of the true way and giving in to intellectual doubt and despair. The Giant deprived Christian and Hopeful of light, and food, and friends; a state of total privation, inducing lowness of spirit and despair of help from others. The only person who could alter this state of mind was the man suffering from it; he was capable of helping himself, in spite of temptations to surrender and die, if only he could bring himself to remember the promises made by God to man. Just in time, Christian did remember that he had the key called Promise—a fact previously obscured by his own state of mind. The symbols stand up well to analysis.

The story as a whole contains a manageable number of characters. Bunyan did not make the mistake of overloading the story with too large a total cast, nor of overcrowding the stage at any one time. Christian and Faithful, together with his successor Hopeful, hold the centre of attention consistently. The rest of the characters appear in small groups, and are quickly and dramatically sketched in for the portion of the story which concerns them. Then they disappear, and the reader is not asked to remember facts about them until they are wanted again. (There are more characters to be remembered in Part II, but there a larger cast is being conducted over a terrain that is already well known; the reader has less to learn in that respect.) The minor characters are drawn from the outside; Christian and his companions are drawn from the inside, and placed well in the foreground, so that they stand out against the host of qualities that are helping or hindering them—for it must be remembered that these minor characters are not people, but tendencies and temptations. They are on a par with Fellow-ship, Goods, Good Deeds, in the play of *Everyman*.

Bunyan's power of presenting character in action is well known. He had a genius for reproducing colloquial speech, a Chaucerian eye for rapid type-characterization, and a sense of humour that set him apart from the gloomy hypocritical Puritan of stage tradition. One example will serve to recall these qualities. At the beginning of Part II Christian's wife is about to set off on the pilgrimage:

> But while they were thus about to be gon, two of the Women that were *Christiana's* Neighbours, came up to her House and knocked at her Door. To whom she said as before. *If you come in Gods Name, come in.* At this the Women were stun'd, for this kind of Language they used not to hear, or to perceive to drop from the Lips of *Christiana*.
>
> The Pilgrim's Progress (1907), p. 297.

Mrs. Timorous was horrified to hear of Christiana's decision; Mercy was half attracted, but had not the courage to say so in the presence of her overbearingly sensible neighbour. So she said:

> *Since she is, as you see, a taking of her last farewel of her Country, I think to walk this Sun-shine morning, a little way with her to help her on the way.* But she told her not of the second Reason; but kept that to herself.
> Tim. Well, I see you have a mind to go a fooling too; but take heed in time, and be wise: while we are out of danger we are out; but when we are in, we are in.
>
> Ibid., p. 299.

With this portentous platitude she left Mercy with Christiana, and went off to tell Mrs. Inconsiderate and Mrs. Lightmind all about it. They decide that a reformed neighbour would be an uncomfortable part of their environment:

> A good Riddance, for my part I say, of her. Should she stay where she dwels, and retain this her mind, who could live quietly by her? for she will either be dumpish or unneighbourly, or talk of such matters as no wise Body can abide.
>
> Ibid., p. 300.

Where Bunyan could use conversation as the medium of his narrative, he was at his best. Where there was less scope for conversation, he sometimes hurried so much over the description of action that he did not make the full emotional impact required by the importance of the event. The fight with Apollyon is summarized, apart from the final bout; this minimizes the intensity and duration of Christian's struggle. The account of Faithful's execution is even more perfunctory; Bunyan simply listed the actions of his tormentors in under six lines. 'Thus came Faithful to his end.' Understatement can be telling, but this passage does not carry the weight of what is left unsaid.

Yet, taken as a whole, *The Pilgrim's Progress* is a great imaginative work which thoroughly deserves its continued reputation. The overwhelming importance of religion to Bunyan is fully communicated. He is felt as a man who has put on the whole armour of God and taken the sword of the Spirit,

> praying always with all prayer and supplication in the Spirit, and watching thereunto with all perseverance and supplication for all saints.
>
> Ephesians vi, 18.

Bunyan's other works have lost much of their force for the modern reader. They can be read, but the emphasis hardly falls where Bunyan intended. *The Life and Death of Mr. Badman* tends to be treated as a novel with an entertaining villain as its hero; Bunyan meant it as the allegorical antithesis to *The Pilgrim's Progress*—a terrible warning to repent in time. The form creates difficulties: the story is related as a dialogue between Mr. Wiseman and Mr. Attentive. They follow the career of Mr. Badman from his earliest youth, through all the variations of his sins, to his lamentable deathbed; as each sin is described, Mr. Wiseman preaches on the corresponding virtue and defines the related vices. Far less of the material is digested into allegory in this book. The reader tends to pass over the moral and concentrate on the vigorous drawing of the character of Badman. He was already very debauched when still young, but in order to marry a rich and pious orphan he pretended to piety himself. Not until they were safely married did his wife discover his real character. He would not allow her to go out to hear sermons; he made fun of the preachers, and tried to circulate scandals about them:

> Now she scarce durst go to an honest Neighbours house, or have a
> good Book in her hand; specially when he had his companions in his
> house, or had got a little drink in his head. He would also, when he per-
> ceived that she was dejected, speak tauntingly, and mockingly to her in
> the presence of his Companions, calling of her his Religious Wife, his
> demure Dame, and the like. . . . If she did ask him (as sometimes she
> would) to let her go out to a Sermon, he would in a currish manner reply,
> *Keep at home, keep at home, and look to your business, we cannot live by
> hearing of Sermons.*
>
> *The Life and Death of Mr Badman* (ed. J. Brown, 1905), p. 76.

There are many vividly told cautionary tales in the book, but it makes
no religious impression.

The Holy War is Bunyan's attempt to write *Paradise Lost* and
Paradise Regained. It is the story of the fall of Mansoul from grace,
his redemption by Emmanuel, and the continuation of the struggle
against the ever-present enemies within. The city of Mansoul is both
the individual soul and the soul of mankind; on a contemporary level it
stands for the various English cities that fell from grace by being on
the side of the King during the Civil Wars, and had to be besieged by
the armies of the Lord. This allegory is less well handled than *The
Pilgrim's Progress*. It contains an enormous number of characters
distinguishable only by name. Bunyan analysed out all the possible
components of the mind, conscience, spirit and will of man, baptized
them in complicated style, and deployed them to the confusion of the
reader. Even Emmanuel himself does not stand out clearly; the characters are not vigorously or individually drawn. The cast is too large for
allegory—or perhaps too quickly introduced, for the sum total of
people engaged is probably no larger than that in Tolkien's *The Lord
of the Rings*. There are moving passages in the book, even though it
does not make an impression as a unified whole. There is a good picture
of the doubts and misgivings of a mind that is afraid it has gone astray
and does not want to acknowledge the fact:

> For now could not *Mansoul* sleep securely as before. . . . For they had
> from the Camp of *Shaddai* such frequent, warm and terrifying alarms;
> yea, alarms upon alarms, first at one Gate and then at another, and again,
> at all the Gates at once, that they were broken as to former peace. Yea,
> they had their alarms so frequently, and that when the nights were at

longest, the weather coldest, and so consequently the *season* most *un-seasonable*; that that Winter was to the Town of *Mansoul* a Winter by it self. Sometimes the Trumpets would sound, sometimes the slings would whorle the stones into the Town. Sometimes ten thousand of the Kings Souldiers would be running round the Walls of Mansoul at midnight, shouting, and lifting up the voice for battel. Sometimes again, some of them in the Town would be wounded, and their cry and lamentable voice would be heard, to the great molestation of the now languishing Town of *Mansoul*.

The Holy War (ed. J. Brown, 1905), p. 235.

That is good allegorical writing; the account is valid whether it is read literally, or metaphorically as an account of a state of mind. It has the vividness and straightforwardness of Bunyan at his best, and it links him with the best qualities of the secular literature of his time. That is the virtue of his style; the virtue of his matter, in so far as they are separable, is that of enlightening the understanding and inflaming the will—two gifts from God which he discusses in *The Heavenly Footman*. His last instructions to the reader in that pamphlet were:

> Be sure that thou begin betimes; get into the way; run apace, and hold out to the end; and the Lord give thee a prosperous journey.

The Heavenly Footman, p. 64.

THOMAS TRAHERNE (1636?–74)

Traherne was a younger man than Bunyan; he was born about 1636, and did not go up to Oxford until the Commonwealth was installed. There he took orders. He lived quietly, first in a little parish in Herefordshire, then, from 1660, as private chaplain to the Keeper of the Privy Seal, in London and at Hampton Court. His life was devotional, and he was beyond the reach of the agitations and dis-illusionments of his day; not because he refused to recognize their existence, but because he knew their unimportance when they were set against the glories of the world as it was originally made by God. All his works were posthumously published, with the exception of one attack on Roman Catholicism. Two devotional works were published later in the century, but the *Centuries of Meditations*, which he wrote for a friend, Mrs. Hopton, and the *Poems of Felicity* remained in manuscript until they were discovered by Bertram Dobell early in the twentieth century. If these had not come to light, he would not have been remembered as a writer. The *Centuries of Meditations* contains his best work. He could write prose of great beauty, but his poetry is nearly always less satisfying; it lacks intensity, and the form and rhythm contribute little to the meaning of the words.

He was a man as intensely religious as Bunyan, but his temperament and outlook were completely different. Because the world was made by God, he valued it; he thought it a sign of wilful ignorance to regard the world merely as a City of Destruction from which to flee. Heavenly felicity was attainable in this life. He was scornful of the Noncon- formists who placed their hopes only in heaven :

> Nor can any reason be given why they should desire it at last, and not now. If they say because God hath commanded them, that is false: for He offereth it now, now they are commanded to have their conversation in Heaven, now they may be full of joy and full of glory. . . . Those Chris- tians that can defer their felicity may be contented with their ignorance.
>
> *Centuries of Meditations* (ed. B. Dobell, 1908), IV, 9.

The difference between felicity on earth and felicity in heaven was only this:

> Heaven is a place where our happiness shall be seen of all.
>
> *Ibid.*, IV, 12.

In the meditations (a form of religious exercise popularized by such men as François de Sales) Traherne revealed his ideas of the world, of the end for which man was created, and of the way in which man could rightly order himself in the universe. He saw God not as the avenger who would send children to hell, but as father, friend and benefactor:

> God is not an Object of Terror, but Delight. To know Him therefore as He is, is to frame the most beautiful idea in all Worlds. He delighteth in our happiness more than we: and is of all other the most Lovely Object.

An infinite Lord, who having all Riches, Honors, and Pleasures in His own hand, is infinitely willing to give them unto me.

Ibid., I, 17.

Superficially this has affinities with the attitude taken later by the third Earl of Shaftesbury, in his cheerful assertion of the goodnaturedness of God. But the tone and feeling are entirely different. Shaftesbury pats his Supreme Manager on the back, whereas Traherne, though not frightened, is filled with wonder and awe.

He saw two co-existent worlds: the world made by God, and the world perverted by man. What he stressed was the continual existence of the world as it was made by God; it could still be perceived by men if they were in the right frame of mind. The world

is a Temple of Majesty, yet no man regards it. It is a region of Light and Peace, did not men disquiet it. It is the Paradise of God.

Ibid., I, 31.

He thought it was possible to see the world in its original splendour and glory, as he had done so easily when he was a child. For him, then,

the corn was orient and immortal wheat, which never should be reaped, nor was ever sown. I thought it had stood from everlasting to everlasting. The dust and stones of the street were as precious as gold: the gates were at first the end of the world. . . . Boys and girls tumbling in the street, and playing, were moving jewels. I knew not that they were born or should die; But all things abided eternally as they were in their proper places. Eternity was manifest in the Light of Day, and something infinite behind everything appeared: which talked with my expectation and moved my desire.

Ibid., III, 3.

There was no need for a grown man to lose this vision even when he had become aware of the miseries of the world as man has made it:

For the very miseries and sins and offences that are in it are the materials of his joy and triumph and glory. . . . Heretofore, to enjoy beauties, and be grateful for benefits was all the art that was required to felicity, but now a man must, like a God, bring Light out of Darkness, and order out of confusion.

Ibid., IV, 21.

If man desired, he could still learn to enjoy the world aright. He had to realize that he alone was heir of the whole world. He must respond to it and take up his heritage with his imagination and feelings as well as with his body. Sensuous satisfaction must be crowned by spiritual appreciation:

> Your enjoyment of the world is never right, till every morning you awake in Heaven; see yourself in your Father's Palace; and look upon the skies, the earth, and the air as celestial joys. . . .
> You never enjoy the world aright, till the Sea itself floweth in your veins, till you are clothed with the heavens, and crowned with the stars.
>
> *Ibid.*, I, 28, 29.

Traherne took pains to show that nothing in God's world could be bettered. He dilated on the virtues of the sun in serving man. God did well to make one sun, not two, for two between them would have dried up the earth; and it was right to make the sun move instead of standing still:

> Did the Sun stand still that you might have a perpetual day, you would not know the sweetness of repose: the delightful vicissitudes of night and day, the early sweetness and spring of the morning, the perfume and beauty in the cool of the evening, would all be swallowed up in meridian splendour: all which now entertain you with delights.
>
> *Ibid.*, II, 9.

The quality of his imagination, and his lyrical powers of expressing what he perceived, set Traherne on a different plane from most of his contemporaries; yet his vision of the world was not divorced from the 'Reason' so much valued in his own times. His vision could be expressed in the form of a theory, clearly thought out and consistent. On the basis of this theory about the nature of the universe Traherne reached conclusions about the nature of man and his satisfactions, and demonstrated how man could attain his ends.

As part of the created universe, man still retained his fundamental virtue; therefore he found his only real satisfaction in loving not only God, but all created things as well:

> But above all by Loving [the soul] does attain itself. Love also being the end of Souls, which are never perfect till they are in act what they are

in power. They were made to love, and are dark and vain and comfortless till they do it. Till they love they are idle, or mis-employed. Till they love they are desolate. . . . Till we become therefore all Act as God is, we can never rest, nor ever be satisfied.

Ibid., II, 48.

This love could have no single object, not even if the object were God:

Were He beloved alone, His love would be limited. He must be loved in all with an illimited love, even in all His doings, in all His friends, in all His creatures.

Ibid., I, 73.

Love had to extend to the universe—that idea followed from the vision of the universe as God originally made it :

He was well acquainted with this mystery—That every man being the object of our Saviour's Love, was to be treated as our Saviour . . . And thus he is to live upon Earth among Sinners.

Ibid., IV, 28.

The love of God led very directly to the love of one's neighbours.

Traherne did not think this love was of value if it was merely instinctive. Faith needed to be turned into assurance, by the riches of knowledge and understanding. Men had to study God. Traherne himself had this wise apprehension of his faith in a high degree. He could give an imaginable explanation of the Trinity, the reasons for the three in one and one in three, in the fortieth meditation of the second century. He could argue the necessity of the invisibility of God:

It is expedient that He should be so [invisible]: for whatsoever is visible is a body; whatsoever is a body excludeth other things out of the place where itself is. If God therefore being infinite were visible He would make it impossible for anything to have a being. Besides, bulk as such in itself is dead. Whatsoever is visible is so in like manner. That which inspireth bulk with motion, life and sense is invisible; and in itself distinct from the bulk which it inspireth. Were God therefore pure bulk, He could neither move, nor will, nor desire anything; but being invisible, He leaveth room for and effecteth all things. He filleth nothing with a bodily presence, but includeth all. He is pure Life, Knowledge, and Desire, from which all things flow: pure Wisdom, Goodness, and Love to which all things return.

Ibid., II, 19.

Traherne's enthusiasm was allied with reason, and he never lost sight of normal life in an ecstasy of transcendentalism. His meditations were directed to the proper end—practical application of doctrine. His view of the universe made sin easier to avoid, since man knew that sin would deform and frustrate him, and make him infinitely odious in the eyes of God. A man who enjoyed the world aright could set a true value on everything; honours and riches would not tempt him when the stars were much more lovely than diamonds, and just as much his own.

Traherne showed a remarkable sense of form. Within the separate meditations a single thought or concept, complete in itself, was propounded, argued through to a satisfying conclusion or amplified to a serene climax. Each meditation was linked in a chain with its predecessor and successor. Each sentence had its place in the total rhythmic pattern; he had a sure sense of balance and cadence. He often left the reader with the feeling that the themes and rhythms of a passage had been followed through as in a choral prelude, exploring every variation and finding their own natural close.

His style was limpid and perspicuous. His plainness was like that of the prose of the Authorized Version; he could rise to nobility in a moment, and return to his norm without any sense of bathos. It was an inclusive simplicity, equally at ease with the splendid and the homely, harmonizing the divergent elements. The basis is simple narrative:

> When I came into the country, and being seated among silent trees, and meads, and hills, had all my time in mine own hands, I resolved to spend it all, whatever it cost me, in search of happiness.
>
> *Ibid.*, III, 46.

Often this style was illuminated by images; both the simple homely analogy that captured the spiritual concept, bringing eternity and infinity for a moment within the reader's grasp and making the strange familiar, and also the image that made the familiar strange, lighting it up with a new kind of wonder.

The homely analogy was frequently employed, just as it used to be by the medieval preachers, or by Latimer in the sixteenth century. When Traherne wished to show the evil influence that one soul could have on another, adults persuading children to prefer rocking-horses and tops before the sun and the wind, he talked in terms of apples rotting in a box:

> My soul was only apt and disposed to great things; but souls to souls are like apples to apples, one being rotten rots another.
>
> *Ibid.*, III, 10.

Again, he was talking of the small importance of life on earth in comparison with the eternal life of man:

> Alas the WORLD is but a little centre in comparison with you. Suppose it millions of miles from the Earth to the Heavens, and millions of millions above the Stars, both here and over the heads of our Antipodes: it is surrounded with infinite and eternal space: And like a gentleman's house to one that is travelling; it is a long time before you come unto it, you pass it in an instant, and leave it for ever. The Omnipresence and Eternity of God are your fellows and companions.
>
> *Ibid.*, I, 19.

He has been talking in terms of distance that are almost meaningless to the ordinary mind; then he suddenly clinches the insignificance of life on earth by this comparison with the single house that you pass in the course of a long journey, and the whole idea is at once imaginable.

The second kind of image, in which Traherne invests the familiar with wonder, pervades the meditations. Here he conveys his direct vision of the world as God originally made it, and communicates both his ever-present delight in its beauty and his feeling of being alive in all created things. One of his most famous passages epitomizes this best:

> You never enjoy the world aright, till the Sea itself floweth in your veins, till you are clothed with the heavens, and crowned with the stars: and perceive yourself to be sole heir of the whole world, and more than so, because men are in it who are every one sole heirs as well as you. Till you can sing and rejoice and delight in God, as misers do in gold, and Kings in sceptres, you never enjoy the world.
>
> *Ibid.*, I, 29.

The images are animated by a super-sensitiveness to all life. To appreciate the loveliness and wildness and 'inscape' of the sea, you must be the sea, and the sea must be in you.

Traherne's kind of wonder made him one of the happiest men of his time. His religion gave him, instead of superficial optimism, an unshakable conviction of the fundamental goodness of the Creator and the creation which enabled him to endure whatever adverse things he encountered, and to take a conscious delight in existence.

THOMAS BURNET (1635?–1715)

Thomas Burnet was not related to his contemporary, Bishop Gilbert Burnet, the Church historian. He came up from Yorkshire to Clare Hall, where he was a pupil of Tillotson. He was greatly attracted by the teaching of the Cambridge Platonists, and when Cudworth transferred to Christ's College, Burnet followed him there. Later, he travelled on the continent as escort to Lord Wiltshire and Lord Orrery. He became Master of the Charterhouse. The early influence of the Cambridge Platonists gave way to the influence of the Deists: he published two treatises against the doctrines of original sin and of eternal punishment.

His most memorable and imaginative work is his *Theoria Telluris Sacra*, published in Latin in 1681. His English translation of the first two books of it followed in 1684, and of the last two books in 1690. This treatise was a monumental attempt to state precisely (without excluding first and final causes) the formal and material causes of what he called 'the Original of the Earth, and of all the General Changes which it hath already undergone, or is to undergo, Till the Consummation of all Things'. In the main, he discussed the creation of the world as Paradise, the Flood, the burning of the world, and the creation of new heavens and new earth.

Burnet's enthusiasm was typical of a mind in transition between the medieval and modern worlds. It was a blend of general intellectual excitement, scientific curiosity and religious awe. He held medieval views on the decay of the world and the littleness of man, but he was modern in his vision of the progressive discovery of truth and in his belief in scientific wonders rather than in miracles. He was always working towards the underlying natural explanation of startling phenomena, but he felt sure that his discoveries did not subvert religious truths; instead, they gave such truths a firm and reasonable basis. While in pursuit of the facts, he never lost his sense of the sublime.

His passion for enlarging the field of knowledge was obvious from the first. He took great delight in the exploration of ideas, in forming new hypotheses and checking them against known facts :

> There is no sort of joy more grateful to the mind of man, than that which ariseth from the invention of Truth; especially when 'tis hard to come by. Every man hath a delight suited to his Genius, and as there is pleasure in the right exercise of any faculty, so especially in that of Right-reasoning; which is still the greater by how much the consequences are more clear, and the chains of them more long: There is no Chase so pleasant, methinks, as to drive a Thought, by good conduct, from one end of the World to the other; and never to lose sight of it till it fall into Eternity, where all things are lost as to our Knowledge.
>
> *The Sacred Theory of the Earth* (1684), Bk. I, p. 6.

Difficulty was a welcome challenge to him. Moreover, he was unafraid of the consequences of discovery. There were no seamarks beyond which man should not venture. He was convinced that scientific truth could never in the last resort be at odds with religious truth:

> We are not to suppose that any truth concerning the Natural World can be an enemy to Religion; for Truth cannot be an enemy to Truth, God is not divided against himself.
>
> *Ibid.*, Preface, sig. a 2 (r).

He scorned men like Donne who felt that Copernicus had destroyed not only the known pattern of astronomy but the whole hierarchical world-order:

> 'Tis all in peeces, all coherence gone;
> All just supply, and all Relation:
> Prince, Subject, Father, Sonne, are things forgot. . . .
> *An Anatomie of the World*, Donne, *Works*
> (ed. Hayward, 1936), p. 202.

He pointed out that it was no compliment to the fundamental strength of religion to be so easily disturbed:

For every new Theory that is propos'd, to be alarum'd, as if all
Religion was falling about our Ears, is to make the World suspect that
we are very ill assur'd of the foundation it stands upon.

Burnet, *op. cit.*, Preface, sig. a 2 (r).

God himself encouraged man to use his reason to examine the works of
God, 'our heritage and habitation'. The last age had made great
progress in these studies, more than all the former ages of the world.
Men were now on the road to finding out

how the Divine Wisdom wrought all these things out of confusion into
order, and out of simplicity into that beautiful composition we now see
them in.

Ibid., Bk. I, p. 53.

This gave Burnet his most satisfying kind of joy in the present world.
He obviously hoped that the pace of recent discovery would be maintained; but he thought that man would never enter completely into his
kingdom of knowledge until he reached heaven, where he would have
the final pleasures of contemplation:

There is no lasting pleasure, but *Contemplation*. All others grow flat
and insipid upon frequent use; And when a Man hath run through a Sett
of Vanities, in the declension of his Age, he knows not what to do with
himself, if he cannot Think. He saunters about, from one dull business
to another, to wear out time; and hath no reason to value life, but because
he's afraid of death. But Contemplation is a continual spring of fresh
pleasures. Truth is inexhausted, and when you are once in the right way,
the further you go, the greater discoveries you make, and with the greater
joy. We are sometimes highly pleas'd, and even transported, with little
inventions in Mathematicks, or Mechanicks, or natural Philosophy; All
these things will make part of their diversion and entertainment in that
state; All the doctrine of sounds and harmony; Of light, colours and perspective, will be known in perfection. But these I call Diversions, in comparison of their higher and more serious speculations, which will be the
business and happiness of that life.
    Do but imagine, that they will have the Scheme of all humane affairs
lying before them: from the Chaos to the last period. The universal history
and order of times. The whole oeconomy of the Christian Religion, and
of all Religions in the World. The Plan of the undertaking of the Messiah:
with all other parts and ingredients of the Providence of this Earth. Do

but imagine this, I say, and you will easily allow, that when they contemplate the beauty, wisdom and goodness, of the whole design, it must needs raise great and noble passions, and a far richer joy than either the pleasures or speculations of this life can excite in us.

Ibid., Bk. IV, pp. 213–14.

Heaven was the Idea of a University, and Burnet knew that there alone could his passion for knowledge be satisfied, and all things understood.

Meanwhile, his *Sacred Theory of the Earth* was intended as a contribution to man's knowledge of the universe in which he lived. As a theory, it had to comply with the dictates of reason, of scientific fact and of Holy Scripture. If it also fitted in with myths and legends of the ancient world, so much the better. His starting-point was the state of the world in which he lived. This he saw as, essentially, a great ruin. Only an orator could describe it as a beautiful and regular globe, the jewel in the firmament. In fact:

'Tis as a broken and confus'd heap of bodies, plac'd in no order to one another, nor with any correspondency or regularity of parts: And such a body as the Moon appears to us, when 'tis look'd upon with a good Glass, rude and ragged.

Ibid., Bk. I, p. 110.

It was divided most irregularly into sea and land, the islands like scattered limbs, long promontories sticking into the sea, long creeks running up into the land. The ocean itself was a prodigious cavity, of unknown depth:

When I present this great Gulf to my imagination, emptied of all its waters, stretching its jaws from one end of the Earth to another, it appears to me the most ghastly thing in Nature.

Ibid., Bk. I, p. 128.

The mountains, to a man who was standing on a summit, would seem strangely rude and ruin-like:

To see on every hand of him a multitude of vast bodies thrown together in confusion, as those Mountains are; Rocks standing naked about him; and the hollow Valleys gaping under him; and at his feet, it may be, an heap of frozen Snow in the midst of Summer.

Ibid., Bk. I, pp. 141–2.

The sight of such things, Burnet thought, made men eager to discover their causes.

He argued that this world was the ruin of a previous world, which we called Paradise. The physical cause of the ruin was the Deluge, which must have covered a world originally smooth, without mountains or oceans. For no forty days of rain could possibly have produced enough water to cover the world and its mountains, even if they were no more than a mile high. It would have required eight times as much water as there is at present in the oceans of the world, allowing for an average depth of a quarter of a mile. Unless the Deluge were a manifestation of divine omnipotence, the original form of earth was smooth. (This was a theory already adumbrated by commentators on the Book of Genesis.) But how was Paradise changed into the fragmented world of the seventeenth century? And what did St. Peter mean by saying that the antediluvian earth perished, or Moses, by recording that the great 'abyss' was broken open at the deluge? Burnet's answer was that Paradise was a shell of dry land enclosing the great abyss of waters that flowed about the central mass of the world; at the Deluge, the shell broke and fell down into the great abyss, and the waters were flung over it.

He explained in great detail how this had come about. When the four elements of which the sphere of the world was composed were cooling down, the earth, being heaviest, sank to the centre; next came the fluids, water underneath and the lighter oils on top. Above these the air circled, but the air still had particles of earth swirling about in it. When these descended towards the solid part, they were trapped in the oily fluid; at first they made only slime spread over the face of the waters, but later this slime hardened into a shell. Burnet was filled with admiration for this architecture:

The whole Globe of the Water vaulted over, and the Exteriour Earth hanging above the Deep, sustain'd by nothing but its own measures and manner of Construction: A Building without foundation or corner-stone. This seems to be a piece of Divine Geometry or Architecture.

Ibid., Bk. I, p. 65.

The world that grew up on this shell was beautiful; a perfect un-
fractured whole, calm and serene. It was moistened by vapours raised
up from the equatorial zone by the sun; they escaped towards the
cooler poles, where they condensed as dew and rain. The earth was an
oval, and its poles lay farther from the centre than did the equatorial
parts; this meant that the poles lay 'higher' than the equator, therefore
there would be a continual flow of water from them towards the
equator, in arteries gradually branching into capillaries and finally
evaporating in the torrid zone. (In fact, in the antediluvian world,
rivers flowed backwards.)

This world was destroyed as a punishment for sin. The immediate
physical cause of the Deluge was that the sun, operating in perpetual
summer, had dried the shell so much that the layer of water beneath
had grown hot, and partially vaporized. The vapour needed more
room than the water it replaced, and thrust through the surface in an
attempt to find it; in this way the shell was broken, and fell into the
abyss. Its collapse gave rise to violent agitation, which subsided
gradually as the waters sank into channels between the fragments of
the former earth, chaotically distributed. Burnet described the process
graphically:

> The pressure of a great mass of Earth falling into the Abysse . . . could
> not but impel the water with so much strength, as would carry it up to
> a great height in the Air; and to the top of any thing that lay in its way,
> any eminency, or high fragment whatsoever: And then rolling back again,
> it would sweep down with it whatsoever it rusht upon, Woods, Buildings,
> living Creatures, and carry them all headlong into the great gulf. Some-
> times a mass of water would be quite struck off and separate from the
> rest, and tost through the Air like a flying River; but the common motion
> of the waves was to climb up the hills, or inclin'd fragments, and then
> return into the valleys and deeps again, with a perpetual fluctuation coming
> and going, ascending and descending, till the violence of them being spent
> by degrees, they settled at last in the places allotted for them; where
> *bounds are set that they cannot pass over, that they return not again to
> cover the Earth.*
>
> *Ibid.*, Bk. I, pp. 75–6.

This tallied with Descartes's account of the formation of the world,
to some extent; he had envisaged it as covered with a thin crust, before
it was inhabited. This crust then collapsed into the abyss and formed

the known world. But Descartes did not identify the collapse with the Deluge.

Burnet's theory satisfied his reasoning powers, and fitted in with the scientific knowledge which he had. If the earth as known to him was of comparatively recent formation, it explained why erosion had not already levelled all the mountains into a plain. The newness of the present earth accounted for the relatively recent development of men's knowledge of geography. The process of the disintegration of the surface of the original earth fitted in with what was known of the effects of heat on various substances. But the theory had also to fit the facts of history as recorded in the Bible. He spent some time relating his hypothesis to texts in the Old Testament. His abyss was clearly what Moses and other prophets called Tehom-Rabba. This was not the sea, but some subterraneous waters, vast in extent, and capable of disruption, since the fountains of it were said to have burst open at the Deluge. There was evidence in the Psalms of David for the original shell of the world, covering the abyss:

> For he hath founded it upon the seas, and established it upon the floods.
>
> Psalm XXIV, v. 2.

> To him that stretched out the earth above the waters: for his mercy endureth for ever.
>
> Psalm CXXXVI, v. 6.

Similar descriptions were to be found in the Book of Job, in Isaiah, and in the Book of Revelation.

He also adduced ancient legends in support of his theory. The lost continent of Atlantis was a memory of the antediluvian world. The myth of the twin children of Chaos, Nox and Oceanus, was relevant to his account of the original creation, for Nox was the dark unpurified air, circling about the waters, and uniting with the ocean to produce their daughter Terra, the dry land. Even the temple of Hieropolis was useful to him, for it was built upon a supposedly bottomless pit, the image of the abyss, in commemoration of Deucalion's flood. This evidence was offered on a less serious level than evidence from the Bible, but it obviously pleased Burnet to see how everything fitted in.

He went on to describe, in the third book, the probable process by which the world would be destroyed, making room for a new heaven and a new earth. It would be consumed by fire, like its emblem the Phoenix, which was fabled to burn and rise renewed from its ashes. He imagined that the fire would begin with a general simultaneous eruption of volcanoes, tearing up the molten roots of the earth. The angels would be engaged in fanning the flames. He gave an orthodox account of the Last Day: the sun veiled and dark; the mountains breathing smoke; earthquakes; the sea retired; flaming meteors and thunder; all the laws of nature seemingly expired. When everything was stricken, the heavens would suddenly burst open and the glory of God would appear. He was far more cautious in describing the future, for which there was no scientific evidence; he recommended modesty and sobriety in the interpretation of scripture, and pointed out that time would undoubtedly modify and correct his predictions.

Obviously his theories are of little importance today, but the imagination that formed them is still impressive. Though he lacked the intellectual power of such men as Descartes and Newton, he grasped the importance of the unity of knowledge. He tried to find a theory that would square with all types of known fact; he was no more depart-mentalized than Sir Thomas Browne had been. In the process of working out his theory he gave himself scope for meditating on the inescapable limits of man's existence, and on the wonders of the creation. He responded emotionally to objects that his critical sense described as ruins. He was fascinated by the caves that were formed when the crust collapsed:

It would be very pleasant to read good descriptions of these Subter-raneous places, and of all the strange works of Nature there; how she furnisheth these dark neglected Grottoes; they have often a little Brook runs murmuring through them, and the roof is commonly a kind of petrifi'd Earth or Icy fretwork; proper enough for such rooms. But I should be pleas'd especially to view the Sea-caves, or those hollow Rocks that lie upon the Sea, where the Waves roll in a great way under ground, and wear the hard rock into as many odd shapes and figures as we see in the Clouds.

Ibid., Bk. I, pp. 115-16.

7

He was awestruck when he thought of the depth and vastness of the sea itself; he imagined it drained of water:

> With what amazement should we see it under us like an open Hell, or a wide bottomless pit? So deep, and hollow, and vast; so broken and confus'd, so every way deform'd and monstrous. . . . 'Tis another Chaos in its kind, who can paint the Scenes of it? Gulfs, and Precipices, and Cataracts; Pits within Pits, and Rocks under Rocks, broken Mountains and ragged Islands, that look as if they had been Countries pull'd up by the roots, and planted in the Sea.
>
> *Ibid.*, Bk. I, p. 132.

He recorded his reactions to the wonders of nature without self-consciousness or embarrassment:

> Next to the great Concave of the Heavens, and those boundless Regions where the Stars inhabit, there is nothing that I look upon with more pleasure than the wide Sea and the Mountains of the Earth. There is something august and stately in the Air of these things that inspires the mind with great thoughts and passions; We do naturally upon such occasions think of God and his greatness, and whatsoever hath but the shadow and appearance of INFINITE, as all things have that are too big for our comprehension, they fill and over-bear the mind with their Excess, and cast it into a pleasing kind of stupor and admiration.
>
> *Ibid.*, Bk. I, pp. 139–40.

Here his prose carried a conviction that Shaftesbury's missed when he wrote his near-blank-verse rhapsodies some few years later. It is interesting to discover that he was responsive to what he had seen of the Alps and Apennines. Most men of his century regarded them as mere obstacles, unfortunately wild; aesthetically, they were 'hook-shouldered heights', asymmetrical failures. Burnet himself had a strong sense of the sublime.

Yet he was painfully aware that all such things were subject to decay; he felt the tragedy of mutability. They could not sustain 'the unimaginable touch of time'. He wrote a noble lament in the third book for the inevitable loss of the glories of the world. It is too long to quote in its entirety; what follows is the conclusion:

> But 'tis not Cities onely, and works of men's hands, but the everlasting Hills, the Mountains and Rocks of the Earth, are melted as Wax before

the Sun; *and their place is no where found.* Here stood the Alpes, a prodigious range of Stone, the Load of the Earth, that cover'd many Countries, and reach'd their Armes from the Ocean to the *Black Sea*; This huge mass of Stone is soften'd and dissolv'd, as a tender Cloud into Rain. Here stood the *African* Mountains, and *Atlas* with his top above the Clouds. There was frozen *Caucasus*, and *Taurus*, and *Imaus*, and the Mountains of *Asia.* And yonder towards the North stood the *Riphean* Hills, cloth'd in Ice and Snow. All these are vanish'd, dropt away as the Snow upon their heads: and swallowed up in a red Sea of Fire. *Great and marvellous are thy Works, Lord God Almighty: Just and true are thy ways, thou King of Saints.* Hallelujah.

Ibid., Bk. III, p. 111.

There is something Miltonic about the grandeur of this roll-call of the high places of the earth. Burnet had an ear for sound and cadence, and he had learned much from the style of the Authorized Version.

His view of man was complex. He was aware of the vast potentialities of the mind of man, but realistic about his weakness and vulnerability. Far from being the master of the universe, man was almost its fool. Burnet gave a medieval account of his frailties:

[He] sees himself every day weak and impotent, hath no power over external Nature, little over himself; cannot execute so much as his own good resolutions; mutable, irregular, prone to evil. . . . Man that comes into the World at the pleasure of another, and goes out by an hundred accidents; His Birth and Education generally determine his fate here, and neither of these are in his own power; His wit also is as uncertain as his fortune; He hath not the moulding of his own Brain, however a knock on the Head makes him a Fool, stupid as the Beasts of the Field. . . .

Ibid. Bk. II. p. 311.

He must not be impudent enough to imagine that the universe was created for the benefit of such a creature. If life on earth were all that man had, his situation would indeed be miserable. He was forced to spend his time on trivialities:

For what is this life, but a circulation of little mean actions? We lie down and rise again: dress and undress: feed and wax hungry: work, or play, and are weary: and then we lie down again, and the circle returns. We spend the day in trifles, and when the Night comes, we throw our selves into the Bed of folly, amongst dreams and broken thoughts and wild imaginations.

Ibid., Bk. III, p. 114.

Yet the capacities of man were greater than this; his expectations should therefore be on a larger scale. This world could not be his only sphere of activity. Man was more than matter in motion, whatever Hobbes and the atomists might say; he was, Burnet strongly hoped, an immortal soul. He must live out his life in the world on this basis:

> Let us be Adventurers for another World: 'Tis, at least, a fair and noble Chance: and there is nothing in this, worth our thoughts or our passions. If we should be disappointed, we are still no worse than the rest of our fellow-mortals: and if we succeed in our expectations, we are eternally happy.
>
> *Ibid.*, Bk. III, pp. 114-15.

Here, eternal values led Burnet to depreciate the delights of the scientist in the wonders of God's creation; his enthusiasm has become more purely religious and transcendental. But his writing is still informed with vigour and a sense of personal commitment. He put his heart into whatever he did. What he imagined was different from what Bunyan or Traherne imagined, but they had in common this passionate excitement in experiencing their respective worlds. Browne might have been speaking of any one of them when he said, 'Life is a pure flame, and we live by an invisible sun within us.'

V

THE MEN OF THE WORLD

IN AN age of strain like the period of the Restoration it is easy to fall into extremes of fanaticism or of triviality. Too many of the Wits had recourse to a policy of 'making the best of it'—ignoring the unpleasant features, and living for personal pleasure. The ability to face the unpleasantness of contemporary life and then to achieve a balance based on this honesty of vision was rare. There are few important men who wrote between 1660 and 1700 who were characterized by level-headedness in combination with moral principles.

George Savile, Marquis of Halifax, and Edward Hyde, Earl of Clarendon, met the problems of their period with more sanity than most of their contemporaries possessed. Their own level-headedness was based on moral principles, but their successes were due to the fact that they realized that many of their fellow men had no principles at all. Both men combined personal integrity with a wise mistrust of human nature. It was Halifax who said, on the subject of credulity, 'Men must be saved in this World by their want of Faith.' Neither of them was a cynic; there were qualities in men for which they had the highest admiration, but they were too wise to believe in the entire goodness of man.

EDWARD HYDE, EARL OF CLARENDON (1609–74)

The Earl of Clarendon began life as Edward Hyde, the son of a country gentleman. He had the normal education at a grammar school and at Oxford, and then came to live in London as a law student. There he became the friend of a group of distinguished men: Ben Jonson, Charles Cotton, the learned John Selden, Lord Falkland, the Earl of

Pembroke and many others. He made friends easily, and he acknowledged the debt he owed to their stimulus and example. He began to make a name as a lawyer. In 1640 he was elected to the Long Parliament. His influence there was soon felt, though he was still only thirty-two: he had a sound knowledge of constitutional matters, which he could expound in an easy and attractive style. He belonged to the more moderate Parliamentarians, who hoped to make a liberal accommodation between the King and the more violent party led by Pym. Unfortunately, Charles's intermittent and ineffective resorts to force made Pym determined to increase the pressure from Parliament until the King capitulated completely. Pym's attitude drove Hyde to support the King. Both during the months of pamphleteering and speech-making before war broke out, and in the early years of the war itself, Hyde was of great service to the King, without becoming a 'royalist' by conviction. Hyde, in the main, composed the King's answers to Pym's attacks; in terms of law, he had the best of the controversy. His appeal was made to the constitution as it was then understood— he said it was better to fight for the known laws of the land than for the New Utopia of religion and government which Parliament was trying to establish in England. When it became clear that the Royalists were losing the war, Hyde obeyed Charles's request to escort his eldest son to the Scilly Isles. Later they went to Jersey. Hyde stayed there for two years, while the Prince went to France. In 1652, after the attempt to restore the monarchy by force had failed, Hyde was called to the court in exile to act as Charles's chief adviser. His political experience made him advise Charles to wait for the most favourable moment for his restoration—the moment when he would be asked to return without conditions. In 1660 Hyde was Chancellor of England. At first he had great power, but it soon began to be undermined by younger men. Charles wanted ministers who were more accommodating, less cautious and restrictive. Men blamed Clarendon for their personal losses and restraints under the Restoration settlement. He was wrongly thought to have advocated the unpopular war with Holland. When, after the miseries of the Plague and the Fire, England was humiliated by the raid of the Dutch up the Medway, it was easy to make a scapegoat of Clarendon. He had antagonized Parliament by implying that the administration, rather than the House of Commons, ought to rule the country. In 1667 he was relieved of his seals of office, and impeached. After a good deal of persuasion he left England for France, and spent the rest of his life in exile. He died in 1674.

It was in the two periods of exile that he wrote his *History of the Rebellion* and his *Life*. He began *The History of the Rebellion* in the Scillies. His purpose was to write down 'with all fidelity and freedom' all he knew of the development of the situation which led to the Civil War, and of the progress of the war, bringing out all mistakes and omissions, so that the chief participants might learn from their mistakes to avoid further disaster. It was never intended for general publication. He began with this purely utilitarian purpose, but as he wrote, he became interested in the literary aspect of writing history; he compared his style and his methods with those of Livy and of Tacitus. The work was unfinished when he returned to England in 1660, and in his second period of exile he was unable to take the manuscript with him. He began, instead, to write a combined history of his own life and times, up to the stage of his second period of exile. In this work he was even more frank, since it was intended only for his own family. He was concerned to vindicate his part in events, and to reveal everything that was of interest. Four years after he had taken up residence in France his son Laurence was permitted to visit him; he brought the manuscript of *The History of the Rebellion* with him. Clarendon then completed this work. His judgment and his vigour of mind were unaffected by his age and situation, and he found it no effort to write.

Clarendon was essentially a man who wrote an apologia for his life and a diatribe on his times. Readers of *The History of the Rebellion* and the *Life* have tended to look at him in one of three ways: as a writer providing material for a definitive modern history of the period; as a historian in his own right who interpreted and judged events according to a pattern (each historiographer sees a different pattern); as a window on some of the gossip of his times. The first two kinds of reader have an incomplete picture, but one which is justifiable for their purposes; the third reader, a dilettante, has a misleading one, since Clarendon appears simply as the collector of anecdotes about the importunate crowd that set on Charles II with demands as soon as he landed at Dover, or about the Queen Mother, who asserted that she would go out of the palace at Whitehall by another door as soon as 'that woman', Ann Hyde, Clarendon's daughter and the Duke of York's wife, dared to set foot inside it. Clarendon took little delight in the vagaries of human behaviour for their own sake; he included them only when they threw light on important historical developments. Clarendon's value as a writer does, of course, consist partly in his qualities as a historian. Mr. Wormald, his most recent critic, has commented on his capacity for historical analysis, his sense of the influence of circumstances on men's intentions and actions, his genuine statecraft, and his perception of what the ideal balance of power within the constitution must be, for his own time. (The terms of the Restoration entirely justified his concept of the English constitution.)

The reader who is most interested in Clarendon's literary value is impressed by these qualities, but others are equally important to him. For him, Clarendon is not primarily the reporter of facts or the interpreter and judge of policy; he is a certain kind of human being writing vividly of what was important to him. The impression is gained less from individual passages (Clarendon does not anthologize well) than from the sweep of the work as a whole—a survey of events made by a man who was at once eyewitness, participant and distanced judge. His writing belonged to his periods of exile, when his comparative leisure gave him an opportunity for contemplation and the attainment of perspective. His position as a historian may be compared with that of Sir Winston Churchill when writing his history of the Second World War. Both men lived through the period of which they were writing, and all the important developments were part of their experience as statesmen at the centre of events. The majority of men who influenced the course of events were personally known to them. Both writers were fortunately placed.

Clarendon strikes the reader (and no doubt he meant to do so) as a man of integrity, drawn into public affairs by a strong sense of duty. He appears clear-sighted and realistic, honest about his own vices and virtues, generous, appreciative of his friends, neither harsh in judgment nor bitter in reaction; a man of feeling who remained loyal to both his Kings, while keenly aware of their defects; a man who wrote with clarity and firmness, and had the ability to underline the point without hammering on the table. The impression he intended to make is most quickly conveyed by two passages from the *Life*. The first is a comment wrung from Charles II in an interview with the Duke of York, when Clarendon was in disgrace, 'His Fault was that He always insisted too much upon the Law'. He never advised the King to overstep his legal rights, and often restrained him from conduct which he considered unprincipled or inexpedient. He took several opportunities of deploring the King's way of life, in audience with him, and was far from being the kind of yes-man that the King would have found more comfortable in office. The other passage is part of a letter from Clarendon to the King, after his seal of office had been taken from him:

> The Crimes which are objected against me how passionately soever pursued, and with Circumstances very unusual, do not in the least Degree fright me. God knows I am innocent in every Particular as I ought to be; and I hope your Majesty knows enough of me to believe that I had never a violent Appetite for Money, that could corrupt me. But alas! your Majesty's declared Anger and Indignation deprives me of the Comfort and Support even of my own Innocence, and exposes me to the Rage and Fury of those who have some Excuse for being my Enemies; whom I have sometimes displeased, when (and only then) your Majesty believed them not to be your friends. I hope They may be changed; I am sure I am not, but have the same Duty, Passion and Affection for You, that I had when You thought it most unquestionable, and which was and is as great as ever Man had for any mortal Creature. I should die in Peace (and truly I do heartily wish that God Almighty would free you from further Trouble, by taking me to himself), if I could know or guess at the Ground of your Displeasure, which I am sure must proceed from your believing, that I have said or done Somewhat I have neither said nor done.
>
> *The Life of Edward Earl of Clarendon, written by himself* (1760), vol. II, p. 413.

Clarendon implied that although the King had turned against him, his own loyalty was as great as ever. He reminded the King obliquely that if he had made personal enemies, it was for the King's sake and in his service. His conscience was clear. He refrained from reproaching the King for his present treatment, and assured him that if his death could do the King service, he would be glad to die. It is not great prose, but it avoids the pitfalls of sycophancy or aggression, and shows Clarendon at his best: dignified, constant, refusing to be terrified by superior power.

The portrait which Clarendon gives of himself may be, in part, historically false. What matters is that it is a convincing presentation, self-consistent and sustained. Clarendon's *persona* is attractive and admirable. He was obviously skilled in the art of ethical rhetoric; he knew how to imply that he was a worthy and likable person, whose view of the events of his day ought to be accepted.

He said himself, 'There was never yet a good History written but by men conversant in business, and of the best and most liberal education.' Certainly he could not be accused of being unversed in business. He excelled in the intellectual virtue of *peritia*—a practical wisdom, based on a realistic appraisal of the situation. This quality is obvious in his conduct both of private and public affairs. He was well aware of the dangers of his own high position, and did his best to escape the charge of being an ambitious and self-seeking man. This was the reason why he refused to be made a Knight of the Garter; why he hesitated for some time before allowing the King to make him an Earl, and regretted his acceptance when he found that his precedence gave rise to jealousy. His anxieties were thoroughly roused by the news that his daughter was secretly married to the King's brother, the heir presumptive. When the Queen Mother's fury on hearing of the marriage was diplomatically diminished by pressure from France, the Chancellor accepted the situation, but was entirely aware of her insincerity. He had an audience with her, in which he 'made all those Acknowledgements which he ought to do', and said, 'He should always depend upon her Protection as his most gracious Mistress'. He could dissemble when it was necessary; but his final comment on the incident ran:

> And from that Time there did never appear any Want of Kindness in the Queen towards him, whilst He stood in no Need of it, nor until it might have done him good.
>
> *Ibid.*, vol. I, p. 273.

The crisis was over, but Clarendon was aware of his continued danger:

> He knew well upon how slippery Ground He stood, and how naturally averse the Nation was from approving an exorbitant Power in any Subject. He saw that the King grew every Day more inclined to his Pleasures,

which involved him in Expense, and Company that did not desire that He should intend his Business or be conversant with sober Men. He knew well, that the Servants who were about the Duke were as much his Enemies as ever, and intended their own Profit only, by what Means soever, without considering his Honour; that They formed his Houshold, Officers and Equipage, by the Model of France, and against all the Rules and Precedents of England for a Brother of the Crown; and every Day put it into his Head, 'That if He were not supplied for all those Expenses, it was the Chancellor's Fault, who could effect it if He would.'

Ibid., vol. I, pp. 273–4.

He knew very well that Charles II trusted him with the main business of government simply because it was, at the moment, easier to do so; he had no confidence that his position would survive the King's discovery of other more congenial men who could take over from the Chancellor:

The Confidence the King had in him, besides the Assurance he had of his Integrity and Industry, proceeded more from his Aversion to be troubled with the Intricacies of his Affairs, than from any Violence of Affection, which was not so fixed in his Nature as to be like to transport him to any one Person.... He would, in a short Time, be acquainted with many, who would by finding Fault with all that was done be thought much wiser Men.

Ibid., vol. I, p. 284.

The King had not yet reached the point of finding the Chancellor more of a hindrance than a help, but he was bound to do so.

Clarendon's judgment was equally good in public affairs. He concerned himself with the springs of action as well as its possible consequences. He knew from experience that certain courses of action would be disastrous; events tended to prove him right. He advised Charles I to tone down the violence of some of his intended replies to his Parliament, and to refrain from provocative action. The Queen gave the opposite advice; unfortunately, Charles vacillated between accepting Hyde's re-wording and taking the Queen's advice about peremptory action. He tried to do both at once, and the combination of a conciliatory tone and the attempted arrest of the Five Members made men distrust him even more. The Chancellor understood why Charles I had found it so difficult to take his advice. He was well aware of the strength of the Queen's influence:

The King's Affection to the Queen was of a very extraordinary Alloy; a Composition of Conscience, and Love, and Generosity, and Gratitude, and all those noble Affections, which raise the Passion to the greatest Height; insomuch as He saw with her Eyes, and determined by her Judgment . . . She had felt so much Pain in knowing Nothing, and meddling with Nothing, during the Time of that great Favourite [Buckingham], that now She took Pleasure in Nothing but knowing all Things, and disposing all Things. . . . And it was her Majesty's, and the Kingdom's Misfortune, that She had not any Person about her who had either Ability, or Affection, to inform and advise her, of the Temper of the Kingdom, or the Humour of the People; or who thought either worth the caring for.

Ibid., vol. I, pp. 121-2.

When the Civil Wars and the Interregnum were over, Clarendon was too good a judge of affairs to share the general opinion that a golden age was at hand. He realized better than most men the kind of moral disruption caused by a civil war. He thought the King's authority was insecure, in spite of the bells and the bonfires. He feared the claims of the Army, the dissensions of the various Puritan sects, the jealousies within the King's own party. Many of his servants were loyal enough, but of weak intellect, or opinionated and unable to get on with one another. The general standard of morals and manners had declined. Reverence and respect in religion had been decried as superstition. Children were not controlled by their parents; servants were not loyal to their masters. This disrespect for tradition and authority had come about when families were split by divided loyalties to King and Parliament, and had fought and spied on one another, 'from whence issued the foulest Treacheries and Perfidiousness that were ever practised'. Moreover, Cromwell, as part of his policy, had encouraged all but his own followers to live vicious lives, so that they might become a public scandal:

In a Word, the Nation was corrupted from that Integrity, good Nature and Generosity that had been peculiar to it, and for which it had been signal and celebrated throughout the World; in the Room whereof the vilest Craft and Dissembling had succeeded. . . . These Dilapidations and Ruins of the ancient Candour and Discipline were not taken enough to Heart, and repaired with that early Care and Severity that they might have been, for they were not then incorrigible.

Ibid., vol. I, pp. 244-5.

Charles II found the problem too large for him, and retired, as far as he could, into a life of pleasure.

Again and again, throughout the *History* and the *Life*, the Chancellor is seen as an accurate judge of men's minds and actions. He understood why there was such difficulty in 1661 in settling the problems of Ireland—the memory of the appalling massacres that characterized the Irish Rebellion was as vivid as if it had happened within the last year, instead of in the early forties:

> And though no Man durst avow so unchristian a Wish, as an Extirpation of them (which They would have been very well contented with); yet no Man dissembled his Opinion, that it was the only Security the English could have in that Kingdom, that the Irish should be kept so low, that They should have no Power to hurt them.
>
> *Ibid.*, vol. I, p. 389.

He felt keenly the humiliation of Charles II's queen, Catherine of Braganza, when shortly after her marriage she was asked by her husband to take his current mistress into her service in the Bedchamber. The Queen became hysterical at the suggestion, and refused to comply. The King was furious at her resistance, and made it clear to the court that she was out of favour. He used all possible means to mortify her, until at last she gave way; not merely accepting the situation, but positively courting the King's mistress and making a personal friend of her. This excessive condescension 'did the Queen less Good than her former Resoluteness had done'. People who had formerly admired her resolution now deprecated her behaviour, and were reluctant to serve someone so inconstant. The King thought her insincere in her first reaction, and congratulated himself on his severity. After this, he never respected her again. Whereas, if she had persevered, there was every likelihood that the King would have desisted, being weary of the struggle and the scandal. Clarendon thought her volte-face most unfortunate.

Clarendon himself wrote the best historical characters in his century. He could appreciate all types of character, and see them as complex wholes. He dissected the man's qualities until he understood his subject, and had grasped his ruling passion or dominant characteristic; then he selected the significant details and fitted them together into a pattern which was calculated to convey his total impression to the reader. He did justice, in the main; he certainly made each man a vivid and individual figure, whether he was giving a thumb-nail sketch of the naval commander, Sir William Penn:

> Pen, who had much the worst Understanding, had a great Mind to appear better bred, and to speak like a Gentleman; He had got many good Words which He used at Adventure; He was a formal Man, and spake very leisurely but much, and left the Matter more intricate and perplexed than He found it.

> *Ibid.*, vol. II, p. 95.

or developing at length the character of Lord Falkland, the man he most admired. Falkland's character must be read as a whole; it is too lengthy to quote here. Clarendon thought his loss at the battle of Newbury one 'which no time will suffer to be forgotten, and no success or good fortune could repair'. His skill in developing a rounded character can be more briefly demonstrated in part of his description of the Earl of Arundel:

> He was generally thought to be a proud man, who liv'd allways within himself, and to himself, conversing little with any, who were in common conversation; so that he seem'd to live as it were in another Nation, his House being a place, to which all people resorted, who resorted to no other place; Strangers, or such who affected to look like Strangers, and dress'd themselves accordingly. He resorted sometimes to the Court, because There only was a greater man than himself, and went thither the seldomer, because there Was a greater man than himself. . . . He was willing to be thought a Scholar, and to understand the most mysterious parts of Antiquity, because he made a wonderful and costly Purchase of excellent Statues whilst he was in *Italy* and in *Rome* (some whereof he could never obtain permission to remove from *Rome*, though he had paid for them) and had a rare Collection of the most curious Medals; As to all parts of Learning he was allmost illiterate, and thought no other part of History so considerable, as what related to his own Family; in which, no doubt, there had been some very memorable Persons.[1]

> *The History of the Rebellion* (1702), Bk. I, i, p. 44.

[1] Clarendon's first editors were a little cautious in their transcription of his manuscript. The original description of the Earl began: 'He was a man supercilious and prowde', and after the phrase 'the most curious Medalls' Clarendon had written: 'wheras in truth he was only able to buy them, never to understande them'.

This catches perfectly the character of a man who lived in pretentious isolation to cover up his deficiencies; who was proud of the wrong things because he had so few genuine qualities of which to be proud. It is a more wounding description for being presented with such surface restraint.

The reader is always conscious of Clarendon's insight into and interest in all types of men; and the vivid detail makes him remember the characters. There is his character of Sidney Godolphin, who was

> of so nice and tender a Composition, that a little Rain or Wind would disorder him, and divert him from any short Journey, He had most willingly proposed to himself. . . . Yet the Civil War no sooner began . . . than He put himself into the first Troops which were raised in the West for the King; and bore the Uneasiness and Fatigue of Winter Marches, with an exemplar Courage and Alacrity.
>
> *Life*, vol. I, pp. 36–7.

There is his affectionate account of William Chillingworth, who loved debate and disputation so much that he had,

> with his notable Perfection in this Exercise, contracted such an Irresolution, and Habit of doubting, that by degrees He grew confident of Nothing.
>
> *Ibid.*, vol. I, p. 44.

He converted himself from Protestantism to Catholicism:

> All his Doubts grew out of himself, when He assisted his Scruples with all the Strength of his own Reason, and was then too hard for himself; but finding as little Quiet and Repose in those Victories, He quickly recovered, by a new Appeal to his own Judgment; so that he was in Truth, upon the Matter, in all his Sallies, and Retreats, his own Convert. . . .
>
> He was a Man of excellent Parts, and of a chearful Disposition; void of all Kind of Vice, and endued with many notable Virtues; of a very publick Heart, and an indefatigable Desire to do Good; his only Unhappiness proceeded from his sleeping too little, and thinking too much; which sometimes threw him into violent Fevers.
>
> *Ibid.*, vol. I, pp. 45–6.

Clarendon impresses the reader not only by his understanding of men and events, but by his personal integrity and courage. He dealt fairly with his colleagues in an age when it was more usual to take advantage of them. When Charles I wanted to make Hyde Secretary of State, in place of Secretary Nicholas, who would be compensated by the gift of the Mastership of the Wards, Clarendon begged the King to desist; he was a friend of Nicholas, and did not wish to see him undone by the change, since he would get no income from the post till the war was over. Hyde went to Nicholas and personally dissuaded him from agreeing to the change, saying, 'it was not the Part of a good Son to undo his Father, or to become his Son that he might undo him'. When he was confronted with the news that his daughter was married to the Duke of York, he advised Charles II to deal severely with the matter. When he realized that the marriage would be countenanced, he asked leave to resign from his post and to leave the kingdom, that it might not be thought that he had engineered the marriage for his own aggrandizement. When the King's association with rakes and atheists laid him open to criticism, Clarendon had the courage to reproach the King for his behaviour in a private conversation with him:

> He did beseech his Majesty not to believe, that He hath a Prerogative to declare Vice Virtue; or to qualify any Person who lives in a Sin and avows it, against which God himself hath pronounced Damnation, for the Company and Conversation of innocent and worthy Persons. And that whatever low Obedience, which was in Truth gross Flattery, some People might pay to what They believed would be grateful to his Majesty, They had in their Hearts a perfect Detestation of the Persons They made Address to.
>
> *Ibid.*, vol. II, p. 267.

The King was not pleased with this plain speaking. Ultimately, Clarendon owed allegiance to principle rather than to authority or expediency. The stand he made became distasteful to both King and Parliament. When the seals of his office were taken from him, he received a great deal of encouragement to leave the country before worse things happened to him. His friends thought he would not be given a fair trial, but would be kept in prison:

> He very resolutely refused to follow their Advice; and urged to them 'the Advantage He should give his Enemies, and the Dishonour He

should bring upon himself, by flying, in having his Integrity condemned, if He had not the Confidence to defend it'. He said, 'He could now appear, wherever He should be required, with an honest Countenance, and the Courage of an innocent Man: But if He should be apprehended in a Disguise running away, which He could not but expect by the Vigilance of his Enemies (since He could not make any Journey by Land, being at that Time very weak and infirm), He should be very much out of Countenance, and should be exposed to publick Scorn and Contempt.

Ibid., vol. II, pp. 411–12.

The only thing that made him change his mind was a message from the King himself saying that it was absolutely necessary he should withdraw; he could not bring himself to defy a royal command. In retrospect, Clarendon condemned himself for his previous want of caution, even though it had been based on his knowledge of his own innocence and his trust in the King:

The Truth is, the Chancellor was guilty of that himself which He had used to accuse the Archbishop Laud of, that he was too proud of a good Conscience. . . . He thought himself very secure in the King's Justice: And though his Kindness was much lessened, He was confident his Majesty would protect him from being oppressed, since He knew his Integrity; and never suspected that He would consent to his Ruin.

Ibid., vol. II, p. 373.

Clarendon made a good hero in his own history.

Perhaps the most impressive quality in Clarendon was his resilience. Publicly disgraced and forced to live abroad at the age of fifty-nine, he built up a new life for himself in France. He was in bad health, but did not allow his circumstances to destroy his spirit:

He began to think of composing his Mind to his Fortune, and of regulating and governing his own Thoughts and Affections towards such a Tranquillity, as the Sickness of Mind and Body, and the continued sharp Fatigue in the six or seven precedent Months, had not suffered to enter into any formed Deliberation. And it pleased God in a short Time, after some Recollections, and upon his entire Confidence in him, to restore him to that Serenity of Mind, and Resignation of himself to the Disposal and good Pleasure of God, that They who conversed most with him could not discover the least Murmur or Impatience in him, or any Unevenness in his Conversations.

Ibid., vol. II, p. 450.

He read a great deal of French, and started to learn Italian. But his main occupation was the writing of his two great histories. The *Life* alone has been calculated at 600,000 words. He had first-class material, and was able to provide full documentation for setting out each stage of the conflict. Moreover, he thoroughly enjoyed writing, and found that words came easily to him. In consequence he was able to fulfil his own idea of the historian's duty. The historian, he said in his essay *On an Active and on a Contemplative Life*, must have 'a lively Perception of Persons and Actions which makes the Reader present at all they say or do'.

So Clarendon became the best memorial of himself and of his age. Not only has his writing the weight of judgment and first-hand knowledge of men and events, but it is enlivened by vivid reporting and by serious wit. His account of such events as the Dutch raid, or the Great Fire, or the sea battles, creates a lively picture in the reader's imagination. Many of his epigrammatic comments on men and affairs stay in the mind. He said of Sir George Downing's powers of argument:

> Assuming all he said to be Demonstration, He wrapped himself up, according to his Custom, in a Mist of Words that Nobody could see Light in, but They who by often hearing the Same Chat thought they understood it.
>
> *Life*, vol. II, p. 200.

Of the Earl of Pembroke's domestic situation:

> In which he was most unhappy, for he payed much too dear for his Wife's Fortune, by taking her Person into the bargain.
>
> *The History of the Rebellion*, Bk. I, i, p. 45.

Of Lord Roberts in the office of Privy Seal:

> Where He was sworn and took his Place; and to shew his extraordinary Talent, found a Way more to obstruct and puzzle Business, at least the Dispatch of it, than any Man in that Office had ever done before.
>
> *Life*, vol. I, p. 374.

Clarendon's prose is in the line that leads from Bacon to Swift; and he is not shamefully overshadowed by either of them.

The writings of Halifax belong to the latter part of the period. He was considerably younger than Clarendon. In his own age he was more famous as a statesman than as a writer. He disconcerted his contemporaries by seeing good points in both the Whig and the Tory party; he did not feel bound to endorse the false judgments of his own side. Although in many respects he agreed with the Whigs about the dangers of letting a Catholic monarch succeed Charles II, he was the champion of order in the Parliament of 1680, which, thanks to him, finally rejected the Exclusion Bill. However, in 1688, when James was in power, and trying to modify the constitution in favour of the Catholics, Halifax became the champion of revolution, and it was largely owing to his efforts that the preliminary negotiations with William of Orange were successful. He refrained from joining in the general witch-hunt against Catholics in the days of the Popish Plot, and when the Whigs were attempting to impeach the elderly Catholic, Lord Stafford, he took Stafford's part. He also defended the Whig, Lord Russell, when the Tories accused him of plotting against the King. Macaulay said that while Halifax was a member of the opposition, his own party suspected him of being a court spy; and when he joined the court party, they were dismayed by his republican doctrines. Halifax himself despised Members who followed the party line instead of thinking for themselves:

> When a Man is drowned in a Party, plunged into it beyond his depth, he runneth a great hazard of being upon ill Terms with good Sense, or Morality, if not with both of them.
> Such a Man can hardly be called a Free-Agent, and for that reason is very unfit to be trusted with the Peoples Liberty, after he hath given up his own.
>
> *Works* (ed. W. Raleigh, 1912), pp. 157–8.

Halifax earned the contemptuous label of 'The Trimmer' for his moderation and willingness to compromise, but a hundred and fifty years later Macaulay praised his impartiality:

195

He was treating of the most exciting subjects in the most agitated times: he was himself placed in the very thick of the civil conflict; yet there is no acrimony, nothing inflammatory, nothing personal. He preserves an air of cold superiority, a certain philosophical serenity, which is perfectly marvellous.

Essays (1883), p. 456.

As a political writer Halifax is remembered chiefly for his *Character of a Trimmer*, written in 1684 and circulated in manuscript. All his work was of an occasional nature, dealing realistically and vigorously with the problems that arose in his time. He avoided laying down fundamental theories about government which would be valid for all times and situations, since he felt that change was an essential of human existence. What he wanted was a working compromise between power and liberty. He based his maxims on his experience of human nature. An idealist might call him a cynic; Halifax would have seen the idealist as a foolish Icarus who would not take into account the realities of the human situation.

For Halifax, moderation was not only an expedient, it was a moral virtue. To be moderate was to be right and just. It meant a due balance between liberty and tyranny; it prevented both the rigid enforcement of abstract principles and the easy-going tolerance that sacrificed all principle. To be a Trimmer was to steer a wise middle course. He took the label as a compliment, and in a famous passage in the introduction to his *Character of a Trimmer* he defined it in this way:

This innocent word *Trimmer* signifieth no more than this, That if Men are together in a Boat, and one part of the Company would weigh it down on one side, another would make it lean as much to the contrary; it happeneth there is a third Opinion of those, who conceive it would do as well, if the Boat went even, without endangering the Passengers.

Ibid., p. 48.

It seemed to him that England herself was the supreme example of moderation:

Our Climate is a *Trimmer*, between that part of the World where Men are Roasted, and the other where they are Frozen; That our Church is a *Trimmer* between the Phrenzy of Platonick Visions, and the Lethargick

Ignorance of Popish Dreams; That our Laws are *Trimmers*, between the Excess of unbounded Power, and the Extravagance of Liberty not enough restrained. . . .

In such Company, our *Trimmer* is not asham'd of his Name, and willingly leaveth to the bold Champions of either Extream, the honour of contending with no less Adversaries than Nature, Religion, Liberty, Prudence, Humanity and Common Sense.

Ibid., p. 103.

These are the values that Halifax stressed throughout his work.

Sometimes, it must be admitted, Halifax laid too much stress on prudence, both as a virtue and as a governing motive of conduct. His assessment of human nature was general, and hardly took into account the occasions when men transcend themselves and sacrifice self-interest in a cause they passionately believe to be just. He referred for his standard to the 'General Consent and Practice of Mankind', and tried to persuade men by telling them of the probable results of their actions. In personal matters, he gave his daughter much advice on cautious conduct. Be generous in your criticism of others, for then people will be less hard in their criticisms of you. Desert your female friends in good time if they are suspected of adultery; if you continue to defend them people will think you behave in the same way. The first recommendation is a good one, but the motive is selfish; the second may have been sensible in Halifax's time, but it is neither generous nor strong-minded. Yet there is a measure of truth in Halifax's idea of human nature:

Temporal things will have their weight in the World; and tho Zeal may prevail for a time, and get the better in a Skirmish, yet the War endeth generally on the side of Flesh and Blood, and will do so till Mankind is another thing than it is at present.

Ibid., p. 85.

However, he was not a materialist. He considered that one of the worst deterrents to being a Catholic in England (at a time when they were debarred from all the professions) was the enforced idleness:

To live at the best an useless, and by others to be thought a dangerous Member of the Nation where he is born, is a burthen to a generous Mind that cannot be taken off by all the Pleasure of a lazy unmanly life, or by the nauseous enjoyment of a dull Plenty, that produceth no Good for the Mind, which will be considered in the first place by a Man that has a Soul.

Ibid., p. 85.

Nor could anyone who was entirely earth-bound write in this strain of Truth:

All the Power upon Earth can never extinguish her; she hath liv'd in all Ages . . . she hath lived very retired indeed, nay sometimes so buried, that only some few of the discerning part of Mankind could have a Glimpse of her; with all that, she hath Eternity in her, she knoweth not how to die, and from the darkest Clouds that shade and cover her, she breaks from time to time with Triumph for her Friends, and Terrour to her Enemies.

Ibid., p. 103.

When Halifax took Nature, rather than the nature of man, as his standard, few would find fault with him. His Nature was not the anarchical state which Hobbes described, but Nature as Hooker understood it—order, virtue and due regulation. Halifax thought England was the best example of obedience to the laws of Nature. She had not made the mistake of having an absolute monarchy—'a thing that leaveth men no Liberty'—nor yet of becoming a republic—'such a one as alloweth them no Quiet'. Neither King nor people had so much power that they could endanger each other's rights or ruin the kingdom. Halifax did not look on this balance of power as a mere mechanical expedient, devised for political ends. He thought of the connexion between King and people as a natural relationship; at its best, it was an organic growth, which had its roots in willingness and affection. Fear and the use of force were a kind of foul-play in such a relationship; they introduced an unnatural element. He had the traditional English preference for ties that grow and develop naturally.

His charity towards men who belonged to other sects was remarkable in an age which had not yet entirely recovered from fanaticism. Men were still inclined to think it was their duty to persecute 'heretics'. Halifax saw that this conviction was rooted in pride:

It is not true Devotion, to put on an angry Zeal against those who may be of a differing Persuasion. *Partiality* to ourselves makes us often mistake it for a *Duty*, to fall hard upon others in that case; and being push'd on by *Self-conceit*, we strike without mercy, believing that the *Wounds* we give are *Meritorious*, and that we are fighting God Almighty's Quarrel; when the truth is, we are only setting out ourselves.

Ibid., pp. 3–4.

Halifax's sanity on this point was based on an assurance that he was right and the heretics wrong, and that the cause of the Church of England would prevail. He did not admit Milton's principle of tolerance and respect for all forms of Protestantism. For Milton, the essence of Protestantism was an acknowledgment of each man's right to interpret the Bible in his own way:

No man, no synod, no session of men though called the Church can judge definitively the sense of Scripture to another man's conscience.

Of True Religion (1673).

Halifax thought that his own Church was right, and that men must be wooed to agree with it. Charity to the erring was the most religious method of reclaiming them. He does not want men punished for their dissent; they must find a welcome in the true Church, and indulgence for their past errors. If persecution is used to change their opinions, the only result will be to strengthen their convictions and increase the sympathy felt for them:

Constancy will be thought a virtue even where it is a mistake: and the ill Judging World will be apt to think that Opinion most right, which produces the greatest number of those who are willing to suffer for it: all this is prevented, and falleth to the ground, by using well-timed Indulgence; and the stubborn Adversary who valueth himself upon his Resistance whilst he is oppress'd, yieldeth insensibly to kind Methods, when they are apply'd to him; and the same Man naturally melteth into Conformity, who perhaps would never have been beaten into it.

Halifax, *op. cit.*, p. 71.

If there must be some anger left still, let it break out into a Christian Revenge, and by being kinder to the Children of Disobedience than they deserve, let the injur'd Church Triumph, by throwing Shame and Confusion of Face upon them.

Ibid., p. 129.

Here, Halifax shows himself as both wise and magnanimous. Generous methods appeal to the best in the Dissenters; and they are the only methods consonant with true Christianity.

Halifax was a sincerely religious man. It is possible to be misled by the quietness and restraint of his feelings when he is discussing the subject of religion. Beside Bunyan or George Fox, he seems to lack tension and passion. Nevertheless his religion was a governing sentiment in his way of life, and he spoke of it in restrained terms because he set a value on self-control in public writings; he had no need to 'spill his soul' or indulge in public catharsis. When he wrote his *Advice to a Daughter*, he spoke first of religion, as the most important factor in life. It was to be the chief object of her thoughts. Since so many writers of his century made religion a thing of terror, he himself emphasized the beauties and attractions of a life based on the Christian religion :

> Nothing is so kind and so inviting as true and *unsophisticated Religion*: Instead of imposing unnecessary Burdens upon our *Nature*, it easeth us of the greater weight of our *Passions* and *Mistakes*: Instead of subduing us with *Rigour*, it redeemeth us from the *Slavery* we are in to our selves, who are the most severe Masters, whilst we are under the Usurpation of our *Appetites* let loose and not restrain'd.
>
> *Ibid.*, p. 5.

> A devout *Mind* hath the Privilege of being free from *Passions*, as some Climates are from all venomous kind of Creatures. It will raise you above the little *Vexations* to which others for want of it, will be expos'd, and bring you to a *Temper*, not of stupid *Indifference*, but of such a wise *Resignation*, that you may live in the *World*, so as it may hang about you like a loose Garment, and not tied too close to you.
>
> *Ibid.*, p. 6.

This passage shows how Halifax is poised and sustained; his moderation and equanimity arise from his firm belief in a benevolent God, and from his conviction that true happiness lies in the service of God. His sense of proportion has a religious origin; it is not merely an Aristotelian avoidance of extremes. Halifax can be wise about his temporal world because he sees it in the light of the eternal spiritual world.

Both by conviction and temperament he was inclined to distrust displays of emotion. Ostentatious devotion seemed suspect to him; those who were really devout did not parade the fact. He commented with amusement on the devices of those who merely wished to be thought religious:

> The next thing to be observ'd to you, is, That *Religion* doth as little consist in loud Answers and devout Convulsions at Church, or Praying in an extraordinary manner. Some Ladies are so extream stirring at *Church*, that one would swear the *Worm* in their *Conscience* made them so unquiet. . . . These affected *Appearances* are ever suspected, like very strong Perfumes, which are generally thought no very good Symptoms in those that make use of them. Let your earnestness therefore be reserv'd for your *Closet*, where you may have God Almighty to yourself: In *Publick* be still and calm, neither undecently *Careless*, nor *Affected* in the other Extream.
>
> *Ibid.,* p. 3.

Although Halifax was no mere man of the world, he had a great capacity for giving sound advice about it. He told his daughter how to handle her husband, how to run her household, how to behave as an individual. The advice is interspersed with satirical portraits of how *not* to behave; Halifax had an admirably light touch, and was well aware of its value in making a point go home. The advice belongs, of course, to the era of 'arranged marriages', alliances between the children of important families, in which the wife, as a superior employee rather than a partner, had many duties but lacked the power to give in her notice. Women must not be the dominant sex; but feminine methods are adequate to persuade a man to do as you wish. Halifax considers the different kinds of fault which she may discover in her future husband. He may be unfaithful; this she must overlook. He may be a drunkard:

> If you will be wise and patient, his *Wine* shall be of your side . . . Others will like him less, and by that means he may perhaps like you the more.
>
> *Ibid.,* p. 13.

Moreover, she can acquire a right of governing in the vacancy—presumably when he is not only drunk but incapable. If he is choleric, she must take advantage of his milder moods to make her just requests to him. If he is a miser, she must wait for the moment when pride or anger or ambition have jolted him out of his normal attitude.

> I am tempted to say. . . . That a *Wife* is to thank God her *Husband* hath *Faults*. . . . A Husband without *Faults* is a dangerous Observer; he hath an Eye so piercing, and seeth everything so plain, that it is expos'd to his full Censure. . . . The *Faults* and *Passions* of *Husbands* bring them down to you, and make them content to live upon less unequal Terms, than Faultless Men would be willing to stoop to.
>
> *Ibid.,* p. 12.

In terms of household economy, the wife must see that things run well and in orderly fashion; too many women are mere visitors in their own houses, and the husband sees 'an empty airy thing sail up and down the House to no kind of purpose'. She must not, however, fall into the opposite error of being so wrapped up in her household and family that she can think and talk of nothing else:

> You may love your *Children* without living in the *Nursery*, and you may have a *competent* and *discreet care* of them, without letting it break out upon the Company, or exposing your self by turning your Discourse that way, which is a kind of *Laying Children* to the *Parish*.
>
> *Ibid.,* p. 22.

Her personal conduct must be above reproach; and she must take pains not to make herself ridiculous in any way. Halifax touches on the unpleasant effect of pride, vanity and affectation in a woman:

> *Vanity* maketh a Woman tainted with it, so top full of herself, that she spilleth it upon the *Company*. . . . The greatest part of her *Fancy* is laid out in chusing her *Gown*, as her *Discretion* is chiefly imploy'd in *not paying* for it. She is faithful to the *Fashion*, to which not only her *Opinion*, but her *Senses* are wholly resigned: so obsequious she is to it, that she would be ready to be reconciled even to *Vertue* with all its *Faults*, if she had her Dancing Master's Word that it was practis'd at Court. . . .
>
> To a Woman so compos'd when *Affectation* cometh in to improve her *Character*, it is then raised to the highest *Perfection*. She first setteth up for a *Fine thing*, and for that Reason will distinguish her self, right or wrong, in every thing she doth. She would have it thought that she is made of so much the *finer Clay*, and so much more sifted than ordinary that she

hath no *common Earth* about her. To this end she must neither move nor speak like other Women, because it would be *vulgar*; and therefore must have a Language of her *own*, since *ordinary English* is too coarse for her. The *Looking-glass* in the Morning dictateth to her all the *Motions* of the Day, which by how much the more *studied*, are so much the more *mistaken*. She cometh into a Room as if her Limbs were set on with ill-made Screws, which maketh the Company fear the pretty thing should leave some of its *artificial Person* upon the Floor. She doth not like herself as God Almighty made her, but will have some of *her own* Workmanship; which is so far from making her a better thing than a *Woman*, that it turneth her into a worse Creature than a *Monkey*.

Ibid., pp. 38–40.

The vividness and vigour of this character-sketch show Halifax at his best.

His penetrative understanding of human nature is most remarkable in his *Character of Charles II*. It is longer and more elaborate than any of the character-studies of Clarendon or Burnet; all the King's qualities are dissected, their origins are suggested and their results portrayed. It is pervaded by Halifax's wit; a wit that does not depend on cruelty or constant depreciation. Halifax was shrewd enough to see the King's faults, but too human to condemn him outright. He drew the picture of a King who was always pleasant, rather lazy, quite a good judge of men and events; but apt to demean himself by too much conversation with his inferiors, by a desire to be thought amusing, and by a bad memory which led him to repeat his anecdotes endlessly. There is a delightful passage where Halifax explains Charles's inclination towards liberality in terms of his hatred of being pestered by requests:

He had as little Eagerness to oblige, as he had to hurt Men; the Motive of his giving Bounties was rather to make Men less uneasy to him, than more easy to themselves; and yet no ill-nature all this while. He would slide from an asking Face, and could guess very well. It was throwing a Man off from his Shoulders, that leaned upon them with his whole weight; so that the Party was not gladder to receive, than he was to give. It was a kind of implied bargain; though Men seldom kept it, being so apt to forget the advantage they had received, that they would presume the King would as little remember the good he had done them, so as to make it an Argument against their next Request.

Ibid., p. 204.

Perhaps the supreme example of the King's *laissez-faire* attitude comes in the section headed 'His Amours, mistresses etcetera'. Halifax proceeds with perfect calm and common sense:

> It may be said that his Inclinations to Love were the Effects of Health, and a good Constitution, with as little mixture of the *Seraphick* part as ever Man had: And though from that Foundation Men often raise their Passions; I am apt to think his stayed as much as any Man's ever did in the *lower Region*. . . . It was resolved generally by others, whom he should have in his Arms, as well as whom he should have in his Councils. Of a Man who was so capable of choosing, he chose as seldom as any Man that ever lived.
>
> *Ibid.*, p. 193.

Amusement is present, but generosity predominated in Halifax's final judgment:

> It is but Justice therefore to this Prince, to give all due Softenings to the less shining Parts of his Life; to offer Flowers and Leaves to hide, instead of using Aggravations to expose them.
>
> Let his Royal Ashes then lie soft upon him, and cover him from harsh and unkind Censures; which though they should not be unjust, can never clear themselves from being indecent.
>
> *Ibid.*, p. 208.

He never allowed his keen insight into men and situations to hurry him into a prejudiced judgment.

Although his primary intention was not to produce a work of art, Halifax was essentially a serious writer. He made more of an effort to analyse and understand the life of his time than did many of his contemporaries who considered themselves to be artists. He was trying to give a picture of the whole of life, instead of an arbitrarily selected scene of sexual or martial conquest. His inclusiveness, his subtlety of apprehension and what Raleigh called his 'practical wisdom' gave his work an artistic truth which is lacking in most of the plays and novels of his time. Not only did he tell the whole truth in so far as he saw it, but he told it with the best kind of wit: wit that sharpened the outlines, instead of calling attention to the writer or to itself. Halifax appreciated the value of wit as a tool when unpleasant truths had to be impressed on apathetic or hostile readers.

It was probably his experience in the House that had taught him how to handle an audience. He might easily have fallen into high-flown dogmatizing on moral topics; he might have been ponderous, melodious, edifying. He avoided the devices of worn-out Ciceronianism, and used the language of conversation, often more colloquial than polite. In this style his lively common sense and his feeling for the absurd were perfectly at home. Addison might have thought him indelicate, if not profane, when he spoke of the 'spiritual cooks' or of 'religion not at cuffs with good humour'. His sentences were often *sententiae* in the Senecan style, on the point of turning into epigrams:

> You must be very undextrous if when your Husband shall resolve to be an Ass, you do not take care he may be your Ass.

> By that time Men are fit for Company, they see the Objections to it.

> Men must be saved in this World by their want of Faith.

> Men often *mistake* themselves, but they never *forget* themselves.

His writing had far more sparkle than Clarendon's; partly because, like Dryden, he had a strong visual imagination. He made the reader see dramatic situations, and then provided a plausible explanation of them. The ludicrousness of the ladies who fidget in church to demonstrate the strength of their religious devotion was excellently conveyed by the ingenuous reason offered—'one would swear the Worm in their Conscience made them so unquiet'. Similarly, in the *Character of a Trimmer*, he showed up the obsequiousness of the silken divines of the English Church 'who, one would think, do practise to bow at the Altar, only to learn to make the better Legs at Court'. He had a quickness of imagination, and his images seemed to rise spontaneously, with his own delight in them still fresh.

In spite of his realistic view of the world it is obvious that Halifax took delight in the process of living—the delight of a man who consciously dealt with the problems of the world, and met them with assurance and spirit. He had not the fullness of delight in life that one meets in certain passages in Traherne or Milton, but in his work he combined sanity with vigour in a manner unequalled in his age.

VI

VIRTUE, GOOD SENSE AND IMAGINATION: THE INFLUENCE OF JOHN LOCKE (1632–1704)

MACAULAY said of the end of the seventeenth century:

> There still lingered in the public mind a pernicious notion that there was some connection between genius and profligacy, between the domestic virtues and the sullen formality of the Puritans. That error it is the glory of Addison to have dispelled.
>
> *Essays* (1883), p. 725.

I think the credit for the change in outlook belongs to John Locke rather than to Joseph Addison. Addison may have reconciled wit with morality, and tempered morality with wit, but it was Locke who took the fundamental step of reconciling good sense and virtue. After Locke, charity, generosity, devotion, reverence no longer sounded absurd or fanatical to the man of good sense. Locke did much to promote the spirit of humane liberalism and tolerance that animated the best of the eighteenth century.

He achieved this by having both an eminent, free-ranging mind, recognized for its influence on the course of philosophical and political thought, and a temperate, humane spirit, capable of affection, humility and faith. D. G. James has described him as 'the apostle of reasonableness', but adds that it would be a mistake to consider him as dull or cold: he had strong feelings which were admirably controlled (*The Life of Reason*, 1949, p. 76). He achieved a golden mean which in lesser men could degenerate into a comfortable and complacent mediocrity.

He was no recluse. He had wide interests and contacts in the worlds of religion, politics, philosophy and science. He had travelled extensively, and lived for periods in various European countries, making use of all his observations in a way that would have delighted Lord

Chesterfield. He was a practical man who worked from experience, distrusting 'systems' and merely intellectual theories. His *Essay concerning Human Understanding* arose from a desire to establish the limits of what man could hope to discover, thereby concentrating his attention on spheres of knowledge where there was hope of success:

> For I thought that the first step towards satisfying several enquiries, the mind of man was very apt to run into, was to take a survey of our own understandings, examine our own powers, and see to what things they were adapted. Till that was done, I suspected we began at the wrong end, and in vain sought for satisfaction in a quiet and sure possession of truths that most concerned us, whilst we let loose our thoughts into the vast ocean of being; as if all that boundless extent were the natural and undoubted possession of our understandings, wherein there was nothing exempt from its decisions, or that escaped its comprehension. Thus men extending their enquiries beyond their capacities, and letting their thoughts wander into those depths, where they can find no sure footing; it is no wonder, that they raise questions, and multiply disputes, which, never coming to any clear resolution, are proper only to continue and increase their doubts, and to confirm them at last in perfect scepticism. Whereas, were the capacities of our understandings well considered, the extent of our knowledge once discovered, and the horizon found, which sets the bounds between the enlightened and dark parts of things, between what is, and what is not comprehensible by us; men would perhaps with less scruple acquiesce in the avowed ignorance of the one, and employ their thoughts and discourse with more advantage and satisfaction in the other.
>
> *Essay concerning Human Understanding*, Bk. I, chap. 1, sec. 7.

The 'vast ocean of being' had had its attractions for men in the seventeenth century; the eighteenth, guided by Locke, was to take a more practical view of life.

Locke had a clear sense of values. In the light of eternity, salvation was the most important end of man; within the world, it was Truth. He believed passionately that every man had an immortal soul, the fate of which depended on his faith and conduct in this world:

> The observance of these things is the highest obligation that lies upon mankind, and . . . our utmost care, application and diligence, ought to be exercised in the search and performance of them; because there is nothing in this world that is of any consideration in comparison with eternity.
>
> *A Letter Concerning Toleration, Works* (1823), vol. VI, p. 41.

He did not believe that any one Church had the monopoly of truth that was valid for salvation. When he arrived at the gates of Heaven, he felt sure that he would not be asked whether he had belonged to the Church of England or to the Church of Geneva, but whether he had loved truth, searched for it and taken hold of it. What was important to truth was not the accessories of the journey—the manner of baptism, fasting, differences in ritual and attire—but the fact that the pursuit was a personal and first-hand one. Locke was essentially Protestant in make-up. He was as sure as Milton had been that faith could only be worked out and won, not accepted on a plate. This theme recurs constantly in his *Letter Concerning Toleration*:

> No man can so far abandon the care of his own salvation as blindly to leave it to the choice of any other, whether prince or subject, to prescribe to him what faith or worship he shall embrace. For no man can, if he would, conform his faith to the dictates of another. All the life and power of true religion consists in the inward and full persuasion of the mind; and faith is not faith without believing.

Ibid., vol. VI, p. 10.

> The care therefore of every man's soul belongs unto himself, and is to be left unto himself.

Ibid., vol. VI, p. 23.

> No way whatsoever that I shall walk in against the dictates of my conscience, will ever bring me to the mansions of the blessed. I may grow rich by an art that I take not delight in; I may be cured of some disease by remedies that I have not faith in; but I cannot be saved by a religion that I distrust, and by a worship that I abhor.

Ibid., vol. VI, p. 28.

The same standards apply in the realm of purely human knowledge. There was no place in Locke's universe for second-hand or implicit knowledge, accepted because someone else had said so:

> Till we ourselves see it with our own eyes and perceive it by our own understandings, we are as much in the dark and as void of knowledge as before, let us believe any learned author as much as we will.

Of the Conduct of the Understanding, *ibid.*, vol. III, par. 24.

He fought a constant battle to make men aware of the deviations from truth which were occasioned by such things as vague definitions of terms, partiality, prejudice, refusal to consider arguments on the other side, reliance on authority, superficiality, sitting on the fence. His *Conduct of the Understanding* is an admirable caveat for those who want to train their minds to avoid such erroneous methods of thinking. Men must examine things as they really are, not their own fanciful ideas of them. Knowledge is sound only when it is well 'bottomed'; that is, grounded on solid first principles. Locke disapproved of the training in logic which was being given in schools and universities. Logic could not lead man to discover truth; it could only confirm his intuitions by setting them out formally. The current habit of training men in logical disputes led to an unfortunate emphasis on victory instead of discovery, and made any genuine conclusion unattainable—for it was always possible to divide any conclusion and object to part of it. Locke was very scathing about these methods in his *Some Thoughts Concerning Education*:

> If the use and end of right reasoning be to have right notions. and a right judgment of things; to distinguish betwixt truth and falsehood, right and wrong, and to act accordingly; be sure not to let your son be bred up in the art and formality of disputing . . . unless, instead of an able man, you desire to have him an insignificant wrangler, opiniatre in discourse, and priding himself in contradicting others; or, which is worse, questioning everything, and thinking there is no such thing as truth to be sought, but only victory, in disputing. . . . Truth is to be found and supported by a mature and due consideration of things themselves, and not by artificial terms and ways of arguing: these lead not men so much into the discovery of truth, as into a captious and fallacious use of doubtful words, which is the most useless and most offensive way of talking, and such as least suits a gentleman or a lover of truth of anything in the world.

Ibid., vol. IX, par. 189.

He applied his own ordinances admirably when conducting an argument. His treatment of the question of toleration showed a genuine attempt to counteract prejudice and make men see not what they had previously believed, but the matter itself, freed from emotional complications. He pointed out, for instance, that all arguments for the persecution of the unorthodox overlooked the basic fact that the

Church was a voluntary society. Men were of necessity part of the civil society in which they lived, and for certain transgressions against that society its magistrates had the right to punish them. They could not in the same sense be said to live in a Church. Of their own free will they joined a Church, and became subject to the spiritual jurisdiction of its clergy. This did not give the civil magistrate any powers over them; his jurisdiction was limited to their civil conduct. If the civil magistrate were to pretend to jurisdiction over men's religious defects— their unorthodoxy, their idolatry—he would also have to undertake to punish such sins as covetousness, uncharitableness, idleness. There was no logical distinction that could be made between the sin of unorthodoxy and the sin of uncharitableness. Legislation against uncharitableness would soon render itself absurd; yet men still arrogated to themselves the power of punishing men for unorthodoxy:

> If any man err from the right way, it is his own misfortune, no injury to thee: nor therefore art thou to punish him in the things of this life because thou supposest he will be miserable in that which is to come.
>
> *Ibid.*, vol. VI, p. 17.

Such clear-sighted setting-out of the basis and implications of popular beliefs helped to persuade the liberal-minded minority who governed the country that toleration was the only just solution to the problem.

The status of Reason was a variable in Locke's universe. Sometimes he spoke of it as 'our only star and compass'; sometimes he acknowledged that it was virtually inoperative in the majority of men. Sometimes he balanced it against faith; sometimes he exalted it and made reason the test of faith. Direct revelation could be accepted only if we were certain that it came from God. Where what was revealed went counter to demonstrable knowledge, revelation must yield to knowledge. 'Faith can never convince us of any thing that contradicts our knowledge' (*Essay concerning Human Understanding*, Bk. IV, chap. 18, sec. 5). Some things, however, were above reason; our normal faculties could not discover them. To these the assent of faith could be given. Such were the doctrines of immortality and of the revolt of the angels:

> Whatever God hath revealed is certainly true; no doubt can be made of it. This is the proper object of faith: but whether it be a divine revelation

or no, reason must judge; which can never permit the mind to reject a greater evidence to embrace what is less evident, nor allow it to entertain probability in opposition to knowledge and certainty.

Ibid., Bk. IV, chap. 18, sec. 10.

'Enthusiasm' entailed the complete abrogation of reason. Some men thought themselves directly illuminated by God:

Reason is lost upon them, they are above it: they see the light infused into their understandings, and cannot be mistaken; it is clear and visible there, like the light of bright sunshine; shows itself, and needs no other proof but its own evidence. . . . Would he not be ridiculous, who should require to have it proved to him that the light shines, and that he sees it? It is its own proof, and can have no other. . . . This is the way of talking of these men: they are sure, because they are sure; and their persuasions are right, because they are strong in them.

Ibid., Bk. IV, chap. 19, secs. 8–9.

Locke had no difficulty in demonstrating the circular nature of this argument: it was a revelation, because they firmly believed it, and they believed it because it was a revelation. In such circumstances reason was paramount.

Locke himself was too sensible to be unaware of the limits of man's reason itself. His whole inquiry into the mind of man was intended to establish precisely those limits. He knew that man's understanding fell very short 'of the vast extent of things'. It was a candle in the universe, fit only for man's immediate purposes: the knowledge of God and of human duties. His mind was narrow, but adequate; he must not be disturbed by the thought of what he could not understand :

Our business here is not to know all things, but those which concern our conduct.

Ibid., Bk. I, chap. 1, sec. 6.

Locke was sure that man's reason could lead him to God:

The same spark of the divine nature and knowledge in man, which, making him a man, showed him the law he was under, as a man. . . . He that made use of this candle of the Lord, so far as to find what was his duty, could not miss to find also the way to reconciliation and forgiveness, when he had failed of his duty.

The Reasonableness of Christianity, Works (1823), vol. VII, p. 133.

There had been, however, a time when man's reason, without the assistance of revelation, had failed to reach the truth. Some of it lay too deep for reason easily to reach 'without some light from above to direct them'. The revelations made through the life and death of Christ had made these truths obvious to all men. Moreover, men had been given an added incentive to virtue. The philosophers had always shown the beauty of virtue, but since human nature was materialistic, few men were attracted to an unendowed bride. Now revelation had 'given the advantage to piety over all that could tempt or deter men from it':

> Virtue now is visibly the most enriching purchase, and by much the best bargain. . . . It has another relish and efficacy to persuade men, that if they live well here, they shall be happy hereafter. . . . Upon this foundation, and upon this only, morality stands firm, and may defy all competition.

Ibid., vol. VII, pp. 150–1.

This is the crux of Locke's marriage of virtue and good sense. Not to be religious was the height of folly, since the result would be damnation; to pursue virtue and believe the simple doctrines set out by Christ was to be guaranteed the joys of eternity. A man of the world could see that this was a good investment, and need not fear that his piety would be ridiculed as unproductive fancy. The tone is reminiscent of Dryden's:

> Faith is the best ensurer of thy bliss;
> The Bank above must fail before the venture miss.
> *The Hind and the Panther*, Bk. I, ll. 148–9.

In fairness to Locke, it must be remembered that this treatise on Christianity was addressed to unbelievers. It was not intended as a full statement of Locke's own religious beliefs and experiences—he was himself intensely pious—but as preliminary instruction concerning the minimum requirements and advantages of Christianity, directed to those whose lack of religion precluded them from responding to any but material stimuli. The marriage did not mean that religion was commensurate with good sense—only that it was consonant with good sense. On this basis, men must build themselves up 'in our most holy faith' and in understanding its mysteries, which were not precluded by its reasonableness.

Locke was essentially a humble man. He knew his own understanding was fallible, and no fit measure of another man's. He would never presume to dictate to others what they should believe. He knew that he was a sinner: he had to work towards 'holiness of life, purity of manners, and benignity and meekness of spirit'. Yet this personal humility was combined with strong faith in the potentialities of man for development in virtue. The Calvinist doctrine of man as a worthless creature tormented by the sin of Adam, and only saved by the especial grace of God, was quite alien to him. He gave this rule, 'Not to think meanly of ourselves, and not to think meanly of others' (*Some Thoughts Concerning Education*, *Works*, 1823, vol. IX, par. 141). He thought men did not inherit Adam's guilt, only his mortality; in fact, they came into the world in a neutral state, on which education and environment were to set the stamp of character. He allowed that they had initial differences of temperament, but the effects of this could be counteracted by training:

> Of all the men we meet with, nine parts of ten are what they are, good or evil, useful or not, by their education.
>
> *Ibid.*, vol. IX, par. 1.

He was deeply concerned to devise a scheme of education which would bring out the best in man. He wanted to mould a virtuous and free-spirited man, capable of self-discipline, whose motives for action were not materialistic. He wanted someone who had developed his intellectual appetite while keeping his physical appetites under control. He wanted to see a certain resilience, rather than over-sensitiveness to the vicissitudes of life. He set a high value on fortitude:

> True fortitude I take to be the quiet possession of a man's self, and an undisturbed doing his duty, whatever evil besets, or danger lies in his way.
>
> *Ibid.*, vol. IX, par. 115.

This really amounts to spiritual independence and self-respect, and completes the picture of a character which can be admired in many ages besides that of John Locke. The temperament which Locke hoped to see coupled with this character was a likable one:

> We cannot but be pleased with an humane, friendly, civil temper, where-ever we meet with it. A mind free, and master of itself and all its actions, not low and narrow, not haughty and insolent, not blemished with any great defect; is what every one is taken with.
>
> *Ibid.*, vol. IX, par. 66.

The real purpose of Locke's educational scheme was to encourage the good qualities latent in individual human beings. His ideal was different from that of the complete gentleman of the Renaissance—an ideal suited to those times, but times had changed. Locke wanted his gentleman to be adapted to the needs of the modern world. He must have perfect command of his own language, and of other modern languages, as well as of Latin. He must study mathematics, geography, history, law, the Bible. He must be up to date in his knowledge of the discoveries of Boyle and Newton. He should learn some kind of manual art to serve as physical recreation—gardening, carpentry, metal-work. Throughout Locke's treatise, however, the main emphasis falls on the overriding importance of cultivating virtue:

> It is virtue then, direct virtue, which is the hard and valuable part to be aimed at in education; and not a forward pertness, or any little arts of shifting. All other considerations and accomplishments should give way, and be postponed, to this. This is the solid and substantial good, which tutors should not only read lectures, and talk of; but the labour and art of education should furnish the mind with, and fasten there, and never cease till the young man had a true relish of it, and placed his strength, his glory and his pleasure in it.
>
> *Ibid.*, vol. IX, par. 70.

So far, Locke's bequest to the eighteenth century was an admirable one. His successors could draw on his sound sense of values, his love of truth, justice, law and liberty. His tolerance and his spirit of moderation were a great improvement on some of the excesses of the earlier part of the seventeenth century, and they were powerful forces in the eighteenth century itself. His endorsement of individual liberties gave inspiration to the leaders of the movement for American independence, and helped to build a new democratic tradition. But his influence on aesthetic thought was less happy. He encouraged some popular views of art; and because his work in other spheres was of such value and importance, his encouragement carried undue weight with the public. Had he thought as the third Earl of Shaftesbury did about aesthetics, he might have freed eighteenth-century writers from some of the difficulties of their position.

Locke did not improve on the more stereotyped aesthetic theories of his age. He was not responsible for them, but his theory of the workings of the mind provided them with a specious philosophical basis. The low value he set on poetry aggravated the situation. Several critical fallacies were encouraged. First, that the imagination was a passive faculty, of a far lower order than reason. Secondly, truth was the end of science, beauty the end of art. Thirdly, figurative language could cheat men into feeling, but only plain language made up of precisely defined terms could arrive at truth. Finally, style was an appropriate garment for thought, not its embodiment.

Hobbes had described the imagination as a purely receptive and associative faculty, combining fading sense-impressions to form compound images. Selection from these belonged to the judgment. Dryden, in his *Preface to Annus Mirabilis*, pictured a peripatetic imagination, but it was more of a collective than a creative one :

> Wit in the poet . . . is no other than the faculty of imagination in the writer, which, like a nimble spaniel beats over and ranges through the field of memory, till it springs the quarry it hunted after; or, without metaphor, which searches over all the memory for the species or ideas of those things which it designs to represent.
>
> *Essays* (ed. W. P. Ker, 1900), vol. I, p. 14.

Locke's subsequent account of the mind as a *tabula rasa* receiving knowledge empirically from a series of impinging sense-impressions endorsed the theory of the relative passivity of the imagination. Its inferiority to reason was stressed throughout the *Essay*. Imagination could never lead to the discovery of truth, because reality was not its material:

But of what use is all this fine knowledge of men's own imaginations, to a man that enquires after the reality of things? It matters not what men's fancies are, it is the knowledge of things that is only to be prized: it is this alone gives a value to our reasonings, and preference to one man's knowledge over another's, that it is of things as they really are, and not of dreams and fancies.

Essay concerning the Human Understanding, Bk. IV, chap. 4, sec. 1.

Here, Locke's reader was asking him to distinguish the degrees of certainty of knowledge; Locke did so, but did not query the basic assumption that the faculty of imagination had little value. Truth for Locke was of one kind: the truth of natural philosophy, based on facts and operating on mechanical principles. Everything else was either a distortion of truth or a fanciful playing with concepts known to be fictional. This attitude was not confined to philosophers: it can be found in such popular manuals as *The Ladies Dictionary* (1694), which used 'poetically' as a synonym for 'untruthfully':

Hylas, going to fetch Hercules some water, fell into the river, or (poetically) was pulled in by the Nymphs in love with him.

The imagination could not provide an alternative route to truth; it was irrelevant to the world of natural philosophy. Sprat, in his *History of the Royal Society* (1667), celebrated the triumph of the world of fact over the former world of the imagination:

But from the time in which the *Real Philosophy* has appear'd there is scarce any whisper remaining of such horrors: Every man is unshaken at those Tales at which his Ancestors trembled: The cours of things goes quietly along, in its own true channel of Natural Causes and Effects. For this we are beholden to Experiments; which though they have not yet completed the discovery of the true world, yet they have already vanquish'd those wild inhabitants of the false world, that us'd to astonish the minds of men.

History of the Royal Society (1667), p. 340, quoted B. Willey, *The Seventeenth Century Background*, p. 213.

The expulsion of the imagination from the world of truth left poetry only the functions of entertainment and wish-fulfilment. Poetry became a very second-class occupation. Locke took the conventional attitude towards it in his *Some Thoughts Concerning Education*:

> If he have a poetic vein, it is to me the strangest thing in the world, that the father should desire or suffer it to be cherished or improved. Methinks the parents should labour to have it stifled and suppressed as much as may be; and I know not what reason a father can have to wish his son a poet, who does not desire to have him bid defiance to all other callings and business: which is not yet the worst of the case; for if he proves a successful rhymer, and gets once the reputation of a wit, I desire it may be considered what company and places he is likely to spend his time in, nay, and estate too: for it is very seldom seen, that any one discovers mines of gold or silver in Parnassus. It is a pleasant air, but a barren soil; and there are very few instances of those who have added to their patrimony by any thing they have reaped from thence. . . . If you would not have him waste his time and estate to divert others, and contemn the dirty acres left him by his ancestors, I do not think you will much care he should be a poet.

> *Works* (1823), vol. IX, par. 174.

Few men in this age had any other concept of the relative value of imagination and reason. Shaftesbury was one of these few: he saw the imagination as an essentially creative faculty, reaching out towards truths that were beyond the scope of natural philosophy. He compared the imaginative mind of the poet with the mind of God:

> Such a poet is indeed a second *Maker*; a just Prometheus under Jove. Like that sovereign artist or universal plastic nature, he forms a whole, coherent and proportioned in itself, with due subjection and subordinacy of constituent parts.

> *Characteristics*, vol. I, pp. 135–6, quoted R. L. Brett, *The Third Earl of Shaftesbury* (1951), p. 105.

John Dennis—who acquired the reputation of impotence, pedantry and dullness merely by virtue of being a critic—also set a higher value on the poet and on the imaginative faculty than was common at the time. He set them less high than Sir Philip Sidney had done, but in his treatise, *The Grounds of Criticism in Poetry* (1704), he acknowledged that poetry had a serious function in human life:

Poetry attains its final End, which is the reforming the Minds of Men, by exciting of Passion. And here I dare be bold to affirm, that all Instruction whatever depends upon Passion. . . . And therefore Poetry instructs and reforms more powerfully than Philosophy can do, because it moves more powerfully. . . . For whereas Philosophy pretends to correct human Passions by human Reason, that is, things that are strong and ungovernable, by something that is feeble and weak; Poetry by the force of the Passion, instructs and reforms the Reason: which is the Design of the true Religion, as we have shewn in another place.

Dennis, *Critical Works* (ed. Hooker, Baltimore, 1939–43), vol. I, p. 337.

Although Shaftesbury had a far better grasp than Locke of the processes of the creation of a work of art, it was Locke's view that prevailed for most of the eighteenth century, and made Akenside, among others, so conscious of the conventional gulf set between Beauty and Truth, and so anxious to bridge it. Much of his poem, *The Pleasures of Imagination*, was devoted to this topic:

> There shall the Virtues, there shall Wisdom's train,
> Their long-lost friends rejoining, as of old,
> Embrace the smiling family of arts,
> The Muses and the Graces. . . .
> Arm'd with the lyre, already have we dar'd
> To pierce divine philosophy's retreats,
> And teach the Muse her lore; already strove
> Their long-divided honours to unite,
> While temp'ring this deep argument we sang
> Of truth and beauty.
>
> > *The Pleasures of Imagination* (1744), Bk. II,
> > ll. 48–51, 62–7.

The division between Beauty and Truth was reflected in the contemporary attitude towards figurative language. Locke allowed that it gave pleasure, but that was all:

But yet if we would speak of things as they are, we must allow that all the art of rhetorick, besides order and clearness, all the artificial and figurative application of words eloquence hath invented, are for nothing else but to insinuate wrong ideas, move the passions, and thereby mislead the judgment, and so indeed are perfect cheats: and therefore however laudable or allowable oratory may render them in harangues and popular addresses, they are certainly, in all discourses that pretend to inform or instruct, wholly to be avoided; and where truth and knowledge are concerned, cannot but be thought a great fault, either of the language or person that makes use of them.

Essay Concerning the Human Understanding Bk. III, chap. 10, sec. 34.

Thomas Baker gave a similar account of the limitations of figurative language, in his *Reflections upon Learning* (1700). Metaphor and symbol could not express the truths of natural philosophy, and the communication of these was the current criterion of linguistic efficiency. Bishop Wilkins's attempt, in 1668, to promote a purely mathematical language in which each 'word' should have only one referent was only an extreme example of a general tendency. Sprat related how the purification of language from metaphor and symbol was one of the aims of the Royal Society:

They have endeavour'd, to separate the knowledge of Nature from the colours of Rhetorick, the devices of Fancy, or the delightful deceit of Fables.

History of the Royal Society (1667), p. 62, quoted B. Willey, *The Seventeenth Century Background* (1934), p. 210.

Symbols were regarded as an imprecise method of expression. No one realized that there were things of importance which could only be expressed in terms of symbols:

The symbolism of the poetic imagination is an attempt to express thought which cannot be put in the conventional language of logical or scientific statement. A poet's thought can be expressed only in the symbolism of his imagery. The reader cannot become acquainted with the thought in any more direct way, though it is sometimes possible for him to go behind the symbols and to perceive what is being symbolized.

Brett, *op. cit.*, p. 107.

For Locke, metaphor and symbol merely denoted inexact concepts; they served to pass off fancies as knowledge :

If all our search has yet reached no farther than simile and metaphor, we may assure ourselves we rather fancy than know, and have not yet penetrated into the inside and reality of the thing, be it what it will, but content ourselves with what our imaginations, not things themselves, furnish us with.

Of the Conduct of the Understanding, Works (1823), vol. III, par. 32.

Language was seen as something separable from the meaning which it expressed. Locke recommended men, when reading, to educate themselves by jettisoning the words of the author, fixing in the mind 'the clear and distinct ideas of the question stripped of words'. They must get rid of 'the false lights and deceitful ornaments of speech'; what they need is purely the gist of the argument (*Ibid.*, vol. III, par. 42). Such advice implies that the meaning is independent of the words in which it is expressed, and that it would not be altered if the words themselves were changed. This is certainly untrue of poetry—though Dryden was obviously operating on that principle when he criticized the language of Shakespeare:

> If Shakespeare were stripped of all the bombasts in his passions, and dressed in the most vulgar words, we should find the beauties of his thoughts remaining; if his embroideries were burnt down, there would still be silver at the bottom of the melting pot.

> *Preface to Troilus and Cressida, Essays* (1900), vol. I, p. 227.

A poem consisted for Dryden of words describing something; it was not a unique work of art. This theory descended directly from the art of rhetoric: *elocutio* was the final stage of putting the invention into words. No one seemed to believe that there was only one true expression of a particular complex of ideas; it was thought that the author had the choice of several methods of wording, within the limits of decorum. Yet, by the end of the seventeenth century, there were critics who grasped the idea that the words were not separable from the thought they expressed; alteration of them would alter the thought itself. La Bruyère, discussing the sublime in literature in his *Caractères*, showed that he understood this idea: only those writers who found '*l'unique expression*', he said, could achieve sublimity. '*Les esprits médiocres ne trouvent point l'unique expression, et usent de synonymes*' (La Bruyère, *Oeuvres*, ed. M. G. Servois, 1865, tome I, p. 145). It is a pity that Locke did not appreciate the significance of this passage;

he had clearly read the *Caractères*, for he praised La Bruyère's views on teaching foreign languages to young children, which came later in the same work (*Some Thoughts Concerning Education, Works* 1823, vol. IX, par. 195). John Dennis, as well as La Bruyère, could see the organic unity of thought and expression. This idea occurred both in his *The Advancement and Reformation of Modern Poetry* (1701) and in his *Preface to Britannia Triumphans* (1704):

> This then is certain, that ev'ry Sentiment or Thought has a Degree of Spirit, or Passion, or Fire, call it what you please, which is proper to it, and every thing above or below that Degree is utterly wrong. Now this is as certain that there is but just one Expression which can convey that Spirit or Passion in its true Proportion. And every thing that is not that one Expression is false, and weakens the Spirit, and obscures the Sentiment.
>
> Dennis, *op. cit.*, vol. I, p. 375.

But the rhetorical view of style as a separate entity prevailed through the greater part of the eighteenth century.

This complex of attitudes towards the imagination and the functions of language naturally influenced the writers of the following century. It created an atmosphere in which men were not easily persuaded to take works of art seriously. They could be enjoyed, but unless they had an obvious moral purpose (of the external kind required by Dr. Johnson of Shakespeare), they failed to merit much consideration. Writers had to struggle to re-establish the standing of literature. Those who rebelled against the philosophers and gave free rein to their imagination were so conscious of their struggle that their writing became extravagant, and merited most of the abuse it attracted from the men of common sense. Their violence was paralleled by the violence of the Wesleyans, who restored superstition and hysteria to religion, as well as a living faith. The pressures of reason produced the cult of the Gothic with its glooms and terrors, and the uncontrolled sentimentality of the novels of feeling. Richard Hurd, in his *Letters on Chivalry and Romance* (1762), lamented the changes that had come about in the cause of philosophic truth:

> Fancy, that had wantoned it so long in the world of fiction, was now constrained, against her will, to ally herself with strict truth, if she would

gain admittance into reasonable company. What we have gotten by this revolution, you will say, is a great deal of good sense. What we have lost is a world of fine fabling.

Letter xii.

In all this we may discern what lay behind Matthew Arnold's assertion that the eighteenth century was an age of prose, unfavourable to genuine poetry, and it must be admitted that Locke's theories left no room for the aesthetic approach to truth. Pope overcame this obstacle, but many of his contemporaries were seriously handicapped by the devaluation of the imagination in the realm of common sense.

Their predecessors were more fortunate. David Hume's view of a terrifying universe of doubt and ignorance, from the barren rocks of his philosophy, was still unimaginable. The men who wrote between 1660 and 1700 could draw on the living tradition of the earlier seventeenth century. The enthusiasm of Bunyan and Burnet was sincere, uninflated, alive with the faith of the Reformation. The wisdom of Halifax was human, not a mechanized principle. The energy of Dryden was spontaneous and secure. In their age, imagination was still part of the world of truth.

VII

APOLOGIA: JOHN DRYDEN

SOMETHING less than justice has been done to Dryden in this book, because several of his qualities have been described only at intervals, and some of them have not been touched on at all. Since his genius had a broad range, instead of being concentrated in one or two perfect works of art, this treatment diminishes him unfairly. Considered as a whole, he emerges as a magnificent figure, uneven in taste and imagination, but large-minded and vividly spoken, combining naturalness with intensity of speech. No other English writer was consistently successful in so many fields: criticism, the new style in prose, various kinds of drama, satire, discursive poetry and translation. He never wrote without genuine gusto, whether he was arguing about true religion, or denouncing rebels, or pleading for a fair judgment on English drama.

His plays were sometimes bad, but he never overestimated them. They were neither flat nor feeble, and at their best they showed liveliness of invention and great vigour of language, in spite of the haste in which they were composed. They always had a full flavour, particularly when he was ramping through a glorious string of couplets, delighting in extravagance, and making great play with his exotic settings in east and west. He has rightly been called the father of English criticism—there were critical essays before his, but he was the first to allow the free play of mind on accepted tenets, and to discourse with such urbanity, vividness and ease. He put forward many new ideas—not as a dictator, but as a reasonable man asking for a hearing in a debate; he was always ready to argue. He emphasized that the real function of the critic was to distinguish the excellencies of works of art, instead of showing his own superiority by pointing out the flaws. He concentrated on talking about the practice of poetry, and spoke from

experience; he was not afraid of giving new advice when his own
experience led him to change his mind on such subjects as the Unities,
or the use of rhyme in plays. He had the taste and insight to appreciate
many of the virtues of such varied writers as Shakespeare, Chaucer,
Horace and Juvenal; he was the first man to write both general and
detailed criticism of the works of English authors. He was the greatest
poetic satirist in his century, unsurpassed in force and imagination.
This quality can be seen not only in his political satires, but in various
passages in *Religio Laici* and in *The Hind and the Panther*. He was a
lively and versatile translator. His better elegies had a dignified simplicity. He had a gift for witty occasional verse which was turned to
good accourt in prologues and epilogues. He embarked on a historical
poem, *Annus Mirabilis*, which contained some impressive heroic
passages. His own prose was entirely lucid and civilized, easy in tone,
free from pedantry, amusing, and lively in phrase and image. He
perpetually enjoyed what he wrote, but he was never content with it,
because he never managed to write the English epic that was his real
aim—and in that sense, like other great men of his age, he was stretching
out towards something beyond his reach.

He could range from the delicate sensibility of the opening of
Religio Laici, where the couplet moves smoothly and gently, without
his usual emphasis on the rhymes:

> Dim, as the borrow'd beams of Moon and Stars
> To *lonely, weary, wandring* Travellers
> Is *Reason* to the *Soul*: And as on high
> Those rowling Fires *discover* but the Sky
> Not light us *here*; So *Reason's* glimmering Ray
> Was lent, not to *assure* our *doubtfull* way,
> But *guide* us upward to a *better Day*.

to the serious note of *The Medall*:

> We loath our Manna, and we long for Quails;
> Ah, what is man, when his own wish prevails!
> How rash, how swift to plunge himself in ill;
> Proud of his Pow'r and boundless in his Will.

or the brilliance of the portrait of Buckingham:

> A man so various, that he seem'd to be
> Not one, but all Mankind's Epitome.
> Stiff in Opinions, always in the wrong,
> Was Every thing by starts, and Nothing long:
> But, in the course of one revolving Moon,
> Was Chymist, Fidler, States-man, and Buffoon;
> Then all for Women, Painting, Rhiming, Drinking,
> Besides ten thousand Freaks that died in thinking. . . .
> In squandring Wealth was his peculiar Art:
> Nothing went unrewarded, but Desert.
> Beggar'd by fools, whom still he found too late:
> He had his Jest, and they had his Estate.

His prose ranged from the broad ridicule of his attacks on Shadwell:

> *Og* may write against the King, if he pleases, so long as he *drinks* for him, and his *Writings* will not do the Government so much *Harm*, as his Drinking does it *Good*: For true Subjects will not be much perverted by his *Libels*; but the Wine-*Duties* rise considerably by his *Claret*. He has often call'd me an *Atheist* in Print; I would believe more charitably of him; and that he only goes *the broad Way*, because the other is too narrow for him.

to the wisdom and ease of his assessment of the progress of a truly original work of art:

> [Virgil] chose to please the most judicious: souls of the highest rank, and truest understanding. These are few in number; but whoever is so happy as to gain their approbation can never lose it, because they never give it blindly. Then they have a certain magnetism in their judgment, which attracts others to their sense. Every day they gain some new prose-lyte, and in time become the Church. For this reason, a well-weighed judicious poem, which at its appearance gains no more upon the world than to be just received, and rather not blamed than much applauded, insinuates itself by insensible degrees into the liking of the reader: the more he studies it, the more it grows upon him; every time he takes it up, he discovers some new graces in it.

One of the best tributes to Dryden's genius came from Congreve, who knew him personally, and loved him as a modest and generous man:

As to his Writings, I shall not take upon me to speak of them; for, to say little of them, would not be to do them right: And to say all that I ought to say, would be, to be very Voluminous. But, I may venture to say in general Terms, that no Man hath written in our Language so much, and so various Matter, and in so various Manners, so well. Another thing I may say very peculiar to him; which is, that his Parts did not decline with his Years: But that he was an improving Writer to his last, even to near seventy Years of Age; improving even in Fire and Imagination, as well as in Judgement.

Works (1923), vol. IV, p. 184.

This was part of Congreve's Preface to the first collected edition of Dryden's plays. Saying little of Dryden's works has not done them right; but justice has been done both by Mark van Doren and by David Nichol Smith to his place in the period of the Restoration.

SUGGESTIONS FOR FURTHER READING

CHAPTER I

HISTORICAL AND SOCIAL BACKGROUND

Sources

Gilbert Burnet: *History of My Own Times* (ed. O. Airy, 1897–1900), 2 vols.

The Life of Edward Earl of Clarendon, written by himself (1759).

John Evelyn: *Diary* (ed. E. S. de Beer, 1955), 6 vols. or (ed. W. Bray, Everyman's Library, 1907), 2 vols.

Celia Fiennes: *Journeys* (ed. C. Morris, 1947).

Samuel Pepys: *Diary* (ed. Wheatley, 1893–9), 6 vols. or (ed. M. Bright, revised J. Warrington, Everyman's Library, 1953), 3 vols.

Sir John Reresby: *Memoirs* (ed. A. Browning, 1936).

Anthony à Wood: *Life and Times* (ed. A. Clark, 1895), 5 vols. or abridged, with introduction by L. Powys, 1932.

Secondary Works

M. Ashley: *England in the Seventeenth Century* (1952).

G. N. Clark: *The Later Stuarts* (1934).

D. Ogg: *England in the Reign of Charles II* (1934), 2 vols.
England in the Reigns of James II and William III (1955).

RELIGIOUS BACKGROUND

Secondary Works

G. R. Cragg: *From Puritanism to the Age of Reason* (1950).

M. Macklem: *The Anatomy of the World: Relations between Natural and Moral Law from Donne to Pope* (Minnesota, 1958).

S. I. Mintz: *The Hunting of Leviathan: Seventeenth Century Reactions to the Materialism and Moral Philosophy of Thomas Hobbes* (New York, 1962).

C. E. Whiting: *Studies in English Puritanism 1660–1688* (1931).

B. Willey: *The Seventeenth Century Background* (1934).

227

SCIENTIFIC BACKGROUND

Sources

Joseph Glanvill: *The Vanity of Dogmatizing* (1661).
   Plus Ultra (1668).

Thomas Sprat: *History of the Royal Society* (1667).

Secondary Works

H. Butterfield: *The Origins of Modern Science* (1949).

R. F. Jones: *Ancients and Moderns* (St. Louis, 1936).

C. Raven: *John Ray, Naturalist, his Life and Works* (1942).

A. Wolf: *History of Science, Technology and Philosophy in the Six-teenth and Seventeenth Centuries* (1938).

THE BACKGROUND OF CRITICISM

Sources

Critical Essays of the Seventeenth Century (ed. J. E. Spingarn, 1908), 3 vols.

John Dryden: *Of Dramatic Poesy and Other Critical Essays* (ed. G. Watson, 1962), 2 vols.

Secondary Works

J. W. Atkins: *English Literary Criticism: 17th and 18th Centuries* (1951).

R. F. Jones and others: *The Seventeenth Century from Bacon to Pope* (Stanford, 1951).

E. R. Marks: *Relativist and Absolutist: The Early Neoclassical Debate in England* (Rutgers, 1955).

W. K. Wimsatt, Jr., and C. Brooks: *Literary Criticism, a Short History* (New York, 1959).

PERSONALITIES

Sources

John Aubrey: *Brief Lives* (ed. A. Powell, Cresset Library, 1949).

Characters from the Histories and Memoirs of the Seventeenth Century (ed. D. Nichol Smith, 1918).

John Dryden: *Letters* (ed. C. E. Ward, Durham, N.C., 1942).

228

History of the Life of Thomas Ellwood, written by his own hand (ed. S. Graveson, 1906).

John Evelyn: *Diary and Correspondence* (ed. W. Bray, 1906).

Lucy Hutchinson: *Memoirs of the Life of Colonel Hutchinson* (Everyman's Library, 1908).

John Locke: *The Correspondence of J. Locke and E. Clarke* (ed. B. Rand, 1927).

Samuel Pepys: *Letters of Samuel Pepys and his Family Circle* (ed. H. T. Heath, 1955).

Thomas Sprat: *An Account of the Life and Writings of A. Cowley* (1668).

Memoirs of the Verney family during the seventeenth century (compiled by F. P. and M. M. Verney, 1925), 2 vols.

Secondary Works

A. Bryant: *Samuel Pepys: The Man in the Making* (1933).
Samuel Pepys: The Years of Peril (1936).
Samuel Pepys: The Saviour of the Navy (1938).

D. Novarr: *The Making of Walton's Lives* (Cornell, 1958).

V. de Sola Pinto: *Enthusiast in Literature, a Portrait of John Wilmot, Earl of Rochester* (1962).

CHAPTER II

THE DRAMATISTS

Secondary Works

F. W. Bateson: 'L. C. Knights and Restoration Comedy', *Essays in Criticism*, vol. VII, no. 1 (1957).

A. Beljame: *Men of Letters and the English Public in the Eighteenth Century, 1660–1744* (ed. B. Dobrée, trans. E. O. Lorimer, 1948). (Originally published in French, 1881.)

B. Dobrée: *Restoration Comedy* (1924); *Restoration Tragedy* (1929).

N. H. Holland: *The First Modern Comedies* (Harvard, 1959).

L. C. Knights: 'Restoration Comedy, the Reality and the Myth', *Explorations* (1946).

C. Leech; 'Restoration Comedy, the Earlier Phase', *Essays in Criticism*, vol. I, no. 2 (1951).

K. Lynch: *The Social Mode of Restoration Comedy* (New York, 1926).

F. H. Moore: *The Nobler Pleasure: Dryden's Comedy in Theory and Practice* (North Carolina, 1963).

A. Nicoll: *A History of Restoration Drama, 1660–1700* (1925).

J. Palmer: *The Comedy of Manners* (1913).

L. J. Potts: *Comedy* (Hutchinson University Library, 1948).

Stratford upon Avon Studies 6: *Restoration Theatre* (ed. J. R. Brown and B. Harris, 1964).

D. Underwood: *Etherege and the Seventeenth Century Comedy of Manners* (Yale, 1957).

J. Wain: 'Restoration Comedy and its Modern Critics', *Essays in Criticism*, vol. VI, no. 4 (1956).

J. H. Wilson: *The Court Wits of the Restoration* (Princeton, 1948).

THE POETS

Sources

Before the Romantics (ed. G. Grigson, 1946).

The Oxford Book of Seventeenth Century Verse (ed. G. Bullough, 1934).

Restoration Verse 1660–1715 (ed. W. Kerr, 1930).

John Dryden: *Poems* (ed. J. Kinsley, 1958), 4 vols.

John Dryden: 'Preface to the Fables', 'Dedication of the *Aeneis*', *Of Dramatic Poesy and Other Critical Essays* (ed. G. Watson, 1962), 2 vols.

Secondary Works

A. W. Allison: *Towards an Augustan Poetic: Edmund Waller's "Reform" of English Poetry* (Kentucky, 1962).

W. Frost: *Dryden and the Art of Translation* (Yale, 1955).

K. G. Hamilton: *The Two Harmonies: Prose and Poetry in the Seventeenth Century* (1963).

R. Hinman: *Abraham Cowley's World of Order* (Harvard, 1961)

A. W. Hoffman: *John Dryden's Imagery* (Florida, 1962).

C. E. Ward: *The Life of John Dryden* (North Carolina, 1962).

C. V. Wedgwood: *Poetry and Politics under the Stuarts* (1960).

THE WRITERS OF FICTION

Sources

Shorter Novels (Everyman's Library, 1930), vol. II.

Secondary Works

L. Bernbaum: *The Mary Carleton Narratives 1663–73* (Cambridge, Mass., 1914).
'Mrs. Behn's *Oroonoko*', *Kittredge Anniversary Papers* (Boston, 1913).
F. W. Chandler: *The Literature of Roguery* (Boston, 1907), 2 vols.

CHAPTER III

Sources

John Dryden: '*Discourse* concerning the Origin and Progress of Satire', *Of Dramatic Poesy and Other Critical Essays* (ed. G. Watson, 1962), 2 vols.
Andrew Marvell: *Poems* (ed. H. M. Margoliouth, 1927).
The Rehearsal Transpros'd (1673).
John Oldham: *Poetical Works* (ed. R. Bell, 1854).
Poems on Affairs of State. Augustan Satirical Verse 1660–1714 (ed. G. de Forest Lord, Yale, 1963), vol. I, 1660–1678.

Secondary Works

J. M. Bullitt: *Jonathan Swift and the Anatomy of Satire* (Harvard, 1953).
V. de Sola Pinto: *Rochester, Portrait of a Restoration Poet* (1935).
T. S. Eliot: 'John Dryden', *Selected Essays* (1932).
I. Jack: *Augustan Satire* (1952).
F. R. Leavis· 'The Irony of Swift', *Determinations* (1934).
J. Middleton Murry: *Jonathan Swift, a critical biography* (1954).
D. Nichol Smith: *John Dryden* (1950).
R. Quintana: *The Mind and Art of Jonathan Swift* (1936).
E. A. Richards: *Hudibras in the Burlesque Tradition* (New York, 1937).
B. N. Schilling: *Dryden and the Conservative Myth: a Reading of Absalom and Achitophel* (Yale, 1961).
M. Starkman: *Swift's Satire on Learning in 'A Tale of a Tub'* (Princeton, 1950).
J. Sutherland: *English Satire* (1958).
M. van Doren: *The Poetry of John Dryden* (1931).

CHAPTER IV

Sources

Richard Baxter: *Autobiography* (ed. J. M. Lloyd Thomas, Everyman's Library, 1925).

Robert Boyle: *The Christian Virtuoso* (1690–1).

George Fox: *Journal* (ed. J. Nickalls, 1952).

John Ray: *The Wisdom of God manifested in the Works of the Creation* (1691).

Selections from the Cambridge Platonists (ed. E. T. Campagnac, 1901).

Secondary Works

M. S. Fisher: *Robert Boyle, devout naturalist* (Philadelphia, 1945).

R. Sharrock: *John Bunyan* (Hutchinson University Library, 1954).

H. Talon: *John Bunyan* (trans. B. Wall, 1951).

B. Willey: *The Eighteenth Century Background* (1940).

CHAPTER V

Secondary Works

W. Raleigh: 'George Savile, First Marquis of Halifax', *Some Authors* (1923).

B. Wormald: *Clarendon* (1951).

CHAPTER VI

Secondary Works

R. L. Brett: *The Third Earl of Shaftesbury* (Hutchinson University Library, 1951).

M. W. Cranston: *John Locke: a biography* (1957).

H. R. Fox Bourne: *The Life of John Locke* (1876), 2 vols.

E. N. Hooker: Preface to *The Critical Works of John Dennis* (Baltimore, 1943), vol. II.

D. G. James: *The Life of Reason* (1949).

J. Sutherland: *A Preface to Eighteenth Century Poetry* (1948).

B. Willey: *The Seventeenth Century Background* (1934).

J. W. Yolton: *John Locke and the Way of Ideas* (1956).

INDEX